GARLAND PUBLICATIONS IN COMPARATIVE LITERATURE

General Editor
JAMES J. WILHELM
Rutgers University

Associate Editors
DANIEL JAVITCH, New York University
STUART Y. MCDOUGAL, University of Michigan
RICHARD SÁEZ, The College of Staten Island/CUNY
RICHARD SIEBURTH, New York University

A GARLAND SERIES

LILLIAN S. ROBINSON

MONSTROUS REGIMENT

The Lady Knight in Sixteenth-Century Epic

GARLAND PUBLISHING, INC.
NEW YORK & LONDON
1985

© 1985 by Lillian S. Robinson
All Rights Reserved

Library of Congress Cataloging-in-Publication Data
Robinson, Lillian S.
Monstrous regiment.

(Garland publications in comparative literature)
Bibliography: p.
1. Epic poetry—History and criticism.   2. Poetry,
Modern—15th and 16th centuries—History and criticism.
3. Women in literature.   4. Knights and knighthood in literature.
I. Title.   II. Series.
PN1317.R63   1985   809.1′3   84-48366
ISBN 0-8240-6709-6 (alk. paper)

The volumes in this series are printed on
acid-free, 250-year-life paper.
Printed in the United States of America

IN MEMORY OF MAYDA ALSACE

FOREWORD

The dissertation that was the origin of this book was written between 1972 and 1974. I successfully defended it at Columbia University, Department of English and Comparative Literature, in May of 1974. In the two years that followed, I revised the text extensively and made some efforts to find a publisher for it. When these efforts were not immediately productive of a contract--although they did yield a certain amount of critical support and some insightful suggestions for further revisions--I returned to other intellectual pursuits. It was always my intention, however, to move this project back onto the "front burner" some day.

In the meantime, I wrote a less technical version of my argument and included it in Sex, Class, and Culture, the collection of my critical essays that was published by Indiana University Press in 1978. It was not until early in 1984, when Garland Press approached me about contributing to their proposed comparative literature series, that I took the work in hand again. This book, therefore, is in several coexisting and, I hope, not inharmonious layers: the core text, from the early 1970's, successive revisions, from the mid to late 70's, and additions, chiefly of a bibliographic nature, from that point to the present.

My basic argument was developed as a challenge to the received interpretation of the Renaissance female warriors that had been part of my own graduate course work. In that view, the lady knights were a symbol of the ideology of marriage for love between women and men who were not only equals but who founded a ruling dynasty on the basis of their militarily demonstrated equality. As I participated in the development of the new interdisciplinary field of women's studies, I was increasingly struck by repeated instances of the contradiction between the actual status of real women and the significance of "woman" as an intellectual or conceptual instrument. If sex equality was not even a visionary ideal, much less a lived reality, in the sixteenth century, and if marriage for love was not yet accepted doctrine or practice, the lady knights cannot be a symbol of equality. In that case, just what is their function? And why is it a courtly compliment for the poet to say to his own patron, "Your (many times great-) grandma wore combat boots"? I sought the answer to these questions in the connection of the lady knights to dynastic issues and, hence, to the problem of the state and the relation to it of a principle defined as feminine. Thus, ironically, investigation of a contradiction that was revealed through immersion in women's studies led me from the study of women's lives to the study of men's minds.

In the years since the dissertation was completed, feminist historians, chief among them the late Joan Kelly, have confirmed and deepened my intuitions about the meaning of the Renaissance period for women. My own debt to their work is reflected in Chapter Two of this study, particularly in its concentration on the public world, the world of economic and political conditions, in which the *idea* of woman came to figure prominently, as the reality of women's role in that sphere tended to diminish.

Because my work was begun so many years ago, I have accumulated an exceptionally large number of debts to teachers, colleagues, and friends. The longest-standing of these

Foreword

are to Dr. Thelma DeGraff, with whom I studied Virgil at Hunter College High School, and Professor Maurice Valency, who introduced me to the Renaissance epic at Columbia. As it happens, one work of each of these scholars is cited in the book, but I owe both of them much more than a footnote. I have moved far away from what they taught me, but never from the love of these poets that their teaching instilled in me.

My dissertation committee at Columbia has also earned my enthusiastic gratitude. James V. Mirollo was my warm and wise mentor, Seth Schein (Classics) was its diligent and enthusiastic second reader, and the defense, chaired by the late William Nelson, was also conducted by Maristella Lorch (Italian) and Joan Ferrante.

In the initial stages of writing the dissertation, I had the good fortune to share an office at MIT with Peter Donaldson, who also shared, as well, his abundant insights into Renaissance theories of government. Next door to us was Richard Koffler, whose generosity in admitting me to his own rich appreciation of Italian and classical literature never failed.

At that time, I was also part of a study group of scholars beginning to do work on women's issues in history and literature. Although I did not bring this manuscript to the group, my approach was and remains influenced by what I learned from interchanges with its members, Mari Jo Buhle, Ellen DuBois, Linda Gordon, Maurine Greenwald, Linda Hunt, Priscilla Long, Meredith Tax, and Lise Vogel.

At the dissertation stage, my sanity and linguistic reputation were preserved by the monumental multilingual proofreading efforts of David Bloom and Judith Treible. I only wish I had them with me now.

In the years of revision, I was invited to present my

developing ideas in seminars taught by Ann Williams and Kathleen McDermott at SUNY/Buffalo and by Dora Janeway Odarenko at Skidmore College. The material on Virgil was presented at Buffalo's conference on Women and Antiquity. Norman Rabkin of the University of California at Berkeley, who reviewed the manuscript for another press, was kind enough to forego the reader's cloak of anonymity and make additional (and very wise) suggestions to me about the direction my revisions should take. Daniel Javitch of New York University proposed further lines to pursue and, some ten years later, recruited the revised manuscript to the Garland series.

Between the first set of revisions and the present version, I participated in a National Endowment for the Humanities Summer Seminar, "Renaissance Self-Fashioning," held at the University of California at Berkeley. Its director, Stephen Greenblatt, helped refine my ideas about the nature of historical myth and the complex relationship between culture and subjective experience, including the (social and subjective) experience of gender.

Not all the individuals named thus far would be equally pleased to have this study in any sense (and to use the most unfeminist possible metaphor) fathered upon them. My intention here is to give them credit for their kindness in helping me avoid mistakes in facts or approach, while I take full responsibility on myself for anything I say that may be wrong or even wrong-headed.

The list of libraries whose resources I have used and whose staffs have been unfailingly helpful constitutes a literal as well as an intellectual itinerary, since I have consulted materials at: Columbia University, Harvard University, the Biblioteca Comunale Ariosteia (University of Ferrara), SUNY/Buffalo, the Bibliothèque Nationale (Paris),

Foreword

the University of California at Berkeley, Stanford University, the University of Pennsylvania, the New York Public Library, and New York University. I have strained the facilities of the Albright College Computer Center and the tolerance of James Belanger and his staff almost beyond their respective limits. In the last stages of bibliographic research, Greg Robinson served as eyes, legs, and occasionally wits for his aunt in the hinterlands.

If the original dissertation had been published, I was planning to end my preface or foreword with an acknowledgement to David Gilden, whose insistent treatment of writing as the most normal of human activities in fact served, during the years of its composition, to keep me human. I am as thankful as ever for that support, but the feeling is dwarfed by the awe and gratitude I feel for his achievement in getting the present text set and printed on inadequate and recalcitrant equipment. Without him, the dissertation would have been done, but less serenely; the book would not have existed at all.

Oley, Pennsylvania
June, 1985

TABLE OF CONTENTS

INTRODUCTION.. 1
CHAPTER I.   VIRGIL: HIC AMOR, HAEC PATRIA
                Introduction............................. 11
                The Education of the Hero................ 15
                Propaganda for Patriarchy................ 22
                Dido and the Education of the Patriarch... 29
                Sexual Expression and the Public Order.... 45
                Lavinia: The Consolation Prize........... 53
                Sex and Social Character................. 59
CHAPTER II.   THE HEART AND STOMACH OF A KING
                Introduction............................. 73
                The Feudal State and the Masculine
                Absolute................................. 75
                The Bourgeois State and the Flexible
                Feminine................................. 80
                The Modern Monarch and the Virgin Queen... 98
                Political Myth and Sexual Reality........105
CHAPTER III.   ARIOSTO: THE DOUBLE STANDARD
                Introduction.............................114
                Dynasty and Destiny......................121
                Reasons of State.........................133
                Ruggiero's Coming of Age.................149
                Bradamante: A Modern Knight..............166
                Marfisa: The New Woman...................179
                Ladies Present...........................188
CHAPTER IV.   TASSO: THE SOCIAL SACRAMENT
                Introduction.............................191
                Man's World, Woman's World, God's World...193

	The Dynastic Didact....................196
	A Political Vision.....................204
	Love and Marriage......................215
	Clorinda: Neither Man nor Beast.........233
	Erminia: The Cloistered Vagabond........252
	Armida: The Limits of Redemption........271
CHAPTER V.	SPENSER: THE MATTER OF BRITOMART
	Introduction..........................286
	The Historical Present................289
	The Queen's Presence..................306
	The Female of the Species.............314
	The Dialectic of Gender...............324
	The Androgynous Potential.............341
	The Anatomy of Love...................355
	With Marriage Meet....................366
	Of Polliticke Vertues.................372
AFTERWORD...387
BIBLIOGRAPHY..392

INTRODUCTION

To investigate the sociology of literature is often to raise more questions than may be responsibly answered. Much of the scholarship under this rubric is simply an elaborate begging of the question, where literary evidence is cited to demonstrate the existence or the nature of a particular social phenomenon, and subsequent discussion relies on that demonstration to explain the appearance or the function of some element in literature. This deliberate circularity is nowhere so apparent as in relations between the sexes. Yet the tension between historical reality and its imaginative translation is most pronounced when it comes to gender. "Woman," as Virigina Woolf put it, "pervades poetry from cover to cover; she is all but absent from history."[1] For this reason, literature has often had to function as an auxiliary history of the female sex and of relations between women and men. Nonetheless, we bring to the reading of such imaginative history a complex of assumptions about historical forces and events that shapes the way we interpret the literature itself.

My present subject, the women warriors in Ariosto, Tasso, and Spenser, reflects the contradiction between social conditions and poetic expression. This study is an attempt to work my way out of the question-begging approach

---

[1] Virginia Woolf, *A Room of One's Own* (1929; rpt. New York: Harbinger-Harcourt, 1957), p. 45.

1

without taking refuge in the contradiction itself, elevating it into paradox, and insisting that henceforth the frontiers of poetry be more rigidly policed. The romance-epic of the sixteenth century was created within certain social circumstances and was itself meant to have an impact on those conditions. It seems to me that these connections may be effectively demonstrated, while acknowledging that the relationship is not literal, but mythopoeic.

The problem arises from the introduction of a substantially new character, that of the female knight, into the tradition to which the romance-epic belongs. Ariosto's Orlando furioso, Tasso's Gerusalemme liberata, and Spenser's Faerie Queene all assign an important place to such a figure.[2] In each poem, a lady of noble rank successfully undertakes a military career and does battle for a cause she considers holy. Although that cause is central to the process of the epic, the poets take pains to let us know that it is not the ladies' sole inspiration for fighting. Ariosto's Bradamante and Marfisa, as well as Spenser's Britomart adopt the lives of knights-errant; in the margins of their more serious struggles, they enjoy casual combat that has no particular moral thrust. Tasso's Clorinda, more removed than the others from the chivalric mainstream, nonetheless has strong affinities with the classic image of the

---

[2] In describing the female warriors as a substantial innovation, I do not mean to ignore their literary antecedents. As this discussion proceeds, it should become evident which elements in the sixteenth-century characters are conventional, which unique. Special notice should be taken of Bradamante, the earliest of these figures, because Ariosto took her, along with much of the machinery for the Furioso, from Boiardo's Orlando innamorato. I begin with the Furioso not simply on grounds of taste, but because I think the motif we are tracing really starts with the way Ariosto interpreted what he found.

Introduction

warrior maiden and huntress. Erminia and Armida, the other two heroines of the Gerusalemme liberata, remain in more traditionally feminine roles, but they also participate in the epic's military action.

Where the Renaissance poets depart from the legends of Penthesilea and Camilla is that their heroines are not Amazons. Despite their masculine role and its trappings, they continue to share the attributes, the sensibility, and the destiny of women. They possess qualities that their culture defines as feminine, their demeanor is characterized as womanly and, most important, they are not alienated from their sexuality. With the exception of Marfisa, who is not Ariosto's chief heroine, each of the knightly heroines engages her lover in battle, on terms approaching equality. Where the military balance between the two combatants is imperfect, in fact, it is because of the disruptive effects of love itself. When a couple duels more than once, it is only the last time that the man wins, and, in any event, his victory is a narrow one.

As I have indicated, Ariosto and Spenser provide for an eventual marriage between the lady knight and her victorious lover. In the dynastic myth each of the epics constructs, these couples become the founders of the ruling house for which the poems were written. Clorinda remains a pagan almost to the end, and she dies at the hand of her lover, Tancredi. There is the suggestion of an eventual reunion in heaven, for, at the last, Clorinda begs and receives baptism from Tancredi. Although Tasso's lovers can thus have no direct place in a dynastic theme, the Gerusalemme liberata is concerned with many of the same political questions that theme serves to reinforce in the other heroic poems. Similarly, the theme of spiritual conversion so central to Tasso's sexual dramas is also highly significant for Ariosto and Spenser.

These two themes are readily defined and mutually dependent. In themselves, however, they do not afford much help in interpreting the female warriors, for neither dynastic legitimacy nor Christian conversion necessarily entails the creation of any such figure. And, without some way of grasping those characters, we lose some of the range and richness of the romance-epic. The most direct approach is to assume that the themes of sex equality, marriage for love, dynastic politics, and religious fulfillment reflect changing attitudes in the society at large and are intended to contribute to the further development of an emerging ideology. From this perspective, the military metaphor, embodied in the person of the virago heroine, would be seen as a particularly forceful expression of equality between the sexes. Superficial acquaintance with literary and historical commentaries bears out such a reading. Discussing Bradamante, for example, Graham Hough calls her the perfect virago, the woman as brave and effective as a man; and he refers to Burckhardt as his source for the information that this ideal was "much cherished in the Italian Renaissance."[3] If we consult Burckhardt himself, however, it turns out that his argument about the virago as a Renaissance ideal relies almost entirely on the poetic evidence of Boiardo and Ariosto.[4]

This is precisely the kind of circular reasoning to which I alluded earlier. If the female warriors are to be understood as representing changes in the status of women or

---

[3] Graham Hough, A Preface to the Faerie Queene (New York: The Norton Library, 1963), p. 29.

[4] Jacob Burckhardt, The Civilization of the Renaissance in Italy (1850; rpt. New York: Random House, 1954), p. 294.

Introduction

the sociology of love and marriage, the interpretation has to rest on stronger evidence for both the historicity of those changes and the forms they assumed. It is here that the research founders, for historians routinely cite literature, quite often the three heroic poems under consideration, to support inferences about changes in Renaissance sexual culture. In fact, however, when the poetic texts are set aside, as constituting part of a scholarly "uncertainty principle," there remains little basis for the claim that social practice or social values were drastically altered. A different critical direction is clearly called for, one that acknowledges and builds on the contradiction between woman as an historical being and as a symbolic instrument.

The problem lies in understanding what kind of myth the romance-epic creates, on what level the symbolism should be apprehended. It is obvious, for instance, that the military motif is largely allegorical. Although the status of women in the Renaissance period may be subject to a wide range of interpretations, I do not think anyone would seriously claim that the profession of arms was a customary--or even conceivable--one for a sixteenth-century lady. No one reads the poems so literally as to believe that they are describing actual women soldiers in masculine attire or advocating any such development.[5] It seems to me almost crude, in the

---

[5] The male-clothing issue is proof, were any needed, that the first readers of the romance-epic knew an allegory when they saw one. If the transvestism necessary to the role of female knight were taken literally, it would raise certain questions of social morality that in fact remain entirely dormant in the poems. Crucial in the case of Joan of Arc, the wearing of men's clothes by women continued, throughout the Renaissance period, to be subject to the severest sanctions. In the seventeenth century, for instance, Catalina de Eranso, for twenty years soldier, mercenary, highway robber, sailor and duelist, needed a special privilege from
(Footnote continued)

absence of any supporting historical evidence, to persist in asserting that female knights, equality, love, and marriage in the poems must stand for the status of women, love, and marriage in real life.

To determine what they do mean, it is useful to consider what the three poems have in common. All belong, first of all, to the same literary "kind," a genre that is, itself, a creation of the Renaissance period. As a form of epic, these works are political, devoted to patriotic expression. They glorify the state itself, as well as the ruling family, its history, and its aspirations; within this context, they also discuss the ideal polity and the individuals who should govern it. It seems worthwhile, therefore, to consider how the lady knights fit into the romance-epic as political poetry and whether the situations they enact are related to ideas about the state that evolved in the period of the Renaissance.

The method I follow in this study is to begin with Virgil's Aeneid, treating it as a limiting case. The action of that epic takes place in a philosophical framework that adamantly denies the compatibility of the state with characteristics perceived as female or with the indulgence of sexual passions. The Aeneid was part of an ideology of government that was taking shape in Augustan Rome, and served much the same function that heroic poetry was to fill in the

---

[5] (continued)
Pope Urban VIII in order to be allowed to retain her cavalry officer's uniform, a right that was granted in recognition of past heroism (See John Laffin, Women in Battle [London: Abelard-Schuman, 1957], p. 23). A more complex literary example is found in the Elizabethan theater, where boy-actors took the parts of female characters whom the vicissitudes of plot often required to masquerade as young men. Here again, the norms of art and life were clearly understood to be distinct and independent.

Introduction

Renaissance period. For, although the Roman state was no Burckhardtian work of art, the political and ideological efforts Augustus made reflected a similar consciousness about what went into the creation of a new public entity.

Moreover, Virgil's immediate political purpose was to honor the house of Augustus and to legitimate its authority by glorifying its founder. The Renaissance, in its revival of ancient culture, was quick to seize on the idea of reviving Roman political power, as well, discovering a ready paradigm in the way Rome used the Trojan legend. For, if the mantle of Troy could fall on her Roman descendants, the legitimacy of a modern state may be (mythically) assured by demonstrating that it is, in turn, the rightful heir of Rome. In Ariosto, the idea of Troy-novant finds its roots in the Carolingian past, where that Holy Roman Empire is secured with the aid of Trojan-descended ancestors of the poet's Este patrons. Spenser combines the theme of Trojan origins (through the Brut for whom the British Isles are named) with the national legend of Arthur, from which potent combination the Tudors claimed descent. Tasso is not so directly genealogical, but his poem, like Ariosto's, does include Estense heros, and his choice of the First Crusade is meant to evoke the contemporary struggles of an embattled Christendom and thus reflect its splendor on contemporary leaders. By choosing what he viewed as a glorious and powerful moment in the history of Catholicism, Tasso was also supplying an honorable pedigree for the Counter-Reformation Church of his own day. For the poets of romance-epic, then, as for Virgil, immediate dynastic issues always form part of a larger statement about the content and direction of government.

Although Virgil was a model and a source for secondary epic as it developed in the sixteenth century, the Renaissance poets transformed his attitudes about sexuality and politics into something very like their opposite. My discussion of Virgil is therefore followed by an examination of the changes that occurred in the sixteenth century concerning the idea and nature of the state. This analysis necessarily involves some consideration of the form and concept of the state as it existed immediately prior to the Renaissance period. The presentation of ideas that are new and sometimes radical in the familiar archaic garb of chivalry makes an understanding of the actual medieval situation particularly important.

These segments of the literary and historical background constitute the essential prelude to a reading of the three romance-epics. Viewed from this perspective, the poems make a rather complex series of statements about government, religion, and sexuality, and about the institution of marriage as a possible locus for reconciling these themes. In the Orlando furioso, both the erotic and political values expressed are modern and secular, tending towards harmony and individual satisfaction. Dynastic issues are in the forefront of the poem, but the politics to which they are linked lack a broad spiritual or imperial scope. As a resolution of the poem's political and sexual dimensions, Ariosto concludes with a marriage between the lady knight and her beloved. In so doing, however, he does not develop a theory about the marriage of lovers and its relation to the public world, or in any way explore the innovation he is perpetrating.

By contrast, Tasso is all too aware of the social and religious implications of a happy ending involving marriage. For him, public and private life, political and sexual concerns, are equally in the service of preeminent spiritual constructs. Rather than mediating between the temporal and

Introduction

religious worlds, marriage represents a threat to the hegemony of holiness and cannot constitute a proper resolution for the love stories in the <u>Gerusalemme liberata</u>. Spenser's political vision embraces both the worldly kingdom of Ariosto and the divine preoccupations of Tasso. He recognizes that sexuality is a potential threat to both kinds of polity, but he develops an elaborate philosophical rationale that distinguishes between destructive lust and the legitimate fulfillments of conjugal love. And he explicitly connects the virtues of harmonious government with balanced relations between the sexes.

It should be emphasized that I am not proposing an interpretation that would constrict our vision of these poems. I am working, rather, within a critical framework that recognizes and stresses the political character of the romance-epic, attempting to determine which aspects of the three poems belong to their "public sector." The readings I suggest are partial and to some extent unbalanced, but I think they afford another, hitherto unexplored approach to the totality of the poems.

CHAPTER ONE
VIRGIL: HIC AMOR, HAEC PATRIA

To begin a study of Ariosto, Tasso and Spenser with a discussion of the <u>Aeneid</u> is an approach whose propriety no one in the sixteenth century would have questioned. For the Renaissance man of letters, Virgil was always the center, the point of reference. His work provided a model for epic poets and theorists alike, and his artistic development was the prescribed pattern for a poetic career. The imitation of Virgil was not limited to working one's way up to the epic through an apprenticeship in bucolic and rustic modes; rather, poets of the sixteenth century looked to Virgil as a source for the scope and themes of national epic.

Roman narrative poetry is characterized by its elevation of national history to the realm of myth, a practice that finds its fullest expression in the <u>Aeneid</u>. To the Renaissance poet who was also attempting to endow myth with historical functions, Virgil offered the means by which the transformation might be effected: a pattern of symbolic incident overlaid with symbolic language.

In the <u>Aeneid</u>, moreover, Virgil elaborated many of the same themes that the authors of romance-epic were to express through the figure of the female warrior. It is, first of all, the epic of imperial destiny, embodying both Roman sovereignty and Augustan pre-eminence, for in establishing the historical myth of Rome as the new Troy, Virgil legitimated the Empire and its ruling clan. The legend of the

Empire's Trojan heritage also presents the ethic of the Roman state, as reflected in Virgil's views of government, warfare, and heroism. At the same time, it contains a conflicting theme, the nature of sexual passion and its controlling female principle. Finally, although seemingly peripheral to these dominant ideas, the <u>Aeneid</u> includes the striking figure of a woman warrior. Virgil's poem thus provides a background against which to understand what happens in the sixteenth-century epic.

In fulfilling his destiny and founding the Roman state, Aeneas must overcome a series of obstacles; more consistently than for any other hero of ancient epic, these obstacles assume a female form and reflect a female motivation. What he rescues from the destruction of Troy is the masculine element: the household gods of the patriarchal family and his own father and son, his dynasty represented in patrilineal terms. The "Oriental" luxury that caused Troy's downfall is allowed to burn with the city. Aeneas never identifies with the sensuous character of Troy, and only his unbalanced rivals Iarbas and Turnus--rivals in the sexual as well as the military sphere--so much as broach the accusation of "effeminate" sensuality.

Trouble, on the other hand, tends to wear a female guise. Juno's unflagging spite is behind most of it, and the other deities she enlists are either female or recruited by means of female sexuality. In the affair with Dido, pivotal event of the <u>Aeneid</u>, a woman and the very fact of sexual passion stand in the way of destiny. Irrational fury drives other female forces that hinder Aeneas: the Harpies, the Trojan matrons, Allecto, her victim Amata, and Juturna. Because Venus' attempts to aid her son so often rely on sexual strategies, her help sometimes creates a temporary barrier and, in any event, is both irrational and inconsistent. In each case, it is a female perceived as such--that is, as a sexual being--who obstructs the hero's orderly progress towards his Lavinian goal.

For Virgil, the female defined by her sexual function is literally hysterical, explicitly Dionysian, and invariably dangerous. In a hero who, we are repeatedly reminded, is goddess-born and through whom the imperial clan paid homage to Venus genetrix, the conflict is particularly bitter. On the private level, it is expressed in the most frequent descriptions of Aeneas, pius, devoted to duty, yet nate dea, goddess-born, where the goddess in question is the patron of erotic love. In the epic macrocosm, the basic tension is between Roman destiny and sexual desire. Expressed in terms of values that inform each side of the contradiction, it is between the state and private needs.

The first half of the epic, the so-called "Odyssean" Aeneid, contains these opposing forces within the consciousness of the hero; in the latter or "Iliadic" half, forces defined as "masculine" and "feminine" do battle in the arena of public life. For this reason, the Dido episode, which properly belongs to neither of the two Homeric categories but is thoroughly Virgilian in inspiration, is the ideological center of the poem.[1] The love affair has been tellingly

---

[1] In using the phrase "thoroughly Virgilian," I do not mean to reopen the controversy about how much Virgil's Dido owes to other sources. The most frequent portrayal of Dido in earlier literature was as the faithful widow of Sychaeus, a queen who never so much as met Aeneas and who committed suicide rather than accept a political marriage with Iarbas. As the tasteless and clearly post-classical witticism expressed it, "maluit ardere quam nubere" [she found it better to burn than to marry.] (On this point see, for example, Alfredo Baccelli, "Il quarto libro dell'Eneide," Studi Virgiliani [Rome: Sapientia Editrice, 1932], II, 82. See also
(Footnote continued)

described as the most critical moment for Rome.² And, although Pöschl calls Dido's internal conflict the "embodiment of what the Aeneid as a whole separates into different forces," he also sees the contrast between the two heroic lovers as "the original tragic conflict between man and woman."³

Potentially, each of these antitheses has its synthesis in the Virgilian scheme. The achievement of Roman destiny entails the sacrifice of Dido, but it also requires the diplomatic marriage with Lavinia. This is a sexual resolution, but one that fulfills the demands of empire, instead of opposing them. Similarly, the figure of Camilla offers the possibility of resolving the conflict between "masculine" and "feminine" values in the state. But both these syntheses are weak and unsatisfying, so that the Aeneid tends to be remembered for its tragic events and autumnal tone. Unlike the epic poets of the Renaissance, Virgil cannot integrate sexual expression or the female principle

---

¹(continued)
Arthur Stanley Pease's edition of Book Four, Publi Vergili Maronis Aeneidos, Liber Quartus [Cambridge, Massachusetts: Harvard University Press, 1935]). Two hundred years before Virgil, however, Naevius mentioned a love-passage between Dido and Aeneas. (Jean Beaujeu, "Le Mariage d'Enée et de Didon et la causalité historique," Revue du Nord, 36, 142 [April-June 1954], 115). Nonetheless, the details and the global significnce of the affair are Virgil's unique contribution. See Thelma B. DeGraff, "Dido--Tota Vergiliana," Classical Weekly, 432 [1949-50], 147-51.)

² Fr. Jose Oroz de la Consolacion, O.R.S.A., "Virgilio, poeta del 'imperium,'" Helmantica, 4 (1953), 264. [emphasis mine]

³ Viktor Pöschl, The Art of Virgil: Image and Symbol in the Aeneid, trans. Gerda Seligson (Ann Arbor: University of Michigan Press, 1962), pp. 91, 47.

into his view of the ideal human order. For this reason, it is useful to examine in detail the shape these conflicts assume in his epic and the limited resolution he does admit.

The Education of the Hero

On the level of epic events, the contest is between Aeneas' imperial mission and his personal fulfillment. Embodying the transition between Troy and Rome, the hero must strain to keep his sense of Troy alive until it can assume a concrete form. (The structure of the poem reflects a similar attempt to balance the Greco-Trojan past, the transitional present, and the Roman future; thus, the first third of the epic is devoted to the Trojan roots of the story, the last third to its Italic conclusion.) For Aeneas, the reconstruction of Troy cannot be merely a matter of reproducing the landscape and architecture of the old city from loving memory. The idea of a new Troy is one that matures and develops within him as he proceeds towards his goal.

Naturally, the former lesson is the easier to learn. Simulacra of the great city appear several times, but they are monuments to grief, not statements of renewed possibility. Praying in Apollo's temple at Delos, Aeneas identifies "home" with Troy:

> da propriam, Thymbraee, domum; da moenia fessis
> et genus et mansuram urbem; serva altera Troiae
> Pergama, reliquas Danaum atque immitis Achilli.
> (III, 85-87)

> O God of Thymbra, grant a home
> And walls to weary men, grant us posterity
> And an abiding city: guard our second

Tower of Troy, this remnant left alive
by Danaan swords and pitiless Achilles.
(III, 118-121)[4]

In reponse to the oracle's advice to "seek out your ancient mother," the Trojans sail for Crete. This is a double misconstruction. First, and obviously, because it is from Italy, not Crete, that Dardanus came, but also because of how they interpret the building of a new Troy. As Aeneas relates it:

> ergo avidus muros optatae molior urbis
> Pergameamque voco, et laetam cognomine gentem
> hortor amare focos arcemque attollere tectis.
> (III, 132-134)

> I could barely wait
> To build our hoped-for city walls, to be
> Called Pergamum, I said. I urged the people,
> Who loved the name, to love their new-found
>   hearths
> And raise a citadel above the town.
> (III, 184-188)

But the Trojans, their cattle, and their crops are alike

---

[4] All citations from Virgil are from the Oxford Classical Texts edition prepared by Frederic Arthur Hirtzel, P. Vergili Maronis Opera (Oxford: The Clarendon Press, 1900) and checked against the edition of R.A.B. Mynors (Oxford: The Clarendon Press, 1969). Translations from The Aeneid are from Robert Fitzgerald's version (New York: Random House, 1983). Since the translation is not a line by line rendering, I have included Fitzgerald's line numbers in each citation.

struck by pestilence, and their fields are barren. Simply reviving the old name and rebuilding is a procedure condemned to sterility.

Even more stagnant is the miniature "Troy" where Andromache now lives in peace with her new husband. Since Helenus was entitled to part of Pyrrhus' estates, the two have been able to build a kind of life-size mausoleum:

> ...qui Chaonios cognomine campos
> Chaoniamque omnem Troiano a Chaone dixit,
> Pergamaque Iliacamque iugis hanc addidit arcem
> ...et parvam Troiam simulataque magnis
> Pergama et arentem Xanthi cognomine rivum
> agnosco, Scaeaeque amplector limina portae.
> (III, 334-337; 349-351)

> He called the plains Chaonian, the realm
> Itself Chaonia--from the Trojan Chaon--
> And built a Pergamum, a citadel,
> Called Illium's, on this ridge...
> I saw before me Troy in miniature,
> A slender copy of our massive tower,
> A dry brooklet named Xanthus...and I pressed
> My body against a Scaean Gate.
> (III, 457-460; 477-480)

Here, despite her remarriage, Andromache remains Hector's widow, childless since the sacrifice of Astyanax. She and Helenus are presumably not to have other children and their settlement will die with them. Aeneas envies them the measure of felicity they have earned for themselves, that they may live out their lives without further turmoil, but he also recognizes the grotesque character of their little

Troy.

Again, after the momentary rebellion of the Trojan matrons and the burning of several of Aeneas' ships, the hero realizes that he can take only the strongest and best-prepared with him, those who can endure the trials in store once they reach Italy. The others are left behind, and another Troy-let is established:

> ...Aeneas urbem designat aratro
> sortiturque domos; hoc Ilium et haec loca Troiam
> esse iubet.
> (V, 755-757)

> Aeneas
> Marked with a plow the limits of the town
> And gave home sites by lot. One place should be
> Called Illium, he decreed, one quarter Troy.
> (V, 983-986)

Inhabited by the old and the unfit, this settlement is clearly no substitute for the re-establishment of Trojan glory and, like the others, has only the name and the superficial form of the fallen city.

Semantically, all these incidents build towards the scene of Juno's final renunciation in Book Twelve, where she states it as her condition that the Latin tribes not be forced to give up their names and that Aeneas' people be called Trojans no longer. Conceptually, the nomenclature reflects the preservation of only that part of Trojan civilization which should be preserved, and its fusion with the new, Roman elements. Troy has not arisen triumphant from her own ashes, but has been reborn better than she was. The Roman conquest of Greece was described by Augustan propagandists as the revenge of Troy's rightful heirs, although it was of course understood more pragmatically. Virgil echoes this explanation, but expresses it in terms of Roman power, the reversal of national fortunes restoring a global balance upset by the sack of Troy.

    The new Troy, furthermore, is to be Aeneas' own city. Augustus cannot be descended from a second-rate hero, nor can the founder of Rome be identified with the decadence of Trojan society by any ties stronger than his painful nostalgia. Thus, the *Aeneid* systematically builds up the past reputation of the hero, linking his name with that of Hector and making Hector recognize that Aeneas is his true successor.[5] Furthermore, just as Aeneas' view of the ideal society does not remain static, fixated on the Trojan past, Virgil makes his hero flexible, capable of learning, so that, in the course of the narrative, and at great personal sacrifice, he develops into a Roman ancestor, possessing all the vaunted imperial qualities.

    Aeneas too frequently is interpreted as blindly obeying the dictates of his imperial fate, or, if a conflict is acknowledged, he is seen as a lifeless marionette dragged now one way, now the other. In fact, beginning with his initial idea that all he need do is establish the Trojan survivors on Crete and name their new capital after the old, Aeneas' vision of his future responsibilities is progressively refined. So, too, is his sense of mission, which outgrows its inital limits through the piecemeal revelation

---

[5] A.J. Gossage, "Two Implications of the Trojan Legend," *Greece and Rome*, 2nd Ser., 2 (1955), 81, 72, 26. See also C.S. Lewis, "Virgil and the Subject of Secondary Epic," from *A Preface to Paradise Lost* (Oxford: Oxford University Press, 1954), rpt. in Virgil: *A Collection of Critical Essays*, ed. Steele Commager (Englewood Cliffs, N.J.: Prentice-Hall, 1966), p. 64.

of a larger destiny. It is in the second half of the poem, after the enlightening visit to the Underworld, that Aeneas' eagerness for Rome crystallizes, encompassing and eventually replacing his memory of Troy. But this shift in allegiance is adumbrated in the first lines of Book One, so that in the early books and, most important, at the time of the encounter with Dido, it already has some substance. At the very least, Aeneas knows, and has known since the night Troy fell, that the destruction of his city was fated. That night, Venus prevented him from revenging himself on Helen, explaining that it was more important to salvage as much as permitted than to dwell on the causes of the tragic event. Moreover, Helen and Paris were not really responsible for what was happening:

>...divum inclementia, divum,
> has evertit opes sternitque a culmine Troiam.
> (II, 602-603)

> The harsh will of the gods it is, the gods,
> That overthrows the splendor of this place
> And brings Troy from her height into the dust.
> (II, 792-794)

Aeneas learned then that since the fall of Troy was the divine will, it would be a sin, <u>nefas</u>, to oppose it or, conversely, to obstruct the rise of Rome.

In fact, it was Virgil's own generation that began to link the two events concretely--the divine inevitability of the first increasingly seeming to necessitate the political course of the second. Thus, the Trojan origins of Rome, which, because of Troy's ultimate fate, had been regarded in the light of an ancestral curse, came to be characterized as the sign of a blessing on Roman endeavors, particularly on the imperial design and its divinely-descended executor. Eventually, the myth of a flawed past, marked by "destruction and rebirth under a sensitive leader," provided the Augustan age with "a parable for its own experience and for its hopes as well."[6]

What is the content of that destiny? And why must it supersede all other concerns? Virgil's reply is not as clear as it might be only because it is not simple. He fully recognizes and communicates the sense of loss entailed in the progress of Roman history, but he embraces the human implications of that loss. And this genuine sensitivity does not mean Anchises is merely mouthing a Party Line when he prescribes the extent of the imperial Roman task:

> excudent alii spirantia mollius aera
> (credo equidem), vivos ducent de marmore vultus,
> orabunt causas melius, caelique meatus
> describent radio et surgentia sidera dicent:
> tu regere imperio populos, Romane, memento
> (hae tibi erunt artes), pacisque imponere morem,
> parcere subiectis et debellare superbos.
>
> (VI, 847-853)

> Others will cast more tenderly in bronze
> Their breathing figures, I can well believe,
> And bring more lifelike portraits out of marble;
> Argue more eloquently, use the pointer
> To trace the paths of heaven accurately
> And accurately foretell the rising stars.

---

[6] Steele Commager, "Introduction," in Virgil: A Collection, p. 4.

> Roman remember by your strength to rule
> Earth's peoples--for your arts are to be these:
> To pacify, to impose the rule of law,
> To spare the conquered, battle down the proud.
> (VI, 1145-1154)

Thus, when Aeneas is learning <u>Romanitas</u>, he is acquiring--or more precisely enhancing--those qualities required to govern an empire <u>and</u> <u>abandoning</u> <u>all</u> <u>others</u>. This process is accelerated once he lands in Italy, for the necessity of its completion is greater, but nowhere in the epic does Aeneas' mission in Italy mean simply locating that ever-receding promised land. He demonstrates his superior inner discipline in contrast to Turnus, but he has already done so in relation to Dido. It is in Italy that he is introduced to the site and the ethos of Rome, but in leaving Carthage he has already shown himself a Roman. In Evander's house he is inducted into Roman simplicity, Roman contempt for Oriental luxury, but, again, his purgation at Carthage was both more personal and more thoroughgoing.

<u>Propaganda</u> <u>for</u> <u>Patriarchy</u>

Just as the Roman Empire involved more than territorial expansion, Italy was never merely a geographical destination for Aeneas. Augustan Rome would have recognized it as a political one. Virgil makes it into an ethical one. The conflict is never between two abstractions called "love" and "duty", but rather between a global concept of the state and those forces that would be fatal to its power. Especially in the last third of the <u>Aeneid</u>, Virgil goes to great lengths to emphasize that tenderness, generosity, and love are not to be banished from the Roman community. But the modes in which these qualities are expressed are severely limited and often highly stylized. In no case do they include open sexual expression.

To explain this, I believe it is essential to understand the function of sexuality in the imperial design. The family was the fundamental sexual institution in Roman society and played a central role in Augustan political thought. The early Empire crystallized a number of changes in Roman marriage. Some of these are regarded by modern commentators as "progressive," representing the breakdown of traditional patriarchal power; others, instituted by law and intended to strengthen the patriarchal system, appear to oppose this tendency. It seems to me that these are not contradictory trends and that both reflect a similar awareness of the state's dependence upon a patriarchal pattern of authority and inheritance. The more "modern" forms are simply the measure of a society that had become sophisticated enough to replace tribal institutions with legal ones more efficiently fulfilling the same function.

The reign of Augustus has been described as one in which less rigid marriages became customary at the upper levels of society. "Free marriage is widely practiced at the beginning of the period...but the old idea of the matron in her husband's power persists."[7] What this rather opaque statement means is that the ceremonial forms of marriage were less important than had been the case earlier, and that it was those rites, confarreatio and coemptio, that had symbolized the transfer of the bride from her father's authority to that of her husband. So-called "free marriage" did not involve such formal transfer, normally requiring

---

[7] Anne (Ruggles) Bromberg, "Concordia: Studies in Roman Marriage Under the Empire," Diss. Radcliffe, 1961, p. 30.

only the statement of intent for its fulfillment, and leaving the bride in her father's power.

Emancipation of the Roman matron was neither the motive nor the result of the decline of specified authority as a component of marriage. The original forms, assuring the husband literal possession of his wife, served to enforce the legitimacy of the heirs and the inheritance of a man's property by his own sons. In matrilineal societies, there are usually few restrictions on women's sexual behavior, since inheritance is assured. It is always possible, after all, to determine who a child's mother is. The fact of fatherhood, however, is a matter of faith, and in societies where all power and property pass through the male line, institutions are devised to justify that faith. Female chastity is essential to such a system and the wife's sexual capacity becomes, itself, a kind of property. Thus, the confarreatio, a patrician marriage form that may eventually have been further restricted to priests, involved a deed of transfer placing the wife under her husband's authority. Coemptio was the corresponding plebian form, being a ritual version of the primitive custom of bride-price, with a stylized "sale" as the basis of the ceremony. The contract was essentially a deed of purchase giving the husband full legal rights over his wife's person and estate. In both cases, the wife's powerless situation was designed to protect the passage of inheritance from father to son. When these forms disappeared and were replaced by somewhat looser ceremonial modes, it was because Roman society no longer relied on the biological bond alone for transferring power to the next generation. Property rights were secured by formal testamentary arrangements and by a body of law relating to bequests and adoption. "From the state's point of view it was essential to get the power and property relations right, since the <u>familia</u> was the basic social unit."[8]

Alterations in the wedding ceremony, therefore, are not an adequate index of the decline of patriarchy. More reliable ones have to do with the possibility of a woman's acting legally in her own right or owning property, the rising divorce rate, the declining birth rate, and the requirement of the bride's consent to a marriage.[9] All of these were contemporary with the adoption of marriage forms that did not place the wife under her husband's authority. Although the main fact, that of inheritance, was still assured, these other changes were widely regarded as indices of social instability. The survival and extension of the Roman Empire required a consistent means of transferring authority and also an ethic of stability. Augustus found both in the myth of the traditional Roman family.

Although new forms were evolving to perpetuate patriarchal power in the private sphere, Augustus understood that those means were insufficient to preserve it in the public realm. If both were to survive, the Roman family had to be imbued with the same sense of solidity and inevitability his propaganda imparted to the Roman state. In this sense, the "reactionary" new marriage statutes complement, rather than contradict more "progressive" marriage trends. Practices had arisen in response to a more complex superstructure that formalized economic arrangements through documents, records, and law courts. Augustus believed it was vital that these

---

[8] M.I. Finley, "The Silent Women of Rome," in <u>Aspects of Antiquity: Discoveries and Controversies</u> (London: Chatto and Windus, 1968), p. 132. On the legal aspects see Percy Ellwood Corbett, <u>The Roman Law of Marriage</u> (Oxford: The Clarendon Press, 1930), especially pp. 71-85.

[9] Bromberg, pp. 32-33. It should be stressed that these social phenomena characterized the propertied classes, not Roman society as a whole.

new practices involve not only the material substance of patriarchy, but the ideology as well.

All the reforms inaugurated by the Emperor emphasized traditional values and their relation to Rome's "greatness." Personal abstemiousness, elevation of public needs over private ones, acceptance of military discipline and administrative authority were the self-proclaimed Roman virtues and were, indeed, foundations of the kind of power Rome exercised. The patriarchal family ideally reflected those virtues and transmitted them, along with the Empire they protected, to the next generation. George Thomson sardonically observes of the probably patriarchal Latins that, because of this system, they were "already one step ahead of the other Italic tribes--the first on the road to world conquest."[10]

In the Augustans' romantic view of the past, the ideal of a solemn marriage in which the wife is chaste, hard-working, fertile, and faithful to death or beyond was sanctioned by national history.[11] Augustan marriage law embodied this view of the tradition. Like the poetry of Virgil, the legislation was apparently intended to have the force of propaganda, rather than more immediate social effects. This body of law reiterated strictures against adultery, which, in practice, was regarded as criminal only if committed by a woman. It penalized childlessness, celibacy, and even tardy remarriage, while it honored producers of three or more children. Order in the family was a social virtue; a disorderly family life was an offence to the state.

---

[10] George Thomson, Studies in Ancient Greek Society: The Prehistoric Aegean, 3rd ed. (New York: The Citadel Press, 1961), p. 99.

[11] Bromberg, pp. 39, 41.

Virgil

Augustan art focused on the same themes as the <u>Leges Iuliae de Maritandis Ordinibus</u>, the imperial marriage code. The identity of Roman destiny and family stability was conveyed through the image of the imperial family itself. Dynastic symbolism combines with the private family virtues and implies a necessary and permanent connection between them. When Bromberg maintains that in visual art "the imperial family usually is represented for dynastic reasons, rather than as embodiments of the value of marriage," she ignores the fundamental unity of these two elements in the Emperor's own thought.[12] The reliefs on the Ara Pacis Augustae, one of the central monuments of the early Empire, give a deliberate prominence to the imperial family. Their presence at the ceremony the sculptor commemorates was significant in itself, particularly in view of the yet-unsettled succession. But their inclusion reflects even more emphatically the idea of the family as a fundamental component of the <u>state</u>, "as basic as the priests, senate, and people or the solemnity of sacrifice."[13] The tensions within Augustus' family and the bitter divisions to which they gave rise were clearly related to the dynastic questions the Emperor faced. But neither the dissension nor its cause has any place in the static Imperial-Family icon as the artist memorialized it.

Virgil's own vision encompassed the more general Roman view of family and state, as well as the specifically Augustan elements. His Fourth Eclogue is based on the figurative association of the New Age with its first-born son. In the course of the Eclogue, the metaphor of childbirth transcends

---

[12] <u>Ibid.</u>, pp. 36-37.

[13] <u>Ibid.</u>, p. 39.

the limits of figurative language and achieves a kind of autonomy, such that the ideas of family, children, the racial future, and the empire come to partake of the same level of reality. In the *Aeneid* itself, there is a moment of even greater complexity. Venus has induced Vulcan to make weapons for her son. Vulcan agrees, receives his sexual reward and, afterwards, falls heavily asleep on his wife's breast. His awakening is described as taking place at the hour

>...cum femina primum,
> cui tolerare colo vitam tenuique Minerva
> impositum, cinerem et sopitos suscitat ignis
> noctem addens operi, famulasque ad lumina longo
> exercet penso, castum ut servare cubile
> coniugis et possit parvos educere natos
> (VIII, 408-413)

> When a poor woman whose hard lot it is
> To make a living by her loom and spindle,
> Pokes up the embers, wakes the sleeping fire,
> Adding some night-time to her morning's work,
> And by the firelight keeps her household maids
> Employed at their long task--all to keep chaste
> Her marriage bed and bring her children up...
> (VIII, 549-555)

In its detail and its subtlety, this image is Dantesque before the fact, and it has attracted the attention of many commentators who sentimentalize Virgil's approach. What happens, in fact, is that Vulcan awakes to set his Cyclopes to work forging arms for Aeneas. These arms include the famous shield, with its sculptured synthesis of future Roman glories. The reference to the working mother and her preparations for the day's tasks are not meant, as some commentators suggest, to show that the "little people" also make their contribution, much less as an earnest of Virgil's all-comprehending soul. If anything, it is a reminder that the imperial grandeur depicted on the shield is in fact structurally dependent on the Roman woman laboring in the domestic sphere to keep herself chaste and her family inviolate.

Dido and the Education of the Patriarch

But the *Aeneid* is a narrative. Unlike sculpture or pastoral, it cannot settle for static pronouncements about the relation between sexual and imperial institutions; it must explore and analyze the question. In the Dido episode, Virgil does precisely this, devoting the greatest energy and sympathy to the forces he must exclude from the emerging Roman state. Because of this very sympathy, many readers have treated the Fourth Book as an attractive and detachable story, one that can be divorced from its epic context. Thus separated from the whole, it became the favorite of the Roman, as well as the modern audience. It has inspired some fifty tragedies and twenty-five operas, works that, whatever their several shortcomings, recognize the essentially dramatic nature of the Book. Virgil consciously imposes the modalities of the drama upon the epic pattern, and it is the poetic success of the Dido story that makes it possible to take it out of context and obscures its wider political significance.

For Virgil's immediate audience, the Book's general politics were reinforced by a topical reference. The figure of Dido stands in some measure for that of Cleopatra. Like

Dido, the Egyptian queen was a towering force in the history of her day. But she was the declared enemy of Octavian, Aeneas' imperial descendant, and represented the power of the East in its struggle with the Augustan West. Her "Oriental" nature, always emphasized in Roman propaganda despite her Greek origin, implied unbridled sensuality. In Aeneas' affair with Dido, the Roman reader saw a threatening parallel with the sexual enslavement that was Antony's supposed fate. The opulence of Dido's surroundings and the magnificence of her passion prefigure that other queen who opposed imperial destiny. Moreover, Virgil's choice of language underlines the similarity. Dido's face as she unsheathes her lover's sword on her funeral pyre is described as <u>pallida morte futura</u> (VIII, 709) [her sick pallor grew/ Before her coming death (IV, 895-896)], a phrase echoed in the description of Cleopatra on the shield that Vulcan makes for Aeneas: <u>pallentem morte futura</u> (VIII, 709) [pallid with death to come (VIII, 960)]. The essence of Cleopatra to Romans living in the wake of her legend was to impede the Empire and destroy the hero; Virgil's public was well prepared to accept the same lesson about Dido and, in so doing, confirm the official version of the Cleopatra story.

The recently-defeated threat from the East only assured a ready comprehension of the Dido episode. It does not explain the scope or the seriousness of the event as Virgil depicts it. Nor does the customary Renaissance interpretation, with its reading of the affair as a temptation that the hero must overcome on his way to spiritual perfection. Such an allegory, suitably purged of its Christian overtones, might have blended well enough with Augustan sexual ideology. But Virgil does not make it that easy. He presents the female possibility in its fullest dimension before he purges it from the imperial state.

Virgil

When Virgil refers to Dido or when Aeneas addresses her, it is most often with the word that names her character as well as her position: <u>regina</u>, the queen. The reader first learns of her when Venus, disguised as a young huntress, tells Aeneas about the city he is approaching. Her story stresses the queen's heroism, courage, cleverness, and inner strength. The tale of her flight from Phoenicia and her precarious establishment of a new city faintly echoes Aeneas' own situation and underlines her similar public role. Dido's first appearance, accoutered like Diana, is splendid, and the joy that it conveys is communal, for she does not merely enter on cue in royal costume, but exercising her state functions:

> regina ad templum, forma pulcherrima Dido,
> incessit magna iuvenum stipante caterva.
> qualis in Eurotae ripis aut per iuga Cynthi
> exercet Diana choros, quam mille secutae
> hinc atque hinc glomerantur Oreades; illa
>   pharetram
> fert umero gradiensque deas supereminet omnis
> (Latonae tacitum pertemptant gaudia pectus):
> talis erat Dido, talem se laeta ferebat
> per medios instans operi regnisque futuris.
> tum foribus divae, media testudine templi,
> saepta armis solioque alte subnixa resedit.
> iura dabat legesque viris, operumque laborem
> partibus aequabat iustis aut sorte trahebat
>   (I, 496-508)

The queen paced toward the temple in her beauty,
Dido, with a throng of men behind.
As on Eurotas bank or Cynthus ridge

> Diana trains her dancers, and behind her
> On every hand the mountain nymphs appear,
> A myriad converging; with her quiver
> Slung on her shoulders, in her stride she seems
> The tallest, taller by a head than any,
> And joy pervades Latona's quiet heart:
> So Dido seemed, in such delight she moved
> Amid her people, cheering on the toil
> Of a kingdom in the making. At the door
> Of the goddess' shrine, under the temple dome,
> All hedged about with guards on her high throne,
> She took her seat. Then she began to give them
> Judgments and rulings, to apportion work
> With fairness, or assign some tasks by lot...
>
> (I, 676-692)

Fastidious critics have found Virgil's appropriation of the Diana image inept. The simile, they argue, is borrowed from Homer's description of Nausicaa and is suitable for the virgin princess, inappropriate for the widowed queen.[14] But the mention of Diana recalls Dido's independence and her voluntary chastity, so unlike Nausicaa's nubile expectancy. It also introduces the hunt motif that characterizes this episode and Dido's downfall, by showing her at the height of her power, as huntress. It also places her law-giving in the context of religious obligation. And, coming immediate-

---

[14] Pöschl, p. 68, recapitulates the orthodox arguments on this issue. It should also be pointed out that Dido's costume, far from being incongruous or harmonizing only with an awkward simile, is accepted Carthaginian garb. As the disguised Venus explains, "virginibus Tyriis mos est gestare pharetram/purpureoque alte auras vincere coturno" (I, 336-337). [Tyrian girls/Are given to wearing quivers and hunting boots/Of crimson, laced on the leg up to the knee (I, 457-459).]

ly after the description of the Amazon Penthesilea, it is an equally strong image, but one that emphasizes that _this_ just and noble ruler is unequivocally a woman.

This last point is important to stress because so many modern writers superimpose their own rigid notions of "masculine" and "feminine" on the character of Dido. There is admiration--but surely no heavy irony--in the famous description, <u>dux femina facti</u>. Some critics, however, speaking of Dido at this stage of her life, are unable to accept that mild verbal paradox. Their view of Dido as reigning monarch is that she is masculine, because the virtues she exemplifies are conventionally manly--and heroic. Thus, upon first hearing of Dido, Aeneas is said to admire the queen's virile energy,[15] and she herself is described as performing the functions of captain, administrator, and judge like one of the old patriarchal kings.[16]

From this perspective, Dido becomes a real woman only when she succumbs to her passion for Aeneas; once more the reader is expected to accept some unspecified (and presumably universal) definition of what is "feminine." Even a critic who sees her as womanly from the first assumes that everyone knows what that means and refers to "la singolare naturalezza, nell'animo della Regina, delle prime impressioni, spiccatamente muliebri." [The remarkable naturalness of the first, strikingly feminine, impressions on the queen's soul.][17] The majority of commentators, however,

---

[15] Alfonso Donato, <u>Didone: o, Amore di terra lontana</u> (Naples, A. Miccoli, 1940), p. 17.

[16] Paolo Fabbri, <u>Virgilio, poeta sociale e politico</u> (Milan: Societa Editrice Dante Alighieri, 1929), p. 215.

[17] Giuseppe Costa, <u>La Psicologia della passione amorosa in Didone</u> (Eneide: libri I e IV) (Padua: G. Pesavento e figli, 1930), p. 8.

agree with Sainte-Beuve that it is love which reveals in Dido "toutes les tendresses et les secrets féminins." This transformation from virile ruler to mere female, through the power of aroused sexuality, apparently has a further stage. For, after her betrayal, "la donna scompare e resta la regina offesa." [The woman disappears and only the offended queen remains.][18] It seems to me that this Protean image of Dido is a simple-minded way of looking at a complex character and that it is wiser to approach her as Virgil did, without reductive categories.

Dido's complexity is reflected in the way she resists her feeling for Aeneas. Forbes is quite alone in his view of her as a widow "desperately lonely for companionship with someone who is her peer," to whom Aeneas "looks like the answer to persevering prayer."[19] Scholarly opinion generally accepts Virgil's picture of her as the ideal one-man woman, refusing to distort her into a pathetic creature unaware of her needs or a conventional dirty joke about the widowed state. In fact, an important element in the poet's vision of her is that initially she is like Aeneas--so much so that their epithets may be used interchangeably. And it is their *pietas*, their devotion to duty, that eventually precludes their love.

For Dido, as for Aeneas, *pietas* involves sexual and political responsibilities, both deriving from her status as the widow of Sychaeus. Venus' first description of the Carthaginian queen reflects a fusion of love and marital morality:

---

[18] Fabbri, p. 217.

[19] Clarence A. Forbes, "Tragic Dido," *Classical Bulletin*, 29 (1953), 58.

Virgil

> huic coniunx Sychaeus erat, ditissimus agri
> Phoenicum, et magno miserae dilectus amore,
> cui pater intactam dederat primisque iugarat
> ominibus...
> (I, 343-346)

> Her husband was Sychaeus, of all Phoenicians
> Richest in land, and greatly loved by her,
> Ill-fated woman. Her father had given her,
> A virgin still, in marriage, her first rite.
> (I, 468-471)

Her devotion was increased by the fact and the manner of his death, and her entire enterprise--the flight from Pygmalion, the theft of her brother's treasure, and the foundation of a new city--was meant to avenge him. Even as she prepares her suicide, Dido considers that part of her life a success:

> urbem praeclaram statui, mea moenia vidi,
> ulta virum poenas inimico a fratre recepi
> (IV, 655-656)

> I built a famous town, saw my great walls,
> Avenged my husband, made my hostile brother
> Pay for his crime.
> (IV, 910-912)

Dido has vowed--not, apparently to her dying husband, but to herself--that she will never remarry. It was her own sense of honor that prompted this resolution, founded on her love for Sychaeus, as well as the political role her widowhood entails. Attracted to Aeneas, she tells her sister:

> si non pertaesum thalami taedaeque fuisset,
> huic uni forsan potui succumbere culpae.
> Anna, fatebor enim, miseri post fata Sychaei
> coniugis et sparsos fraterna caede penatis
> solus hic inflexit sensus animumque labantem
> impulit...
> ille meos, primus qui me sibi iunxit, amores
> abstulit; ille habeat secum servetque sepulcro.
>
> (IV, 18-23; 28-29)

> Had I not set my face against remarriage
> After my first love died and failed me, left me
> Barren and bereaved--and sick to death
> At the mere thought of torch and bridal bed--
> I could perhaps give way in this one case
> To frailty; I shall say it: since that time
> Sychaeus, my poor husband met his fate,
> And blood my brother shed stained our hearth gods,
> This man alone has wrought upon me so
> And moved my soul to yield...
> That man who took me to himself in youth
> Has taken all my love; may that man keep it,
> Hold it forever with him in the tomb.
>
> (IV, 22-31; 38-40)

Underestimating Dido once more, Forbes says that she took her vow of faithfulness "in a frenzy of emotion and devotion."[20] In fact, the frequent references to Sychaeus thoughout Book Four are eloquent reminders of the difference between neurotic turmoil and ethical conflict. If he does

---

20 Forbes, p. 53.

not quite join "the characters and...[serve] as the third member of a love triangle," Sychaeus is nonetheless present as a moral force.[21] It is in the little chapel dedicated to him that Dido, defeated in love, seems to hear him calling her and resolves on suicide as the only honorable course. She inveigles Sychaeus' old nurse, whom she has adopted as her own, into helping her prepare for death. And in the Underworld, where she refuses to speak to Aeneas, she has been reunited with her husband, aequatque Sychaeus amorem [and Sychaeus returned her love].

Dido's mission, which she abandons for her passion and its consequences, is a political one. Like Aeneas, she has responsibilities as leader of her people, responsibilities to Carthage. In Book One, before Cupid carries out his mother's shortsighted strategy, Dido belongs unambiguously to her state function. That function is what gives her situation its dimension of classical tragedy, its "certain magnitude." It also removes the characters from a hackneyed situation in which the woman represents purely domestic emotions, while the public ones are upheld by the man. In Dido's case, moreover, the personal faith she has pledged to Sychaeus was not based on any conscientious principle, and, however genuine, would be insufficient in itself to justify the inner conflict she experiences.

The broken vow to Sychaeus has immediate political effects. Readily swayed by Anna's argument that an alliance with Aeneas would be the best thing for Carthage, Dido seeks confirmation of the gods' approval. At the same time, she escorts the Trojan hero around the site of her city. Carthage no longer seems to her a worthy end in itself, but a

---

[21] Edward Phinney, Jr., "Dido and Sychaeus," Classical Journal, 60 (1965), 357.

lure with which to attract Aeneas. In the somewhat longer run, that attempt would prove successful, for the wanderer who envied people who had a home before he even knew them is vulnerable to the appeal of a new city. At first, however, Dido's feeling is one-sided, and a few lines after she has proudly displayed the wealth of Phoenicia and the potential of Carthage, she loses interest in the whole operation:

> non coeptae adsurgunt turres, non arma iuventus
> exercet portusve aut propugnacula bello
> tuta parant: pendent opera interrupta minaeque
> murorum ingentes aequataque machina caelo.
> (IV, 86-89)

> Towers, half-built, rose
> No farther; men no longer trained in arms
> Or toiled to make harbors and battlements
> Impregnable. Projects were broken off,
> Laid over, and the menacing huge walls
> With cranes unmoving stood against the sky.
> (IV, 121-126)

The union of Dido and Sychaeus, as Virgil describes it, corresponds to Roman values about marriage and government. Dido's assumption of leadership after her husband's death is a legitimate continuation of that union--although on a more heroic scale than the Romans might find comfortable in a real woman. The widow of Sychaeus performs her public role as part of her heritage from him and as fulfillment of vengeance for his death. In the Augustan view, this is a proper extension of marital duty to the state, a correct resolution of sexual and territorial obligations. (Aeneas' marriage to Lavinia is, of course, to be another such resolution.)

After their love is consummated, Dido and Aeneas destroy this balance: She retreats from her responsibilities to Carthage and he eagerly assumes some of them. In fact, he is inspecting the renewed building activities when Mercury arrives and urges him to continue his own mission. The messenger's sardonic speech accuses Aeneas of a dereliction of duty that is simultaneously sexual and political:

> ...tu nunc Karthaginis altae
> fundamenta locas pulchramque uxorius urbem
> exstruis? heu regni rerumque oblite tuarum!
> (IV, 265-267)

> Is it for you
> To lay stones for Carthage's high walls,
> Tame husband that you are, and build their city?
> Oblivious of your own world, your own kingdom!
> (IV, 361-364)

Dido's chaste reign and Aeneas' eventual marriage place sexual relations at the service of political ends. But it is worth noting that the illicit love between Dido and Aeneas, which upsets the moral equilibrium, involves a similar fusion of sex and politics.

This message is extended through the identification of Dido with the later destiny of her city. Virgil and his audience interpreted her unfaithfulness to Sychaeus as foreshadowing the perfidy that characterized Carthage in Roman versions of history; her curse was seen as an invocation of the Punic Wars. More important, Dido's suicide prefigures Carthage's destruction. Virgil expresses it in a simile:

> non aliter quam si immissis ruat hostibus omnis
> Karthago aut antiqua Tyros, flammaeque furentes
> culmina perque hominum volvantur perque deorum
> (IV, 669-671)

> As though all Carthage or old Tyre fell
> To storming enemies, and, out of hand,
> Flames billowed on the roofs of men and gods.
> (IV, 927-929)

These lines not only anticipate what Rome was to do to Carthage, but justify it. For Dido's crime, sexually expressed, is whatever is inimical to the interests of Rome. The lesson is particularly clear for any reader to whom the simile evokes Virgil's description of Troy's fall and who recalls which elements the official ideology purged from Rome's Trojan heritage.[22]

Through Dido, Virgil makes a clear statement about the transforming power of sexual love and the danger it does to the state. Dido's own degradation is expressed in the extended metaphor of the hunt. At her first appearance, she is like Diana, in her chastity as well as her choice of sport. When she gives way to her feeling for Aeneas, Virgil

---

[22] Inheritiors of the post-Gibbon tradition may find this an unfamiliar view of Roman sexual morality. It should be borne in mind that that morality failed to include many areas of experience, especially for men. Thus, prostitution, concubinage, bisexuality, and the debauching of slaves were not forbidden to ruling class Augustan males. Excess, however, was frowned on, and for precisely the same reason that women were confined to their roles within the family unit: that _some_ kinds of sexual expression could endanger public order. M.I. Finley's article, cited above, is very useful on this issue.

Virgil

describes her as if she were literally smitten:

> uritur infelix Dido totaque vagatur
> urbe furens, qualis coniecta cerva sagitta,
> quam procul incautam nemora inter Cresia fixit
> pastor agens telis liquitque volatile ferrum
> nescius: illa fuga silvas saltusque peragrat
> Dictaeos; haeret lateri letalis harundo.
> (IV, 68-73)

> Unlucky Dido, burning, in her madness
> Roamed through all the city, like a doe
> Hit by an arrow shot from far away
> By a shepherd hunting in the Cretan woods--
> Hit by surprise, nor could the hunter see
> His flying steel had fixed itself in her:
> But though she runs for life through copse and
>   glade
> The fatal shaft clings to her side.
> (IV, 95-102)

The huntress in full command of her condition has herself become a helpless, wounded animal, the prey of an unconscious hunter; she flees, but bears her fatal pain within her.

At length, the passionate consummation occurs during a hunt. The sound of horses and riders in pursuit of wild game combines with that of the thunderstorm to create a background of heightened expectation for the sexual scene inside the cave. As the day begins, Dido appears dressed for sport, but the richness of her garb overpowers its specific function, and this time a comparison with Diana would be forced. It is Aeneas' appearance, in fact, that earns the equivalent simile:

> qualis ubi hibernam Lyciam Xanthique fluenta
> deserit ac Delum maternam invisit Apollo
> instauratque choros...
> ipse iugis Cynthi graditur mollique fluentem
> fronde premit crinem fingens atque implicat auro,
> tela sonant umeris: haud illo segnior ibat
> Aeneas, tantum egregio decus enitet ore.
> (IV, 143-150)

> Think of the lord Apollo in the spring
> When he leaves wintering in Lycia
> By Xanthus torrent, for his mother's isle
> Of Delos, to renew the festival...
> ... the god walks the Cynthian ridge alone
> And smooths his hair, binds it in fronded laurel,
> Braids it in gold; and shafts ring on his
>   shoulders.
> So elated and swift, Aeneas walked
> With sunlit grace upon him.
> (IV, 199-202; 205-209)

Dido is still magnificent, but she is not the one who recalls a divinity summoning dancers to greet the Spring.[23]

Although the cave scene is an essential part of the narrative, it also conveys some of the same symbolism as the motif of the hunt. On the literal level, the couple seeks

---

[23] Significantly, however, the Homeric description of Apollo evoked in these lines is that of the god as agent and bearer of death. (See Georg Nikolaus Knauer, <u>Die Aeneis und Homer: Studien zur poetischen technik Vergils mit Listen der Homerzitate in der Aeneis</u> [Gottingen: Vanderhoeck und Ruprecht, 1964], p. 386.)

shelter in the same cave and, while the storm rages, they finally break the sexual barriers between them. Thereafter, Dido is not concerned with keeping the affair secret, for she calls it a marriage. The reader has witnessed negotiations between Juno and Venus that have also mentioned marriage, one that would seal an alliance between the exiles from Tyre and those from Troy. Juno makes the initial offer. Since Dido has been poisoned by love, she says,

> liceat Phrygio servire marito
> dotalisque tuae Tyrios permittere dextrae.
> (IV, 103-104)

> let the queen
> Wait on her Phrygian lord, let her consign
> Into your hand her Tyrians as a dowry.
> (IV, 146-148)

She describes her plan for the actual wedding and, although the two principals are to arrive there by apparent chance and no ceremony is planned, she stresses the legitimacy of the proceedings:

> speluncam Dido dux et Troianus eandem
> devenient. adero et, tua si mihi certa volulntas,
> hic hymenaeus erit.
> (IV, 124-127)

> As Dido and the Trojan captain come
> To one same cavern, I shall be on hand,
> And if I can be certain you are willing,

> There I shall marry them, and call her his.
> A wedding, this will be.
>
> (IV, 173-177)

The goddesses still have different intentions, but the people whose interests they direct have even less control over what is happening to them. Once more, as in the simile of the doe, Dido acts wildly, out of her response to unseen forces. Juno is Dido's sponsor at her marriage and Nature assists but, although the queen later accepts it as a marriage, she is unaware at the time that she is enacting a ceremony. Aeneas, like the shepherd who does not know his bolt has found a target, is once more an unconscious agent of the same forces. He has no idea he is committing himself to anything more formal than the seemingly casual encounter in the cave. And thus, according to Roman law and his own conscience, he was in fact making no such commitment, however correct the invisible ritual may have been.

The moral decline reflected in the hunt motif is also manifested in Dido's outward behavior. Her desperate alternation of pleas and rages when she learns Aeneas is leaving is not on the elevated level of her earlier bearing and discourse. As H.L. Tracy expresses it, her character has undergone a "falling-off in quality," such that even when it again rises to the heroic, one feels Dido's suicide partakes as much of frenzy as of honor.[24] Nonetheless, she regains her former greatness through the act, because it restores her dignity. Her curse, her final speech, and her situation in the Underworld make it clear that, whatever its origin, her suicide <u>becomes</u> a moral rather than an emotional ges-

---

[24] H.L. Tracy, "<u>Aeneid</u> IV: Tragedy or Melodrama?" <u>Classical Journal</u>, 41 (1946), 201.

ture. Pöschl sees the matter in a similar light:
> The curse, besides being an expression of love become hate, restores her lost dignity. To the ancient man [sic] revenge meant restoration of his spiritual existence...the queen's pride, her self-respect, her sense of dignity...all demand her death...The very character of Dido demands that she not seek death because of lost love but because of the consciousness of her deep fall. That Queen Dido should commit suicide because of frustrated passion would seem far from great to Virgil.[25]

Sexual Expression and the Public Order

The basic question for our understanding of Virgil's intent is how much of Dido's experience takes the form it does because of her gender. Pöschl's reply is categorical: "A balance is struck between Dido and Aeneas, and the inferiority of the queen can be traced to her femininity."[26] I believe that the issue is somewhat more complicated. It is not her sex that weakens her, but her sexuality. That is, Dido is not simply a woman, but a woman in the throes of overwhelming love, and that causes her degeneration, with all its political consequences. Of course, Virgil thought that such frenzy was inherent in female sexuality. But it is important to go through these steps, as the poet did, rather than attributing to him summary conclusions about the innate temperaments associated with gender.

Such generalizations only blur Virgil's specific focus

---

[25] Pöschl, p. 86.

[26] Ibid., p. 138.

on sexuality. Forbes, for instance, sees the entire struggle as one between love and duty, wherein Dido, as a woman, inevitably chooses love, and Aeneas, a man, chooses duty.[27] Donato carries this interpretation into the realm of political hindsight, asserting that the ancestor of the race divinely destined to rule the world could not fail to place duty before love.[28] It seems to me that Aeneas does experience an inner conflict, but Virgil says nothing to suggest that love is a protagonist in that struggle. The compassion and remorse Aeneas suffers over what he does to Dido are hardly the kind of primary emotions that overcome religious and patriotic necessity. If, as Parry maintains, piety meant devotion to persons as well as to the gods and the state, Aeneas fails in his own principal virtue.[29] In comparison with Dido's torrent of feeling, his approach is emotionally shallow. This is not to say that Virgil assigns any moral superiority to Dido because of her greater capacity to feel and to express her emotions. Rather, he explicitly attributes this capacity to female nature, where that is clearly understood as a biological, not a psychological category. Thus, Dido's physical abandon is more extreme after the encounter in the cave. As Fama reports it:

> nunc hiemem inter se luxu, quam longa, fovere

---

[27] Forbes, p. 53.

[28] Donato, p. 45. The entire passage is worth reproducing, I think, if only for its devastating lack of irony about the Roman destiny: "Per il progenitore dei dominatori del mondo, per l'Eroe latino, c'era oltre l'amore, piu che l'amore, c'era cosa austera, terrible, il dovere, l'ubbidienza al Nume; non Cartagine, Roma doveva unificare il mondo e dare al mondo unificato, sue giuste leggi."

[29] Adam Parry, "The Two Voices of Virgil's Aeneid," Arion, 2 (1963), rpt. Virgil: A Collection, pp. 119-20.

Virgil

> regnorum immemores turpique cupidine captos.
> (IV, 193-194)

> They reveled all the winter long
> Unmindful of the realm, prisoners of lust.
> (IV, 264-265)

Actually, this is one of Fama's mixtures of fact and fancy. Aeneas may be neglecting his own particular mission, but not the duties of royalty. He is behaving as if the fates, no longer insisting that he pursue his search for Italy, had relaxed his destiny and granted him Carthage instead. Mercury rebukes him for abandoning his own predestined kingdom in favor of Carthage and for exercising in Dido's realm the leadership he should be reserving for his own. Dido, on the other hand, has apparently relinquished state power: While they are together, she does not fulfill her role as a queen at all, but lives through her relationship to Aeneas, through her sexuality. Similarly, the queen's grief at Aeneas' departure is expressed both in terms of the political situation in which he leaves her and her lack of a baby to comfort her. Her arguments about the legitimacy of their marriage, the threat of war, and the absence of a child by the man she loves are intertwined--as if her thinking about each is governed by the same passion.

The irony of applying Mercury's disingenuous stricture on female fickleness to the character of Dido is doubled by the way that pronouncement is often taken as a summary of <u>Virgil's</u> attitude towards her. In fact, Virgil never renders moral judgement on Dido--much less on womankind--but rather on erotic love itself. This view of sexuality is echoed elsewhere in Virgil's poetry. Almost every speech Turnus utters, for instance, contains a reference to the

<u>sexual</u> insult he feels Aeneas is offering him. He regards the struggle as primarily a battle for Lavinia's body, a prize that has no intrinsic (sexual) significance to Aeneas. Although Turnus has been, throughout, a man possessed by demoniacal forces, it is only at the last that his love and his madness are fused. Preparing for the final combat, he sneers at Aeneas as an effeminate Phrygian, and Virgil describes the extent of his obsession:

> his agitur furiis, totoque ardentis ab ore
> scintillae absistunt, oculis micat acribut ignis:
> mugitus veluti cum prima in proelia taurus
> terrificos ciet atque irasci in cornua temptat
> arboris obnixus trunco, ventosque lacessit
> ictibus aut sparsa ad pugnam proludit harena.
> (XII, 101-106)

> To this length driven by passion, he gave off
> A sparklinhg glow from his whole face, and fire
> Flashed from his eyes, as a wild bull at bay
> Will give a fearsome bellow and whet his horns
> To fury on a tree-trunk, striking blows
> Against the wind, kicking up spurts of sand
> In prelude to the fight.
> (XII, 142-148)

Turnus, like Dido, is an impressive and tragic figure. But the love that transforms him serves only to enrage and brutalize.

In the <u>Georgics</u>, this message is even more explicit. The rape of Eurydice is responsible for the hive's destruction, and the dangerous sexuality of Helen and Cleopatra is suggested. Virgil's description of love's effects on humankind is not unlike the throes conventionally depicted by Renaissance poets. Conspicuously absent, however, are those refining and ennobling qualities the sonneteers attributed to the passion:

> quid iuvenis, magnum cui versat in ossibus ignem
> durus amor? nempe abruptis turbata procellis
> nocte natat caeca serus freta; quem super ingens
> porta tonat caeli, et scopulis inlisa reclamant
> aequora; nec miseri possunt revocare parentes,
> nec moritura super crudeli funere virgo.
> (<u>Georgics</u>, III, 258-263)

> Think of a young man, burning with cruel love to
>   the bone:
> Think of him, late in the blindfold night swimming
>   the narrows
> That are vexed by headlong gales, while above his
>   head the huge
> Gates of heaven thunder and the seas collide with
>   a crash
> Against the capes: powerless to recall him his
>   sorrowful parents
> And the girl who is soon to die of grief over his
>   body.
> (<u>Georgics</u>, III, 258-263)

No distinction is made here between the affective and the erotic aspects of love. Both are experienced sexually, their violent effects on the individual foreshadowing their impact on public order.

    This passage is all the more striking in that it appears in the midst of a catalogue of animals on whom lust has damaging effects. Virgil begins with a generalization:

> ...non ulla magis viris industria firmat
> quam Venerem et caeci stimuilos avertere amoris,
> sive boum sive est cui gratior usus equorum.
> (<u>Georgics</u>, III, 209-211)

> ...the most effective way to reinforce their
>   strength
> Is to bar them off from the passion and blinding
>   goads of lust,
> Whether your fancy is the breeding of bulls or
>   horses.
> (<u>Georgics</u>, III, 209-211)

He proceeds to describe the combat of two jealous bulls, enamored of the same cow, in terms reminiscent of the simile used for Turnus. The sexual force is the same in other animals, with devastating effects on the global harmony of life:

> Omne adeo genus in terris hominumque ferarumque
> et genus aequoreum, pecudes pictaeque volucres,
> in furias ignemque ruunt: amor omnibus idem.
> tempore non alio catulorum oblita leaena
> saevior erravit campis, nec funera vulgo
> tam multa informes ursi stragemque dedere
> per silvas; tum saevus aper, tum pessima tigris
> (<u>Georgics</u>, III, 242-248)

> All manner of life on earth--men, fauna of land
>   and sea,
> Cattle and coloured birds--

Virgil

> Run to this fiery madness: love is alike for all.
> At no season but love's does the lioness so
>   neglect
> Her cubs and range so savage over the plains, or
>   the clumsy
> Bear deal out such wholesale death and destruction
>   in the woods;
> Then is the boar morose, the tigress in a wicked
>   temper
>
>   (<u>Georgics</u>, III, 242-248)

Sexual torments of the stallion and the youth come next, but the mare, whom the wind itself can impregnate, is the worst afflicted. The concluding lines of this remarkable excursus are devoted to that racing amorous beast, her passionate energy and baneful genital secretions.

Virgil himself admits that the entire section, occupying some seventy-four lines, is a digression. I have cited it at such length because it is clearly a significant one, affording insight into a constellation of inter-connected personal and social attitudes. This view is further reinforced by considering Virgil's ideal commonwealth:

> illum adeo placuisse apibus mirabere morem,
> quod neque concubitu indulgent, nec corpora segnes
> in Venerem solvunt aut fetus nixibus edunt;
> verum ipsae e foliis natos, e suavibus herbis
> ore legunt, ipsae regem parvosque Quirites
> sufficiunt, aulasque et cerea regna refigunt.
> saepe etiam duris errando in cotibus alas
> attrivere, ultroque animam sub fasce dedere:
> tantus amor florum et generandi gloria mellis.
>
>   (<u>Georgics</u>, IV, 197-205)

> Most you shall marvel at this habit peculiar to bees--
> That they have no sexual union: their bodies never dissolve
> Lax into love, nor bear with pangs of birth their young.
> But all by themselves from leaves and sweet herbs they will gather
> Their children in their mouths, keep up the queenly succession
> And the birth-rate, restore the halls and the realms of wax.
> Often, too, as they wander they bruise their wings on hard
> Rocks, happy to die in harness beneath their burdens--
> Such is their love for flowers, their pride in producing honey.
>
> (<u>Georgics</u>, IV, 197-205)

It would be frivolous, I think, to mine these passages for speculations about Virgil's psychic makeup or the degree of pathology it included. What is important is to understand the politics that inform his expression. The comparison of Dido to a wounded animal and Turnus to a maddened one seem far less fortuitous in the light of the <u>Georgics</u>. Moreover, in these lines, Virgil identifies lust as a fever that attacks and degrades both sexes, to the detriment of collective discipline and the common good. And it is in this context that Dido's condition must finally be situated.

Virgil

Lavinia: The Consolation Prize

Unlike the fortunate bees, human beings have to live with their sexuality and must develop structures where it can be expressed in ways that support, rather than weaken, the social fabric to which they are committed. As I have indicated, the Augustans perceived the Roman family as such an institution. Within the epic, Aeneas' marriage to Lavinia is intended to resolve the conflict between the state and human sexuality. This solution had historical implications, as well, becuase the imperial dynasty that Aeneas founds is similarly portayed as the natural focus for reconciliation of opposing forces.

In this regard, it is appropriate that Creusa, ancestress of the imperial family, plays the role she does in the narrative. She has borne Aeneas a son, from whom the ruling class will descend, reinforcing the Trojan roots of the imperial clan. This assured, she disappears during the flight from Troy, so that the family as rescued from the burning city reflects its Trojan origin in a strong, exclusively male line. Moreover, at the end of Book II, her apparition tells Aeneas about his future in the Western land. Because she understands his mission, she also understands why she has no part in it:

> illic res laetae regnumque et regia coniunx
> parta tibi
>
> (II, 783-784)

> the years will bear
> Glad peace, a kingdom, and a queen for you.
>
> (II, 1016-1017)

As Creusa suggests, the marriage to Lavinia is not a dynastic arrangement, but a territorial one--an imperial one. From the first, the Latin princess is identified with the land where Aeneas is to settle; their union does not signify the joining of two peoples and cultures so much as the hero's final arrival at his destination. The opening lines of the epic define that goal, employing the adjective in its neuter form, so that the name "Lavinia" appears at the very beginning. Rhetorically, as Commager points out, Lavinia is "little more than an eponym for the Italian land, Lavinium."[30] But this nomenclatural situation was by no means unique. For centuries, at a time when men were given personal names, Roman women's names were simply tribal ones with a feminine ending. Finley asserts that the resultant confusion must have been welcome, since the situation would otherwise have been easy to remedy. "It is as if the Romans wished to suggest very pointedly that women were not, or ought not to be, genuine individuals, but only fractions of a family."[31] By a similar extension, Aeneas' bride is not meant to be an individual, but a symbol of her country.

The personality that Virgil assigns her accords well with this iconological function. We learn little about Lavinia in the course of the poem, except what confirms an initial sense of her role. She is Latinus' only surviving child, his sole heir, and *iam plenis nubilis annis* [already of fully marriagable age]. It is interesting that these facts are related without the daughter's name being mentioned at all. (It first occurs some twenty lines later.) In the same expository passage, Amata is alluded to as *regia coniunx* [the royal spouse], but she is not named either.

---

[30] Commager, p. 11.
[31] Finley, p. 131.

Virgil

Certain commentators--principally Italians writing in the Mussolini period--have made a virtue of Lavinia's very colorlessness. She is supposed to be the model bride for the Roman state, dedicated to hearth and home, subject to the authority of both father and husband.[32]

Lavinia's situation also makes it clear that bonds of affection and sexual attraction have nothing to do with the intimate relationships on which the state is founded. Although Hughes speaks of Virgil's "care in the twelfth Aeneid to make us feel the love between Aeneas and Lavinia," most commentators agree that he treats that feeling with such subtlety as to render it invisible.[33] The only emotions Lavinia displays are directed towards her mother and Turnus. Filial love is the stronger of these passions and, because of Amata's manipulations, is even reponsible for some of the warmth the princess feels for her original suitor. There is certainly no implication that the defeat of Turnus and the consequent marriage to Aeneas are as catastrophic for Lavinia as they would be had Turnus' passion been mutual. When her parents beg Turnus not to fight Aeneas, Lavinia responds with silent emotion:

> accepit vocem lacrimis Lavinia matris
> flagrantis perfusa genas, cui plurimus ignem
> subiecit rubor et calefacta per ora cucurrit.
> Indum sanguineo veluti violaverit ostro

---

[32] See, for instance, Fabbri, especially pp. 221-2. Fabbri also observes that because Lavinia does not emerge from the shadows, she is "più respettabile e come sacra." He also makes the curious suggestion that her silence and docility were Virgil's rebuke to the great freedom allegedly permitted to unmarried girls in his own day.

[33] Merritt Y. Hughes, "Our Virgil?" University of California Chronicle, 32 (1930), 442.

> si quis ebur, aut mixta rubent ubi lilia multa
> alba rosa: talis virgo dabat ore colores.
>
> (XII, 64-69)

> Lavinia, listening to her mother, streamed
> With tears on burning cheeks; a deepening blush
> Brought out a fiery glow on her hot face.
> As when one puts a stain of crimson dye
> On ivory of India, or when
> White lilies blush, infused with crimson roses,
> So rich the contrast in her coloring seemed.
>
> (XII, 92-99)

At this moment, manifesting her feeling for the doomed captain she is not to marry, Lavinia appears at her most beautiful. But to yield a true estimate of Lavinia's involvement, the restraint of this portrait has to be contrasted with the depiction of Turnus as enraged bull, which follows almost immediately.

All the images of Lavinia are negative: not speaking, not demonstrating individual traits, not showing deep feeling. The effect is one of tremendous passivity, aptly corresponding to her political role. Lavinia is a pawn in the struggle between her parents, just as she is in the larger struglge that engenders it. Even the moment when her destiny is revealed shows her basic lack of autonomy:

> praeterea, castis adolet dum altaria taedis,
> et iuxta genitorem astat Lavinia virgo,
> visa, nefas, longis comprendere crinibus ignem
> atque omnem ornatum flamma crepitante cremari,
> regalisque accensa comas, accensa coronam
> insignem gemmis tum fumida lumine fulvo

Virgil

> involvi ac totis Volcanum spargere tectis.
> (VII, 71-77)

> While the old king lit fires at the altars
> With a pure torch, the girl Lavinia with him,
> It seemed her long hair caught, her head-dress
>   caught,
> In crackling flame, her queenly tresses blazed,
> Her jewelled crown blazed. Mantled then in smoke
> And russet light, she scattered divine fire
> Through all the house.
> (VII, 94-100)

The gods mark Lavinia as they did Ascanius on the night Troy burned. For her, as for him, the miraculous fire presages a glorious individual destiny within a national calamity. When Iulus is touched by the divine fire, however, it is a sign of hope for his family, and stirs them to the action that makes it possible to fulfill his destiny. Lavinia's more dramatic flaming only heightens the sense that she is helpless and acted upon by fate. Throughout the *Aeneid*, we encounter characters whose personal and social destinies are determined by fate; we watch them as they try to learn what the future holds, as they struggle with its implacable conditions, and are controlled by irresistible forces. Lavinia is the only one who, in the face of destiny, appears to abdicate her own autonomy.

This resigned powerlessness reflects the function of Lavinia in later Roman rhetoric. In the *Silvae* of Statius, for example, the newly married bride is described in terms of Ilia, Lavinia, and Claudia. Venus is not present at the wedding, and the goddess of love is invoked only as *genetrix Aeneia*. Trojan descent and dynastic stability are the values sustained in the epithalamion, within which Aeneas' Latin bride takes her rightful place. Marriage to Lavinia means Rome's retention of the heritage of Trojan legitimacy, strengthened by both the purging of Eastern elements and the union with the Italic soil. This is the public myth to which Virgil's narrative contributes.

But it is hardly a satisfying solution. What happens to Dido is an aesthetic as well as a historical necessity. The second half of the epic contains many elements that make up for the missing fire of the earlier books. Aeneas' marriage with Lavinia is not one of them, for it does not fully resolve the questions Virgil has raised so poignantly. Parry makes an observation about the larger political issue that also applies to this aspect of it:

> The explicit message of the Aeneid claims that Rome was a happy reconciliation of the natural virtues of the local Italian peoples and the civilized might of the Trojans who were to found a new city. But the tragic movement of the last books of the poem carries a different suggestion: that the formation of Rome's empire involved the loss of the pristine purity of Italy.[34]

In much the same way, the formation of Rome's empire demanded the loss of Dido, abandonment of the sexual and emotional power she embodies. The dynamic of the poem prepares us to accept that. But Virgil is eloquent about what he excludes from the Roman state, pallid about what he admits. Ending up with Lavinia in no sense compensates for the sacrifice.

---

[34] Parry, p. 110.

Virgil

<u>Sex</u> <u>and</u> <u>Social</u> <u>Character</u>

A similar drama of inadequate resolutions occurs on another plane, where opposing <u>qualities</u> are identified as male or female, and where the figure of Camilla is supposed to represent a successful balance. The masculine side of this conflict is more readily defined, for Virgil was working within a cultural tradition that "knew" what manliness was. Moreover, Aeneas himself possesses most of the virtues that comprise that masculine profile. He is courageous, but he is not a "wild man." His conduct in battle, as in personal life, reflects dignity, control, strength and reserve; where these break down, as in the epic's final scene, it is because he is overcome by passionate loyalty. Devotion to honor and duty, with all the concrete implications these abstractions entail, characterize his moral life.

Other instances are called for, however, to flesh out and enrich the personification of the male principle. Thus, for instance, the funeral games that occupy most of Book V extend the vision of manhood Aeneas' character affords. It is significant that these games appear <u>where</u> they do. Although they mark the anniversary of Anchises' death, they occur just after Dido's suicide. Hers is the death that is fresh in the reader's mind, with its details of feeling and gesture circumstantially rendered. That was the extreme of feminine expression. The games, part of a patriarchal ritual, are the masculine response. There is great energy, along with magnificent order and discipline, in the contests. The spirit of competition is high and enthusiastically encouraged, although success crowns those efforts that demonstrate piety and self-control, along with the desire for glory. Ascanius and the other boys conclude the event with a complex cavalry exercise and mock-battle. Virgil's audience would have recognized these boys as representatives of the major Augustan clans; the youths also reflected the masculine Roman virtues at their best and thus embodied the promise of the national future. Here, at the games dedicated to Anchises, they make their contribution to patriarchal and dynastic continuity, for:

> hunc morem cursus atque haec certamina primus
> Ascanius, Longam muris cum cingeret Albam,
> rettulit et priscos docuit celebrare Latinos,
> quo puer ipse modo, secum quo Troia pubes;
> Albani docuere suos; hinc maxima porro
> accepit Roma et patrium servavit honorem;
> Troiaque nunc pueri, Troianum dicitur agmen.
> hac celebrata tenus sancto certamina patri.
> (V, 596-603)

> This mode of drill, this mimicry of war,
> Ascanius brought back in our first years
> When he walled Alba Longa; and he taught
> The ancient Latins to perform the drill
> As he had done with other Trojan boys.
> The Albans taught their children, and in turn
> Great Rome took up this glory of the founders.
> The boys are called Troy now, the whole troop
>   Trojan.
> (V, 770-777)

The tale of Nisus and Euryalus, in Book IX, provides a romantic and more directly military setting for the manly virtues. Courage is underscored, to the point of savagery and recklessness, for it is inspired by loyalty to the Trojan cause and its leader. The two are remarkable, however, for their devotion to each other, which is the affective basis of the episode. Their mutual attachment serves to reinforce their patriotism and thus strengthen the evolving idea of Rome. That is the vein in which, after describing their death, Virgil memorializes them:

> Fortunati ambo! si quid mea carmina possunt,
> nulla dies umquam memori vos eximet aevo,
> dum domus Aeneae Capitoli immobile saxum
> accolet imperiumque pater Romanus habebit.
> (IX, 446-449)

> Fortunate, both! If in the least my songs
> Avail, no future day will ever take you
> Out of the record of remembering Time,
> While children of Aeneas make their home
> Around the Capital's unshaken rock,
> And still the Roman Father governs all.
> (IX, 633-638)

It is worth observing that this is the kind of love that Virgil considers proper and holy, love that finds its outlet in service to the beloved and the state, rather than in sexual expression. It is also noteworthy, I believe, that the protagonists are both male. Ironically, this incident contains one of the poem's last references to Dido, as Ascanius offers as reward to Nisus and Euryalus, the fortunate pair who earn their death together, <u>cratera antiquum quem dat Sidonia Dido</u> [the ancient winebowl that was Sidonian Dido's gift].

Both of these archetypally "masculine" events have their "feminine" counterpoint in the narrative. The description of funeral games, preceded by Dido's despairing suicide, is immediately followed by the rebellion of the Trojan women. While the men parade their athletic prowess in honor of the dead patriarch, the women mourn Anchises in their own way, weeping and remembering. The malevolent Juno sends Iris among them, disguised as an elderly matron, Beroe, who is respected by the others for the losses she has suffered. Speaking to the very real frustration and misery these women have experienced, Iris encourages defeatism, suggests remaining where they are and, to accomplish this, urges them to burn the Trojan ships, the "cause" of their ceaseless wanderings. Pyrgo argues that the speaker is not really Beroe, but a divine visitor; her emphasis on the ailing Beroe's desire to be present and pay her duty to Anchises implies that if Iris' true (if divine) identity were known, her advice would be spurned. Yet the women waver <u>inter amorem/praesentis terrae fatisque vocantia regna</u> [half in unhappy love/of landscape there before them, half still bound/to fated realms calling them onward] until the goddess reveals herself and flies upward, upon which a wild frenzy takes hold of them:

>   cum dea se paribus per caelum sustulit alis
>   ingentemque fuga secuit sub nubibus arcum.
>   tum vero attonitae monstris actaeque furore
>   conclamant, rapiuntque focis penetralibus ignem
>   (pars spoliant aras), frondem ac virgulta facesque
>   coniciunt. furit immissis Volcanus habenis
>   transtra per et remos et pictas abiete puppis.
>   (V, 657-663)

>   The goddess on strong wings went up the sky
>   Traversing a great rainbow under clouds.
>   Now truly wrought upon by signs and wonders,

Virgil

> Wrought to a frenzy, all cried out together,
> Snatching up fire from hearths, despoiling altars,
> Taking dry foliage, brush, and brands to throw.
> And Vulcan, god of fire, unbridled raged
> Through rowing thwarts and oars and piney hulls.
> (V, 850-857)

In the grip of their madness, the matrons act without reason, attacking the Trojans' only means of reaching the promised kingdom. The assault is short-lived and is quelled by Ascanius almost before his father, interrupted at the solemn memorial rites, arrives on the scene. As Aeneas enters and the fire rages on, the women flee:

> ast illae diversa metu per litora passim
> diffugiunt, silvasque et sicubi concava furtim
> saxa petunt: piget incepti lucisque, suosque
> mutatae agnoscunt excussaque pectore Iuno est.
> (V, 676-679)

> But the women scattered here and there in fear
> Along the beaches, in the woods, wherever
> They could take cover in rock caves, ashamed
> To face the daylight, face what they had done--
> For now they knew their own, and their shocked
>   hearts
> Were free of Juno.
> (V, 875-880)

In their fury, the matrons were less than human; in their shame, they are like frightened children or household pets. Their legitimate grievances are submerged in the total irrationality of their action, and when the passion leaves them, nothing is left but a few dispersed, cowering creatures.[35] The word Virgil most often uses for the ladies is <u>matres</u> [mothers], which in this context conveys no sense of dignity and status. These women are the mothers of the tribe and their behavior here is functionally linked to their biology; it is "hysterical."

A milder form of this female disease mars the manly exhibition of grief at the death of Nisus and Euryalus. Ascanius and his comrades are shocked to see the heads of the dead youths mounted on the Rutulians' spears, but the normal response in their culture would be to avenge them, as Aeneas was to avenge Pallas in the epic's final slaying. But the mother of Euryalus intrudes a note of hysteria:

> ...at subitus miserae calor ossa reliquit,
> excussi manibus radii revolutaque pensa.
> evolat infelix et femineo ululatu
> scissa comam muros amens atque agmina cursu
> prima petit, non illa virum, non illa pericli
> telorumque memor
>
> (IX, 475-480)

> Then all at once warm life drained from her body,
> Shuttle and skein unwound dropped from her hands.
> She flew outdoors, all wretchedness, and wailed

---

[35] In the end, of course, they get what they want, for the destruction of several ships means that some of the Trojans, including the weary matrons, <u>have</u> to stay behind. It is not in the epic vein, I suppose, to wonder what would have happened had the <u>matres</u> offered this as a suggestion to begin with. As it is, a female seer lays out the plan, whose wisdom is then confirmed by the shade of Anchises. It should be noted that this is the only time in the poem that Anchises' judgment (as distinct from the foreknowledge he reveals in Book VI) is correct.

Virgil

> As women do, tearing her hair, and ran
> To reach the rampart, in mad haste, to reach
> The front line, paying soldiers there no heed,
> No heed to danger, none to missiles.
>
> (IX, 673-679)

Worse yet, her loud lamentations influence the troops, who forget momentarily how a soldier and a real man behaves:

> hoc fletu concussi animi, maestusque per omnis
> it gemitus, torpent infractae ad proelia vires.
>
> (IX, 498-499)

> All hearts were shaken by her cries, and groans
> Of mourning came from all, their strength for
>   battle
> Broken and benumbed.
>
> (IX, 705-707)

Like the matrons who burned the ships, this unnamed woman is a Trojan mother whose motherhood has been outraged, who has endured great sorrow and incredible deprivation. She reflects the human side of war, the common pain that gives Virgil's writing its tragic undertone. Yet her behavior, again like that of the frenzied arsonists, is treated as a departure from proper norms, a lowering of the epic tone.

This is the view of female nature that pervades the poem, creating its effect even where there is no corresponding image of Roman maleness to set it off. Juno, of course, is the Trojans' major antagonist. The source of her enmity is loosely political, in that it is connected to her supporting Argos against Troy, and Carthage against Rome. But it also involves her as a female:

>   (necdum etiam causae irarum saevique dolores
>   exciderant animo; manet alta mente repostum
>   iudicium Paridis spretaeque iniuria formae
>   et genus invisum et rapti Ganymedis honores)
>   (I, 25-28)

>   the origins of that anger,
>   That suffering, still rankled: deep within her,
>   Hidden away, the judgement Paris gave,
>   Snubbing her loveliness; the race she hated;
>   The honors given ravished Ganymede...
>   (I, 38-42)

We are reminded throughout that Juno's animus assumes the forms it does because of her gender, especially after her strong identification with the unhappy Dido.

Unlike Odysseus in his wanderings, Aeneas does not encounter a variety of monsters and demons; his trials tend to come in more human shapes. It is particularly significant, therefore, that the only "traditional" horrors he has to face are female. There are, first of all, the dread Harpies:

>   tristius haud illis monstrum, nec saevior ulla
>   pestis et ira deum Stygiis sese extulit undis.
>   virginei volucrum vultus, foedissima ventris
>   proluvies uncaeque manus et pallida semper
>   ora fame.
>   (III, 214-218)

>   No gloomier monster, no more savage pest
>   And scourge sent by the gods' wrath ever mounted
>   From the black Stygian water--flying things

With young girls' faces, but foul ooze below,
Talons for hands, pale famished nightmare mouths.
(III, 297-301)

Allecto, who acts through Amata, is a similar demoniacal being, an outcast even among outcasts, seeming, like the Harpies, to be even more monstrous because she is female. Juno summons Allecto, creatress of grief, from the depths. Allecto,

...cui tristia bella
iraeque insidiaeque et crimina noxia cordi.
odit et ipse pater Pluton, odere sorores
Tartareae monstrum: tot sese vertit in ora,
tam saevae facies, tot pullulat atra colubris.
(VII, 325-329)

Grief's dear mistress, with her lust for war,
For angers, ambushes, and crippling crimes.
Even her father Pluto hates this figure,
Even her hellish sisters, for her myriad
Faces, for her savage looks, her head
Alive and black with snakes.
(VII, 445-450)

Allecto is the source of Amata's madness, which builds on the queen's preference for Turnus and her idea that he was her promised son-in-law. The latter is a self-delusion, like Dido's notion that she was realy married to Aeneas, but it is not madness. Amata is also susceptible because of her sex: She is in a state of rage over the broken "betrothal" to Turnus and full of a (natural) concern Virgil calls "feminine" over what the Trojans' arrival portends. When the poison takes hold, she runs wild, racing about the city and fleeing to the woods. Her frenzy is Dionysian:

> quin etiam in silvas simulato numine Bacchi
> maius adorta nefas maioremque orsa furorem
> evolat et natam frondosis montibus abdit,
> quo thalamum eripiat Teucris taedasque moretur,
> euhoe Bacche fremens, solum te virgine dignum
> vociferans: etenim mollis tibi sumere thyrsos,
> te lustrare choro, sacrum tibi pascere crinem.
> (VII, 385-391)

> she feigned
> Bacchic possession, daring a greater sin
> And greater madness. Off to the woods she ran,
> Into the leafy hills, and hid her child
> To snatch a marriage from the Teucrians
> Or to postpone the wedding. "Evoe,
> Bacchus," she shrilled out, and then cried again
> That you alone, the god, deserved the girl,
> Who held an ivy thyrsus in your honor
> And danced for you, and let her hair grow long,
> Sacred to you.
> (VII, 530-540)

This is the sole imaginable alternative to the hearth and the patriarchal family: wildness, savagery, and the rituals of an abandon whose only "normal" analogue is unbridled sexuality. Amata's expression of her grief is reminiscent of Dido's when she learns that Aeneas is planning to steal away from Carthage. Dido too runs distracted through the streets, and she, like Amata, is compared to a Bacchante at the orgies on Cithaeron.

Virgil

If individual women aroused to fury resemble one another, so do groups of frenzied females. Amata leads the Latin matrons to behavior that is as wild as her own and that echoes the riot of the Trojan matrons:

> fama volat, furiisque accensas pectore matres
> idem omnis simul ardor agit nova quaerere tecta;
> deseruere domos, ventis dant colla comasque;
> ast aliae tremulis ululatibus aethera complent
> pampineasque gerunt incinctae pellibus hastas.
> (VII, 392-396)

> As word of this went round,
> Laurentine mothers fired by sudden madness
> Felt the same passion to acquire new homes.
> They left the old ones, baring to the wind
> Their necks and hair, while some in fawnskin dress
> Filled heaven with long quavering cries and bore
> Vine-covered wand-spears.
> (VII, 541-546)

This time, Virgil does not simply refer to them as matres; he has Amata conjure them by their motherhood, by their female sexual capacity, to throw off their bonds, loosen their hair, and join her outrageous primitive rites. And it is through their sexuality that they respond and join her in the woods.

Finally, there is Juturna, goddess of pools and rivers, who holds this high office in exchange for her virginity. She is Turnus' sister and, urged on by Juno, she takes an active part in the final battle, bravely adding to the chaos and bloodshed and protecting her brother as long as possible. In the Virgilian moral vocabulary, both the fierceness of her attachment and the way it is expressed are thoroughly feminine.

What alternatives does Virgil offer to the rampaging female condition? On the one hand, there is Lavinia, submitting with equal docility to Bacchic rituals or political marriage. On the other, there is Camilla, the warrior maiden. Camilla is often regarded as an androgynous figure, combining the virtues of both sexes. In fact, she is so striking and impressive a personality precisely because Virgil deliberately removes her, if not from the fact of gender, from the realm of sexuality.

Nearly half of Book XI is devoted to Camilla, whom Turnus invites to share command over the Italian troops. The scenes in which Camilla appears are among the freshest in the epic, presenting the vigor and excitement of battle without Virgil's usual lurking horror at the realities of war. Her progress is pure and beautiful, like her body, so that both terms in the phrase "virgin warrior" are equally significant.

Her character is similarly undefiled. As a soldier, she is fearless and highly skilled, the incarnation of the goddess who protects her. Unlike Turnus and most of the other soldiers Virgil depicts, she is not cruel, although, like them, she rises to glorious rage. She is a strong and inspiring leader in battle and she is straightforward, guileless. Camilla must die defending the old, purer Italy, but she reflects the moral ideal of Virgil's Rome, an ideal that was always envisaged as masculine.

What, then, is feminine about her, aside from her unquestioned membership in the female sex? When Chloreus appears on the battlefield shimmering with gold and bronze, Camilla is attracted by his accouterments and makes him her target. This is her undoing, for Chloreus, aided by Apollo

Virgil

and by his own relative purity in not seeking spoils, hurls the javelin that kills her. Virgil himself calls her eagerness for the bright plunder "feminine," an occasion Sainte-Beuve seizes upon and elaborates: "On a beau être amazone et guerrière, on est toujours femme."[36] But, as Virgil himself points out, that hunger for the pretty spoils of war is common to all soldiers, particularly the young and beautiful. It was, after all, the gleaming helmet he could not resist that betrayed Euryalus to the enemy. And it is his arrogant flaunting of Pallas' glittering belt that is responsible for the death of Turnus, for the sight of it enrages Aeneas and makes him deny a request to spare the enemy for the sake of his aged father.

What is far more important is that Camilla is not a sexual being. Dido's appearance in the costume of Diana is meant rhetorically, to demonstrate the height from which her sexuality causes her to fall. But Camilla really is a huntress and a devotee of the virgin goddess. That, and not her womanhood, is what inspires all her acts. Nor is there any suggestion that her virginity is a temporary state, that she is awaiting completion through love. Fabbri compares her with Tasso's Clorinda, declaring that Camilla is closer to "our" hearts because she is simpler and "più fanciulla"[37] [more of a maiden]. She is perpetually _fanciulla_. The Renaissance heroines who derive from her are all chaste, but they are capable of love and preparing to join their lovers in combat or marriage. They succeed because they are women;

---

[36] C-A Sainte-Beuve, _Etude sur Virgile_, 1855-56, 2nd ed. (Paris: Michel Frères, 1870), p. 182.

[37] Fabbri, p. 219. For a view of Camilla's virginity and her military role as unnatural rejections of feminine virtue, see Sister Mary Ste. Therese Wittenberg, S.N.D., "Virgil's Camilla," _Classical Bulletin,_ 42 (1966), 70.

Camilla succeeds because, by Virgil's own standards, she is not one.

In Camilla, Virgil once more presents us with a figure who is expected to resolve the conflicts between masculine and feminine elements. Instead, she reinforces the poet's view, repeated throughout the epic, that the only way to reconcile the female principle, the principle of sexuality, with the state is to purge it.

CHAPTER TWO

THE HEART AND STOMACH OF A KING

For the woman warrior to move from the periphery of the epic to its narrative and conceptual center, a dislocation of values had to occur. As a consequence of that dramatic shift, the Renaissance heroines modeled on Camilla, while retaining the Volscian princess' military prowess and commitment, also figure in the epics' amorous adventures. Their sex is emphasized; it is central, not marginal, to their heroic identity. At the same time, the female came to represent the resolution of social conflict, instead of its embodiment. This transformation did not take place because hysteria had replaced good order as a public virtue, but rather because the same "feminine" characteristics that Virgil decried had been reinterpreted in a far more favorable light.

Even within the framework established by the Aeneid, it would be possible to perceive female behavior very differently from the way Virgil construes it. Not only might Dido be understood sympathetically, with emphasis on her qualities of loyalty and passion, but the other women characters could also be redefined. Instead of stressing the uterine frenzy of the Trojan and Latin matrons, for example, one might reexamine the motives of their revolt, finding them admirable and even moving. These are women deeply concerned with maintaining a balance between private feelings and public life, unwilling to continue sacrificing the concrete and personal to an abstract masculine politics. Of course, such an attempt to "rehabilitate" characters that quite clearly represent destructive forces would be a grotesque anachronism. The real problem is to understand what made sixteenth-century writers reconsider the qualities defined as feminine and regard them as capable of making a positive contribution to the commonwealth.

So stated, the issue is immense. It is almost as if one were asking, "What was the difference between the Renaissance period and the early Roman Empire?" And that question is not merely unanswerable, it is the wrong question. In discussing the Aeneid, after all, it was not necessary to retrace Roman civilization as a whole, but rather to examine those cultural elements that informed sexual ideology in the epic and to which the poem itself was intended to contribute. The sexual values communicated by the Renaissance epic should be interpreted with reference to the same social categories: the idea of the state, the idea of the female, and the ways in which they interact. Through these definitions, it should be possible to approach the question of what it meant, in literary and social terms, for a poet to say to his patrons, "Your ancestors accomplished certain glorious, pious deeds; and, what is more, you are descended from a couple that married for love on the basis of equality demonstrated through military combat."

It is important to recognize that the social definitions at issue were not static. The period of the Renaissance was preeminently and self-consciously a time of transition, and its literature reflects the actual process of change, as well as its results. The heroic poems of Ariosto, Tasso, and Spenser provide a particularly sensitive measure of evolving ideology because their composition and publication span almost the entire course of the sixteenth century. More important, they were created with an explicit ideological function. They were not intended simply to "reflect" ideas that were being generated and implemented somewhere else in the society. Rather, they represent contributions to the development of social thought, and, as such, they played an active, albeit mythopoeic, part in the historical process.

The Feudal State and the Masculine Absolute

Ariosto, Tasso, and Spenser employed a medieval setting and a chivalric motif for the communication of ideas that belonged to their own Renaissance period. This deliberate archaism cannot be understood without some inital grasp of the medieval reality onto which the Renaissance conceptions were grafted. And chivalry itself cannot be grasped as a literary device without prior reference to chivalry as a cultural formation, a response to the institutions of feudal society. Only then can the lady knight, the particular object of our scrutiny, be understood in her complex relations to chivalry, as it was and as it was imagined, to her female contemporaries, and to their ancestresses--as those women were and as they were imagined.

The code and the practice of chivalry are abstractions from social reality, ideal expressions of the relationships that constitute feudalism. As such, they are stylized and insubstantial. To recognize that chivalry serves a culturally symbolic function does not mean that the symbol itself is randomly chosen or inexactly applied. In fact, the chivalric metaphor was an entirely apt figure for a system whose basic economic and political institutions each had their military aspect, and in which all fundamental social relationships had their military dimension.

MONSTROUS REGIMENT

Within the feudal class, the mutual bonds of lord and vassal were based on both economic and military dependence. Although the system thus provided "machinery for cooperation between members of the land-holding strata," it also had built into it elements of perpetual discord, since the same structures that established the pattern of land-tenure also entailed the interlocking private armies that challenged and defended property rights.[1] Government was not the province of a central state, but was largely carried out through the basic socio-economic relationships. Moreover, the medieval state, where it was monarchic, was a _feudal_ monarchy, in that the head of state was at once a king and a feudal suzerain, the nobles simultaneously subjects and vassals; although the kingship was a state offfice, the kingdom was property, landed property. These dualities made for a peculiar kind of absolutism wherein the king held all the powers of the state, but those powers were not, themselves, closely defined, so that there was in fact a diffusion of authority among the large landowners. Medieval ideas about government were categorical, but they reflected a rigidity applied to the body of law, not to the state; indeed, the state had no independent conceptual existence, being perceived simply as the means of enforcing the law, which was set above it.[2]

---

[1] Sydney Painter, "Individualism in the Middle Ages," _Feudalism and Liberty_, ed. Fred A. Cazel, Jr. (Baltimore: Johns Hopkins University Press, 1961), pp. 256-59.

[2] Friedrich Meinecke, _Machiavellism: The Doctrine of Raison d'Etat and Its Place in Modern History_, trans. Douglas Scott (London: Routledge and Kegan Paul, 1957), p. 27. See also S.B. Chrimes, _English Constitutional Ideas in the Fifteenth Century_ (Cambridge: Cambridge University Press, 1936) p. 14. Discussing a somewhat later period, Rowen makes the point that "absolutism meant that the king held all the powers of the state, but not that the state
(Footnote continued)

Heart and Stomach of a King

As Painter observes, feudalism was anarchic in that it presupposed a more or less permanent state of war.[3] All the internal and external relationships that characterize the feudal mode are founded on the use or channeling of force. Not only was subordination of the serfs maintained by forcible means, but disputes within the feudal class, even when of a juridical nature, could be settled by combat. This intrusion of military practice into the fabric of daily life gave rise to a cultural situation in which, although actual wars continued to be waged on a large scale for material and political motives, and there is no doubt that the architects and participants of those wars understood what they were doing, many medieval descriptions of warfare portray it as a simple extension or multiplication of individual combat. This mode of perception meant that political difficulties and even international disputes could be resolved, the "right" side determined, and large-scale conflict averted by single combat between two rulers who were principals in the "dispute." It does not matter how frequently or infrequently combat between two champions actually took the place of judicial proceedings, battles, or wars. What is important is that the metaphor at once reflected and influenced the way people thought about real political and military events.

Warfare was an exclusively male pursuit and supported a

---

[2] (continued)
held all the powers in and over society." (Herbert H. Rowen, "Kingship and Republicanism in the Seventeenth Century: Some Reconsiderations," in From the Renaissance to the Counter-Reformation: Essays in Honor of Garrett Mattingly, ed. Charles Howard Carter [New York: Random House, 1965], p. 424.)

[3] Sydney Painter, "Feudalism and Western Civilization," Feudalism and Liberty, p. 4.

77

"masculine" structure of values. Whether one views this warfare as a series of cruel and brutal events or superimposes on one's insight the comparative restraint and regulation of the chivalric myth, the manifest norm hinged on a definition of virility. For, in either case, prowess, strength, and bravery were a knight's major virtues. Where the chivalric code was applied, these qualities had to be further refined by adherence to rules of fair play, abstemiousness, loyalty, and honor. Insofar as chivalry actually contributed to the formulation of the laws of war, it also played a part in defining a public expression of manhood in the state. Furthermore, writers of history in the Middle Ages used the chivalric myth as a unifying principle to explain the events they described. Through that fiction, "history was reduced for them to a grave spectacle of honor and virtue, to a noble game with edifying and heroic rules."[4] The desirability of perpetuating an illusion in this fashion is not at issue here, but rather the influence of an essentially masculine ideal upon historical consciousness.

None of this should be construed as implying that members of the female sex had no function under feudalism. Women of the villein class did productive work in agriculture and in various kinds of domestic manufacture. Among landowners, women were valued for their marriage-portions, their skill in household management, and their ability to provide heirs. In an economy based upon land itself, the productivity of the estate, and the security of inheritance, a woman's dowry, her housewifery, and her fertility all in

---

[4] Johan Huizinga, "The Political and Military Significance of Chivalric Ideas in the Late Middle Ages," in Men and Ideas: History, the Middle Ages, the Renaissance (London: Eyre and Spottiswoode, 1960), p. 198.

fact constituted direct, material contributions to the life of society. When Painter deprecates the qualities for which women were valued, claiming that the feudal system had no place for anyone who could not fight, he is actually referring to the absence of an ideological rather than a social role.[5] Feudal society was defined by a set of economic relations, more or less clearly established depending on the place and time, maintained by a set of military relations. Both aspects--the force by which the means of production were acquired, augmented, and defended, quite as much as the productive process itself--constitute the material basis of feudalism. Although the collective forms and the personal relations that operated in the economic sphere were certainly reflected in cultural life, their ideal expression is not as universally available in medieval culture as is the translation of military relations into the realm of ideas and the modalities of art.

Women of all classes played an essential part in the productive experience of feudalism; although their work might be sex-specific, the cash market and wage labor had not, as yet, created a separation between the home and "the world" as economic locations, and, in that process, redefined women's work as non-productive. The most glaring sex division of labor did not occur between the home and the field, the workshop, or the marketplace, but between all of these and the field of battle. A woman's place might be in any or all of the former list, but it stopped short of the military sphere. Thus, when social experience was perceived and depicted in terms borrowed from the dominant military forms and when the metaphors of chivalry became literary

---

[5] Painter, "Feudalism and Western Civilization," p. 10.

motives embodying one way European culture saw human relations, a perspective was being applied from which the female contribution was excluded. The vision of public life, the theory of the state that is latent in all this is as absolute--and as stylized--as the world-view represented by a chess-board set up for play. With the distinction that this situation is even more of a man's world.

This is not to say that women were entirely cut off from the exercise of either feudal or governmental power. The point is rather that a woman who held such power was essentially an "homme d'occasion," an honorary man.[6] If she did her job well, she was said to exemplify masculine virtues, so that her performance in no way influenced the social definition of what was appropriately feminine. Again, the emphasis must be on the female as she appears conceptually, in her relation to other political concepts, and the political experience of exceptional women did not influence that ideology.

The Bourgeois State and the Flexible Feminine

Medieval government can be outlined in the kind of generalizations I have employed because it did not involve an explicit global theory of the state. In terms recognizable to a modern observer, people of the Middle Ages hardly possessed the concept of the state at all.[7] By contrast, the Renaissance period witnessed changes in social and con-

---

[6] This very apt phrase is borrowed from Maurice Valency, In Praise of Love (New York: Macmillan, 1961).

[7] Garrett Mattingly, "Changing Attitudes Towards the State During the Renaissance," in Wallace Ferguson, et al., Facets of the Renaissance (New York: Torchbooks-Harper, 1959), p. 26.

stitutional structures that were particularly marked, though by no means identical, in Italy and England. At the same time, the state itself became a subject of serious intellectual concern. In its condition of flux, it attracted writers intent on discussing it both analytically and prescriptively. Whereas the center of a medieval treatise on government might be the proper conduct of kingship, sixteenth-century realists like Commynes and Machiavelli described the principles of <u>effective</u> rule. The former approach did not require any concern with the actual nature or functioning of the state; the latter demanded that these matters become a writer's principal focus.

Garrett Mattingly has succinctly summarized the political changes accompanying the transition from feudalism:

> the replacement of feudal and communal militia by mercenary troops, the adoption of advanced diplomatic techniques including the employment of resident ambassadors, the growth of a civil bureaucracy with businesslike methods and permanent records, and the rise of sentiments favorable to the moral autonomy of political behavior.[8]

Mattingly's list was kept deliberately terse in order to deflate the pretensions of scholars whose claims for the Renaissance are more sweeping. Yet the changes thus schematically presented remain thoroughgoing enough to imply a massive reordering of public life. And it is evident that

---

[8] Garrett Mattingly, "Some Revisions of the Political History of the Renaissance," in <u>The</u> <u>Renaissance:</u> <u>A</u> <u>Reconsideration</u> <u>of</u> <u>Some</u> <u>of</u> <u>the</u> <u>Theories</u> <u>and</u> <u>Interpretations</u> <u>of</u> <u>the</u> <u>Age</u>, ed. Tinley Helton (Madison: University of Wisconsin Press, 1964), p. 11.

none of these innovations was spontaneous or accidental; they resulted from the action of more fundamental forces. To arrive at a just evaluation of the governmental changes, it is essential at least to identify those forces that brought them into being, and to examine the superstructural forms they assumed. Only then can we return to the question of the female character and what it has to do with modifications in the state itself or in the way men thought about it.

In the area of political economy, the transitional nature of the period cannot be overemphasized. Commentators are in almost unanimous agreement about the breakdown of feudal institutions leading to the transition.[9] They disagree, however, about what stage it had reached by the sixteenth century, particularly in England, where many of the contradictions were sharpest. At one extreme, there is a postion that maintains that virtually until the end of the century, depite the obvious decline of the system, the ruling class remained essentially feudal. As the expression of that class, the state must, therefore, have still been a feudal state.[10] By concentrating on strictly economic factors, this explanation makes no attempt to account for the

---

[9] When I speak of the unanimity of commentators, I am referring, of course, to those scholars who continue to make use of feudalism as a historical category. It has become fashionable to deny that such a system existed. (See, for example, Elizabeth A.R. Brown, "The Tyranny of a Construct: Feudalism and Historians of Medieval Europe," American Historical Review, 79 (1974), 1063-88. It seems to me that this article, which sets up and proceeds to demolish a series of straw-men, reflects a professional unwillingness to acknowledge the historicity of feudalism--perhaps in order to avoid coming to terms with the reality of capitalism.)

[10] Maurice Dobb, "Reply to Sweezy," in The Transition from Feudalism to Capitalism (New York: Science and Society, 1954), p. 26.

large-scale changes that did occur in government apparatus prior to 1600. At the other extreme is the version of history that takes Italy for an advance model of European development and considers that, by the period of the Renaissance, social and economic power had passed to a non-feudal middle class. According to this view, political power in other parts of western Europe, as in Italy, now rested in a thoroughly non-medieval institution, the sovereign territorial state.

The truth probably lies somewhere between these two extremes. But it is not immediately obvious what it means to lie between them. As Paul Sweezy describes the problem:

> We usually think of a transition from one social system to another as a process in which the two systems directly confront each other and fight it out for supremacy...Transitional forms are thought of as mixtures of elements from the two systems which are vying for mastery...[but, in fact] feudalism in western Europe was already moribund, if not actually dead, before capitalism was born. It follows that the intervening period was not a simple mixture of feudalism and capitalism: the prominent element was <u>neither</u> feudal <u>nor</u> capitalist.[11]

It seems to me that this is much more than a sectarian quarrel about technical labels. If we are to understand a sixteenth-century poem that takes place in the medieval past and that adopts certain modes out of that past, it is impor-

---

[11] Paul Sweezy, "Critique of Dobb's <u>Studies in the Development of Capitalism</u>," in <u>The Transition from Feudalism</u>, pp. 14-15.

tant to know what currency those aspects of medieval culture had in the Renaissance period and what they meant when employed symbolically. Moreover, the <u>Orlando furioso</u>, the <u>Gerusalemme liberata</u>, and <u>The Faerie Queene</u> themselves contribute to our understanding of the historical forces at work, for they reflect precisely that balance of conflicting class interests and ideologies implied by Sweezy's theory of the transitional period.

In the economic sphere, both the conflict and the balance are evident. The period from the fourteenth century through the seventeenth was marked by an equilibrium between cash values and land values, although the significance of this situation was vitiated by the fact that agriculture was coming increasingly to be dominated by the modalities and constraints of capitalist exchange. Because of this, there was tension not merely between some decaying feudal aristocrats and the rising bourgeoisie, but among several social groups: aristocrats whose capital in land had come to represent something quite different from what it had in feudal times, several levels of the bourgeoisie, and the newly enlarged class of gentry, whose situation, a contradiction in terms, was essentially that of a rural bourgeoisie. Moreover, there were inter-connections and overlaps, as well as conflicts, among these groups. At the onset of its development, a capitalist class has to accumulate capital, that is, acquire certain assets and means to wealth, and it has to do so as cheaply as possible. The dissolution and redistribution of the monasteries under Henry VIII was a classic case of accumulation of such assets without investment. This had the dual effect of making a landed class out of many who had previously dealt in a cash market and, at the same time, of placing landed property in the hands of those who managed it according to the principles of such a market. Frequent intermarriages further sealed the developing connections between the gentry and the bourgeoisie in this period. It was an age of "new fortunes and new men" who had ties to older classes and more particularly to the crown and its centralized power.[12]

But it was not all peaceful integration. As a period of inflationary expansion, the sixteenth century was marked by a movement in which the entrepreneurial class became increasingly wealthy and powerful in contradistinction to (aristocratic) landowners, on the one hand, and to wage earners and producers, on the other. Yet it was a mark of the large-scale social movement within early modern Europe that much of the profitable economic activity was in fact supported or carried out by members of the aristocracy.[13] There was cultural conflict, as well, since the prevailing ethical systems still condemned or at least failed to sanction some of the most lucrative activities of the newly powerful money-makers. (Indeed, it was a function of political poetry in this period to rationalize the new behavior according to new values. And one way of doing so was to demonstrate mythopoeically that such activities were actually the highest realization and fulfillment of <u>old</u> principles--for example, by clothing the female knight, the representatative of modern statecraft, in paraphrenalia of chivalry, or by disguising bourgeois meritocratic arguments about personal fitness to rule as arguments for the reten-

---

[12] J.E. Neale, "The Elizabethan Age," in <u>Essays in Elizabethan History</u> (London: Jonathan Cape, 1958), pp. 30-31.

[13] Lawrence Stone, <u>The Crisis of the Aristocracy, 1558-1641</u>, (Oxford: Clarendon Press, 1965), pp. 335-85.

tion of hereditary aristocratic power.)[14] Thus, when Lawrence Stone argues that despite the growing wealth of new classes, the dominant value system in sixteenth-century England remained that of the landed gentleman, he fails to take account of the ways that value system itself was being changed by the ascent of the bourgeoisie. Similarly, when Stone mentions that it was precisely the frenetic mobility up and down the class scale that motivated intensive propaganda efforts in favor of rigid class divisions, he fails to acknowledge that such ideological efforts often worked dialectically.[15]

The state was at once the sphere in which these social conflicts were expressed, and a participant in them. It retained, of course, the support of the propertied class; but, just as in the Middle Ages the king had also been a feudal overlord, so now the crown became an owner of the new, mercantile property. In fact, mercantilism entailed the action of the national state in the economic realm in order to increase its own power and prosperity. Thus, although the state was the equilibrant among the social forces at work in the society, it was operating in a system in which the revelation of actual and potential wealth had altered all the old balances and where its own interests at times required the subordination of citizens' economic

---

[14] Stone (pp. 22-23) points out the way this myth worked outside the realm of poetry: "Because of...[the] crushing burden of belief in the need for social stability, all change had to be interpreted as the maintenance of tradition. In religion, the reformation was defended as a return to the early church; in politics, parliamentary sovereignty was defended as the enforcement of fourteenth-century customs; in society, the rise of new men was disguised by forged genealogies and the grant of titles of honour."

[15] Ibid., pp. 36, 39.

claims to those of the state itself.

Beyond this broadest level, attempts to generalize about the Renaissance state--whether viewed administratively or theoretically--often founder upon local variations. In connecting a significant motif in our three poems to contemporary conceptions of the state, there is some danger of ignoring the fact that two of them were written in Italy (in fact, in Ferrara), one of them in England. Conversely, there is danger in assuming that conditions under the Estensi and the Tudors were so different as to negate any notion of a common "Renaissance" trend within the state. According to this latter view, similarities among the three poems--particularly between Spenser and his Italian models--can be explained in terms of genre and literary influence, whereas only their differences need by ascribed to national history. Actually, the Italian and English political experiences have enough in common to support a number of generalizations and to explain certain correspondences among the poems themselves.

The most striking feature of the Italian political scene, as it would remain until late in the nineteenth century, was, of course, its fragmentation. Dante expressed a sense of cultural unity that transcended the immediate situation when he said of the Italians, "curiam habemus, licet corporaliter dispersa" [we have a court, although it is physically dispersed].[16] The continued dispersion of the Italian "court" did not mean that government failed to change--and, indeed, rather early on--from its medieval modes. Although "Italy had her Prince only in the pages of Machiavelli," the emergence of a principiate occurred at the regional level much as it did on the national level in those

---

[16] Dante, De Vulgari Eloquentia I, xviii, 5.

countries that were developing out of conventional feudal forms.[17]

In fact, it was the absence of traditionally-defined feudalism in most of the Italian peninsula that was responsible for the character the modern state assumed there. Only Sicily and those parts of southern Italy that the Normans conquered ever came under the dominance of the feudal system as it was practiced in the rest of Europe. Elsewhere in Italy, even where agriculture was the principal source of income, it was carried out largely under the economic and political influence of the towns. Rome's material legacy to Italy meant that even when battles were fought over land and the fortified castles that protected it, Italian economics and culture had an essentially urban basis. "The nucleus of political life in Italy was the town, not...the castle.[18] At a time when most of western Christendom remained feudal, the Italian bourgeoisie were already on their way to shaping the first truly temporal state in modern Europe.

The state had, at first, a distinctly medieval character, based on the corporate and guild structure devised by the municipal ruling class that controlled the communes. By mid-fifteenth century, however, the old communal system was well on the way to transformation to a more unitary kind of government. Instead of retaining their previous position in a complex interlocking hierarchy of special powers and separate jurisdictions, roles that were analogous to those assigned to members of various rural classes under feudalism,

---

[17] Denys Hay, "Introduction" to The Renaissance, Volume I, The New Cambridge Modern History, ed. G.R. Potter (Cambridge: Cambridge University Press, 1964), pp. 7-8.

[18] Denys Hay, The Italian Renaissance in its Historical Background (Cambridge: Cambridge University Press, 1962), p. 30.

"men began to take on the appearance of citizens in the eyes of a state."[19] The state itself became larger, a territorial rather than a municipal unit, but increasingly directed from the municipal center. This entailed a growth in bureaucratic structure, economic and juridical restructuring aimed at eliminating pockets of redundant power, and, with these, a tendency for control to rest with the central adminstration. That this process was not carried to its furthest extent is one effect of Italy's disunification and the foreign domination to which it gave rise. But the sixteenth century was also a period of intense concern about governmental theory in Italy, owing precisely to the political disorders that were overwhelming her; and the programs evolved by both "realists" and "utopians" tended to emphasize systems that were even more advanced examples of the centralized bureaucratic commonwealth than any yet in existence.

In England, the transition from the feudal to the modern state is recognized as a Tudor achievement. Elizabeth's style of government, one of the forces that shaped Spenser's political thinking, was highly centralized and paternalistic. The full development of that structure would not have been possible, however, without the reforms instituted during her father's reign. England was unlike Italy both because it had been organized as a feudal territory and because, in the sixteenth century, it was developing as a _national_ state. At this stage, however, the net effect of these different histories was much the same. Thomas Cromwell's political philosophy may well be summarized, as Elton

---

[19] David L. Hicks, "The Sienese State in the Renaissance," in _From the Renaissance to the Counter-Reformation_, pp. 76-77.

claims, in the words "empire" and "commonwealth."[20] But, in England as in Italy, those abstractions were translated concretely into centralization, bureaucratization, and specialization at home, professional diplomacy abroad.

Examination of each of these categories will illuminate both the nature of the state and contemporary thinking about it. Employing those terms Elton ascribes to Cromwell, one may say that the condition of the commonwealth determined the possibility for empire. Cromwell himself, by personal occupancy of key offices and control of administrative detail, represents the Renaissance practice of centralization most vividly. The historic trend towards consolidation was equally marked, however, in situations where there was no single figure to personify it, and even where, as in hamstrung Italy, it was impossible for centralization to create a state that was also modern in other ways, and thus able to take its place among the nations of Europe. Other contradictions were created by the progress of this trend in England, where the central government was unable to establish a national bureaucracy that could embrace local affairs. Centralization of power in England did eradicate certain local privileges, however; national application of the law meant control of aristocratic violence that had been locally protected, but it also meant the destruction of the surviving remnants of local democracy.[21] At the same time, it made for concentration of patronage under royal or court control, which, in turn, added one more impetus to the flowering of court life.

---

[20] G.R. Elton, *The Tudor Revolution in Government: Administrative Changes in the Reign of Henry VIII* (Cambridge: Cambridge University Press, 1962), p. 302, n. 1.

[21] Stone, *Crisis of the Aristocracy*, p. 31.

The advance of bureaucracy that characterized Renaissance government meant that matters of state depended increasingly on an office, rather than an individual. Cromwell's peculiar situation does not contradict this generalization, for, intensely personal and detailed though his administration was, it was based precisely on his tenure and execution of certain state offices. By the end of the sixteenth century, the spirit of methodical administration had taken hold all over Europe. It was most advanced in Spain and her American colonies, which is, perhaps, one reason why the Spanish system proved so attractive to Italians like Machiavelli. Such theorists perceived the governmental process as an interaction between the prince's highly personal leadership, on the one hand, and an effective bureaucracy, on the other.

Just as feudalism and the governmental forms associated with it had a characteristic (indeed, an intrinsic) form of warfare, so, too, did early capitalism. Changes in the way violence was expressed on both the personal and the public levels also led to changes in the way military matters were used as conceptual or metaphorical instruments. The professionalization of military service, paralleling the other developments I have traced, combined with advances in military technology to create a situation in which "war was no fun anymore."[22] For many, the moral equivalent of war and its former "fun" was to be found in the law courts, which, like war, combined elements of boredom, difficulty, strategic planning, and sheer luck, and which offered the same perilous prospects of defeat and victory. The notion of personal and military service owed to a member of the landed

---

[22] Ibid., p. 295.

class was rapidly disappearing, and with it the band of retainers and the private army. Stone maintains that "the key" to English society in the early and mid-sixteenth century lies in the word "manred" which means "control over persons for military service," a word, which, significantly enough, had disappeared from the English language by the middle of the seventeenth century. Its place in the scale of aristocratic values was taken by rent, "even rack-rent."[23]

The affective and ideological ties that bound vassal to lord in a relation involving, among other obligations, military service, was thus replaced by a cash nexus. For the aristocrat, his own military obligations to the prince came increasingly to be translated into an ideal of service in the government or at court, an ideal that was strengthened by the greater secularization and bureaucratization of the state and the desire on the part of conservatives to assure that the new posts created by this expansion be occupied by the aristocracy. Though noble birth was an asset, the nature of these positions meant that in qualifying for them and filling them adequately, there was more emphasis on book learning and less on adherence to an essentially medieval code of honor than had formerly been the case.

New codes were also taking shape within the realm of combat itself. On the global level, this development involved codification of the rules of war. In interpersonal relations, it had to do with the definition of the duel. The latter regulation had greater literary influence, and the romance-epic reflects the kind of change that occurred. The fundamental weapons of combat at the beginning of the

---

[23] Ibid., p. 264.

sixteenth century were a heavy sword with only one cutting edge and a buckler or shield, armaments that promoted a style of fighting that was satisfyingly dramatic without being overly hazardous to life and limb. The rapier, a far deadlier weapon, came into common use in Italy by the middle of the sixteenth century, and had been adopted in England by the 1580's. With this new destructive capacity, there developed two formations reflecting the new culture that was being defined by capitalism: technique and regulation. The former was manifested in the establishment of schools of "defence" (what we would call "fencing") with accredited masters, styles, and degrees of skill, whereas the latter found expression in the "theological rigidity" of a dueling code that attempted to cover all personal and social eventualities.[24]

From the literary point of view, these developments are worth noting. The kind of combat that took place when the opponents were armed with single blade and buckler, combat that was energetic without necessarily (or even probably) proving fatal, is the sort that is practiced in the poems of Ariosto, Tasso, and Spenser. By the time the _Gerusalemme liberata_ and _The Faerie Queene_ were written, they described not only bygone times and heroes, but bygone methods of conducting the wars that constitute each poem's principal context. I suspect that some of the careful definitions and inflexible rulings that the three poets attribute to the obsolete chivalric code are actually inspired by the emerging contemporary code of the duel. Moreover, with the art and the "laws" of dueling so elaborately advanced, the poets retained a model of single combat as a way of settling per-

---

[24] _Ibid._, pp. 243 ff.

sonal and political scores. Indeed as real warfare became increasingly impersonal, the metaphor of two champions working out their differences face to face on the field became increasingly apt, since the dueling field and the tiltyard replaced the battle site for most men, and the duel was a form of combat involving the principals alone, not a band of their friends, family, and retainers.

This individualistic approach was mirrored, as well, in the evolving vision of the ruler and his relation to the growing complexity of government. To the extent that it was centralized at all, medieval government had placed responsibility on the king and his immediate entourage. Early modern government was more nearly autonomous, divorced from the royal household and individual whims, but with bureaucratic departments responsible to the central authority of the prince. Obviously, this involved a new definition of the prince, a concentration on the personal qualities that would make his rule effective. It is important to recognize, however, that all theoretical attempts to define the ruler and his new role presupposed the support of a functioning bureaucratic administration.

A salient feature of bureaucracy is specialization. As the ruler, in principle, became less specialized, government offices became much more so. Each department had its function, its particular jurisdiction and area of control, and organizational reform in the sixteenth century always meant greater definition of function and further specialization, in the interests of bureaucratic order. The professionalization that accompanied this development was also evident in the sphere of international relations. Diplomacy became a full-time occupation, akin to the civil service in the assumptions that were made about the specialization, the expertise, and the national loyalties of the ambassador.

Heart and Stomach of a King

The feudal states of medieval Europe had paid lip-service, at least, to the notion of an ambassador as serving the collective welfare of the entire Christian commonwealth. By the Renaissance period, his duty was understood as owing exclusively to his own state. This situation was only underscored by the occasional appointment of nonprofessionals, chosen from the higher strata of society, for special, short-term diplomatic missions involving personal representation of their sovereigns. It would be premature to describe the view of the state implicit in all this as nationalistic, especially since it was not territorial entities, but the city-states of Italy, that refined the modern notion of diplomatic service. What is essential about the way the Renaissance diplomat looked at the map of Europe is not yet nationalism, but secularism.

This same secular attitude prevailed in another major thrust of international relations, the codification, mentioned earlier, of the usages of war. Appeals to religious duty and the vision of a universal Christendom were no longer effective in the altered political and ideological situation of the sixteenth century. Thus, the new rules of war evolving in the Renaissance period came to acknowledge the conception of teritorial sovereignty and rely on the idea of a common secular law, the ius gentium.[25] A similar principle was applied to the notion of a balance of power among the major European countries and within a given state. From the Italian point of view, of course, the sixteenth-century experience made it clear that such an equilibrium, internationally, was as good a fate as Italy could hope for. In the fifteenth century, the same result had been achieved

---

[25] J.R. Hale, "International Relations in the West: Diplomacy and War," New Cambridge Modern History, p. 290.

internally, through the system of the five strongest states keeping one another in check, so that, until its vulnerability to foreign intervention destroyed it, the situation was "somewhat balanced."[26] Citing the consequence before its cause makes it evident, I trust, that the balance of forces was not exactly an unqualified success as a political principle. But it also demonstrates that it *was* a principle that political thinkers invoked.

Utopian theorists tended to base their notion of the ideal polity on a double aspiration: law and order in public life supported by the elimination of the most striking inequities engendered by the rise of new productive relations. Although the latter goal, particularly, ran counter to the tenor of the times, it is significant that the idea of a just balance is once more the controlling one. On the governmental plane, the essence of the English system, as established under the Tudors, was a balance of the forces representing class interests that were not, in fact, about to be reconciled by any utopian redistribution of income. The monarch's role was "the procuring of support in the Commons by adjustments in policy and by the managerial enterprise of creating a strong Crown interest in the Commons."[27] Although it was not always coherently or consistently expressed, the concept of equilibrium recurs in a wide range of Renaissance political contexts. "Balance" was clearly perceived as a vital political factor and the way in which it was employed bears particularly on the reasons for introduction of a female principle into the state.

---

[26] Meinecke, p. 29. The quoted remark is from Machiavelli.

[27] G.R. Elton, "A High Road to Civil War?" in *From Renaissance to Counter-Reformation*, p. 329.

Another idea to which I have made repeated allusion is that of the "state" itself, a principle often as abstract as the idea of balance within it. In fact, it is impossible to discuss the Renaissance concept of the state without underlining the novelty of there being such a concept at all. In Renaissance rhetoric, the state came to possess an identity, almost an autonomy that dictated its own moral code. Christian tradition supplied moral standards meant to hold for both the individual and the state; this is the justice that prevails in More's Utopia. In Renaissance Europe, however, as in the pages of Machiavelli, what More called the justice of princes reigned supreme. Although "Machiavelli never forgets what is 'good'...from the standpoint of personal morality...he insists on a clear-cut distinction between that and what is 'good' in public policy."[28] In practice, this meant that Machiavelli considered public safety the highest good and arrogated to the state the power to protect it. Preservation of the state itself thus became a moral goal, for goodness and justice were forthcoming only from that source. This form of statism applied to the prince himself and to his methods. That is, the prince's rule might be absolute, but the test of his competence was his ability to serve the state, by changing with times and conditions, just as the test of the state was its ability to survive and expand.

I do not mean to make a case for Machiavelli as representative of the political thought of his time. But references to what he thought about the constellation of forces he called the state are included because they are the period's clearest expression of the state-as-concept. And

---

[28] E. Harris Harbison, "Machiavelli's *Prince* and More's *Utopia*," in *Facets*, pp. 60-61.

it is necessary to establish that the Renaissance period fostered the view of the state as a moral entity, separable from other categories, a potential political object or agent. This intellectual autonomy leads to personification and anthropomorphizing, reflected in the way Mattingly conceptualizes the state when, in describing the doomed Concert of Italy, he speaks of "the natural egotism of a political organization with no higher end than its own self-perpetuation and aggrandizement" and reiterates that in these circumstances "the state could think only of itself."[29]

The Modern Monarch and the Virgin Queen

Since it is a commonplace among historians that the fifteenth and sixteenth centuries were the age of kings, it is important to examine what kingship was coming to mean during those years. The tendency to conceive of the state as an organic, conscious being reinforced and was reinforced by new definitions of the person who was the head of state. Indeed, the Renaissance was the first period in which it is appropriate to apply that term to a European ruler. This concept of "head of state" implies an interplay between absolute power and administrative flexibility. It means that the monarchy itself was one of the forces that needed to be accommodated in order to achieve social balance and, at the same time, constituted the principal locus of that balance.

Although most commentators agree that the monarch's role was changing along with the apparatus and concept of the state, Rowen maintains that the medieval elements remain

---

[29] Garrett Mattingly, _Renaissance Diplomacy_ (London: Jonathan Cape, 1955), p. 91. On these points, see also his "Changing Attitudes," p. 36.

fundamental.[30] I think it is important to stress the transitional nature of the role, rather than cavil about the stage at which it had arrived in the sixteenth century. Rowen provides useful warnings about interpreting words like "kingship," "republic," and "state" as if they had the same meaning for the Renaissnce period as they do for us. But all his caveats about drawing inferences from unexamined use of terms fail to explain how an essentially medieval king could have presided over a rapidly modernizing state apparatus.

A solution to this problem lies in Rowen's own assertions about the tension inherent in the office of king. The conflict he describes is between the monarch's service to himself or his own interests and service to others or the common good. This contradiction arises, according to Rowen, because of the notion of the state as a form of property. As property, he claims, it may legitimately be used for the benefit of the person who owns it. But it is a special kind of property, in that it involves power over others, including power to affect interests that conflict with those of the king as property-holder. It seems to me that Rowen's very lucid statement of the case weakens his own thesis about the survival of medieval patterns of kingship. For this is a thoroughly modern description of property itself and the rights and relationships adhering to it. It is a definition of property under capitalism, of "private property," a concept that makes sense only in a system motivated by profit. By contrast, although the medieval king was both monarch and feudal overlord, it would not have been possible to describe his suzerainty as a relationship involving

---

[30] Rowen, p. 427.

property in the capitalist sense or to perceive a <u>material</u> contradiction between his two roles.

One effect of the conflicting pressures operating on the leader was a new style of kingship, frequently described as "personal monarchy." This style represented a dynamic relationship between royal power as one of the opposing forces in the state and royal power as the source of resolution. As J.E. Neale describes it, "under personal monarchy, the machinery of government was the ruler's. In theory it was intimately linked with royal prerogative, while in practice there was a flexibility which permitted and even demanded constant intervention from the centre."[31]

This dynamic underlies Machiavelli's concentration on the individual prince, his qualities, and his tactics. He does not personify the state in the figure of its leader, nor does he identify the two. Rather, he expresses the relationship by a fundamentally naturalistic image of the state, utilizing metaphors of the human life-cycle as if they were not figures of speech but political facts. The state acquires a kind of humanity, for him, as the product of human effort and will, particularly the effort and will of the prince. The nature of personal monarchy, properly understood, thus makes it both possible and necessary for him to talk about the whole state process through the medium of its leader.

The duality of the ruler as agent and equlibrant found its fullest expression within the structures of government. The king "not only led but also fought" the various political interests within the state, and the relationship itself was complex, changing, and contradictory, comprising both

---

[31] Neale, p. 37.

"domination and dependence."[32] This was a task best accomplished by a sovereign who was guided by the spirit of compromise and flexibility, but who could devise means to express those qualities in a forceful and even autocratic fashion.

Throughout this discussion, I have used the words "king" and "prince" the way sixteenth-century writers did, as synonyms for "ruler." But the concept of personal monarchy is well exemplified by the reign of Elizabeth, a sovereign who was neither king nor prince. (It should be stressed, I suppose, that there is no single "best" example of this mode of government; nor can any one monarch's particular style be considered "typical.") From its inception, Elizabeth's rule bore her individual stamp and was marked, as well, by that peculiar intercourse between the roles of the sovereign as participant and mediator in political disputes that characterizes Renaissance kingship.

Both despite and because of her control of factions, the hallmark of Elizabeth's reign was balance--a balance achieved through moderation rather than coercion. Thus, Elizabeth attracted and retained the support of the "radical" Protestants while utilizing her concentrated power to enforce the High Anglican policies they found abhorrent. Elizabethan England was thus able to enjoy "the advantages of the liberals coupled with the dynamic of the fanatics."[33]

Neale's interpretation of her success gives a great deal of credit to consummate political art, proportionally little to the historic forces that shaped Renaissance monarchy. It is Elizabeth's uniqueness, rather than her participation in a contemporary pattern, that he appreciates. He

---

[32] Rowen, p. 427.
[33] Neale, p. 42.

also makes the rather curious claim that her achievement rested on her solitary condition, indicating the "stark fact that her votaries had no alternative person to worship. To be 'England's Eliza' she had also to be England's Virgin Queen."[34] Leaving aside the unanswerable question of whether Elizabeth would have been as effective a sovereign if, for example, she had borne an heir to the throne, we are faced with the assertion that the queen's sexual status was somehow responsible for her success. To be sure, Neale links it to the isolation implicit in celibacy, not the celibacy *per se*. Emphasis is often placed on Elizabeth's (rhetorical) virginity as the factor that removed her from the female condition and made her an exception to commonplaces about women *or* men. But frequently her gender is regarded as being responsible for her remarkable reign, and more particularly for its admirably flexible and balanced character, while the virginity is seen as simply an act of supererogation.

Elizabeth as an *idea* has always had a powerful appeal for historians and political commentators. Her sexuality is almost always an important part of the conceptual framework. The recurrent theme of these discussions is the "lasting wonder that in so masculine a society, a woman, and one so young, managed to formulate policy and dominate those about her."[35] Yet it is clear that the fact of her womanhood also helped shape her policy of domination.

To Sir Robert Cecil, Elizabeth "was more than a man and (in troth) sometymes less than a woman." It was customary for her subjects to address her in political contexts with

---

[34] Neale, "The Accession of Queen Elizabeth," in *Essays*, p. 58.

[35] *Ibid.*, p. 55.

the language of impassioned courtship, and any interpretation of her style as queen must take into account the significance and function of that convention. Nor was the sexual reference all in one direction. The queen herself made rhetorical use of her female identity in political situations, combining the language of personal affection with the conventional formulae of diplomatic letters and state documents. Although perhaps "less than a woman," she constantly reminded those around her that she was more--and quite definitely other--than a man. By asserting that she was equal to all the demands of monarchy, she was actually assuming superiority, since she was a _female_ who nonetheless commanded masculine virtues. It was a device she apparently resorted to when the matter at hand was really important to her. Speaking about the succession, for instance, she declared, "For myne owne part I care not for death, for all men are mortall, and though I be woman I have as good a courage, answerable to my place, as euer my ffather had."[36] At Tilbury, when the Spanish Armada threatened, she is supposed to have addressed her people in this vein:

> I know I have the body but of a weak and feeble woman, but I have the heart and stomach of a king ...to which, rather than any dishonour shall grow by me, I myself will take up arms, I myself will be your general, judge, and reward of every one of your virtues in the field.[37]

---

[36] Elizabeth's address on the limitation of the succession, 5 November 1566, is quoted in _English Historical Review_, 36 (1921), 516.

[37] Quoted in Neale, "The Sayings of Queen Elizabeth," _Essays_, p. 104. This speech is preserved in popular tradi-
(Footnote continued)

To the reader of sixteenth-century epic, this description has a familiar ring, for, supported by the flexibility and balance of Elizabeth's reign, it sums up all of Renaissance statecraft in the image of a female warrior. But Ariosto published the Orlando furioso before Elizabeth was born, and her example could hardly have served as Tasso's inspiration, either. Even Spenser, who derived much of the ideology in The Faerie Queene from his specifically Elizabethan ambience, found the figure of the lady knight in the pages of the Italian poets rather than in the court around him. My purpose in discussing Elizabeth's queenship and its sexual concomitant was to suggest a less direct connection with the lady warriors: I believe that both the quality of Elizabeth's rule and the figure of the female knight have a common historical and ideological origin.

In the Middle Ages, the form and concept of the state were ideally complemented by the masculine character-profile. As in Augustan Rome, the proper conduct of government was seen as incompatible with sexual indulgence, which was dehumanizing in a woman, "feminizing" in a man. The values of medieval Christianity had merely intensified the sexual polarization clearly apparent in Virgil, identifying the female as a temptation to lust and self-destruction, even when she herself was not a prey to vice. The changes that took place in the Renaissance period altered the nature of the state, moving it away from the stringencies of medieval thought. Terms like "statecraft" and "statesmanship,"

---

[37](continued)
tion, but many historians doubt its authenticity. Neale accepts it as a good record or approximation of the Queen's remarks. To his historical documentation might be added the less weighty evidence of style: The periods certainly sound like those in the well-attested speech before Parliament cited above.

that came into being out of the imperatives of the early modern state, imply a transcendence of absolutes. They connote manipulation, flexibility, compromise, balance, control. The institutions of government that arose in response to changing historical conditions--phenomena like centralization, bureaucracy, and diplomacy--are based on such flexibility. At the same time, the state in the transition from feudalism made new demands on the individual leader, demands that called for flexibility of temperament, as well as of institutions. To use the kind of anthropomorphic metaphor a sixteenth-century theorist might have approved, the state underwent modifications in its "personality." Government was still a masculine pursuit, and the exceptional women who ruled did not hold office by virtue of some collective decision that female nature was better suited to the new conditions of government. But the new character of the state no longer harmonized with the absolutes of the masculine stereotype. It was not <u>women</u> the Renaissance state required, but a principle that the culture defined as female.

Political Myth and Sexual Reality

Thus far my attention has been directed to the intersection of two Renaissance concepts: the state and the female character. This emphasis was dictated by the conclusions I expect to draw about the lady knights. In discussing the state and female as ideas, I connected those ideas to changing political conditions; similarly, had I interpreted the women warriors as being about sex equality, I should have examined not only what the poems themselves have to say about these subjects, but also the contemporary sociology of love in its relation to the institution of marriage. A brief consideration of the issue will explain why I lay less stress on that approach and on the interpretation of history that underlies it.

It seems to me undeniable, first of all, that something was happening to the ideology of love and marriage in the Renaissance period. Whereas the conventions of courtly love tended to assume an adulterous relationship, whether or not it was consummated sexually, sixteenth-century inheritors of that tradition admitted the possibility of marriage with the beloved. Although it was by no means a universal assumption, Renaissance literature begins to suggest that marriage is the proper culmination of true love; some literature even asserts the converse, that love is a necessary condition for marriage. Castiglione's courtier, for example, is instructed to address his love-making only to a lady who is eligible for marriage. The patterns of courtship in a book like *Il cortegiano* are of course symbolic representations of human intercourse, not norms for its actual conduct. But, although the immediate conventions are literary, rather than social, defining the new courtly love as a search for a suitable marriage partner does give that advice a certain practical status.

At the same time, theorists of love were increasingly dependent on a popularized neo-Platonism, which appropriated ideas about love of the good impelling one up the ladder of love towards spiritual transcendence; the beloved, ideally, was the equal or superior of the lover. The homosexual element in Plato's theory was invariably purged, however, so so that the love explored in Renaissance theory was heterosexual and not necessarily removed from actual relationships. Thus, the theoretical possibility emerges of a woman who is regarded as an equal participating in an ideal love that leads to honorable marriage.

Heart and Stomach of a King

Now, in the <u>Orlando furioso</u>, the <u>Gerusalemme liberata</u>, and <u>The Faerie Queene</u>, there appear ladies who are at least the equal of their men and who manifest that fact in the most concrete and challenging arena, the field of battle. The love they experience is true and profound, and in the two cases where such a result is possible, they marry the men they love. It would not be unreasonable to assume that the romance-epics were part of a more sweeping literary movement that reversed traditional assumptions about the separation of the world of love from the world of marriage. Or to conclude that this literary movement was the expression of a deeper shift in social values and practices.

Unfortunately, the second part of this hypothesis has no basis in history. Renaissance literature did begin to assert the ideal of true love leading to marriage, but the declaration remained a purely literary phenomenon. There is no evidence to support the view that most sixteenth-century marriages were based on love between the partners or even upon their more than perfunctory consent. Nor was love-marriage a recognized principle to which even lip service was paid, especially for members of the class to which the heroic poems were chiefly addressed.

If anything, the conditions and arrangements of matrimony were becoming increasingly remote from personal concerns and goals. The dowry remained a central institution, but its meaning was altered in a money economy. Whereas the feudal bride brought land on her marriage and her worth might be identified with that land, a Renaissance marriage-portion tended to be in cash or in property that was either convertible to cash or perceived in terms of cash yield. It was therefore movable, transferable, marketable. Through our period, the size and strategic importance of dowries increased; their size relative to that of the "jointure" reserved as support for the bride's possible widowhood also increased; marriages among the possessing classes were arranged and even consummated at very young ages; and there was a heavy traffic in wardships, entailing right of bestowal in marriage, of wealthy minors. The socially ambitious bourgeoisie, with greater access to cash and with daughters to use as commodities, did much to inflate the market in marriage portions for the daughters of land-holding classes, as well.[38] The influence of mercantilism was not limited to such competition, however. Rather, it is important to understand the extent to which the mercenary values imposed by the bourgeoisie affected the family as well as public economy. Thus, whereas the motives for aristocratic marriage in pre-capitalist Europe involved a number of social and political factors, and preservation of the class itself was a primary concern, in our period alliances within the aristocracy came increasingly to be dominated by strictly pecuniary considerations.[39]

By the early seventeenth century, however, there was widespread criticism of marriage for money, and Stone speculates that this disapproval may well have increased in proportion to the frequency of the practice.[40] Only as paternal authority came to be eroded--and to some extent

---

[38] Stone, Crisis of the Aristocracy, pp. 640 ff., especially pp. 646-47. See also p. 182. For a popular summary of some of these issues, see the first several chapters of Maurice Percy Ashley, The Stuarts in Love: With Some Reflections on Love and Marriage in the Sixteenth and Seventeenth Centuries (London: Hodden and Stoughton, 1963) and Lawrence Stone, Family and Fortune: Studies in Aristocratic Finance in the Sixteenth and Seventeenth Centuries (Oxford: Clarendon Press, 1973).

[39] Stone, Crisis of the Aristocracy, p. 618.

[40] Ibid., p. 617.

replaced--by that of the state itself, whose image and surrogate it had always been, did an element of choice begin to enter the marriage arrangements for youth of the upper classes. This "choice" tended to be limited to the power of veto (something the church, in theory, had always required), and this, in turn, to an absence of positive antipathy. A second marriage, where amiable companionship, if not love, was the goal, was often the first time either sex really got to exercise a personal option.

Generally speaking, the medieval economy had drawn rigid class lines, but allowed highly flexible sex lines.[41] Establishment of capitalist exchange removed social production (and hence the male entrepeneurs and wage earners engaged in it) from the home, and conversely, removed domestic economy from the realm of social production. Both of these factors materially lessened the chances for women of the artisan or trading classes to participate in the wider commonwealth. At the same time, the new economic conditions created and enforced a new leisure for upper-class women, and awarded social prestige to the acquisition of this leisure. The "mechanical state" postulated by seventeenth-century social theory as the appropriate expression of capitalist economic relations, considered the individual the fundamental unit of society, rather than the family--a situation that redefined women's role within the family as a set

---

[41] Mary Beard, _Woman as Force in History_ (1946; rpt. New York: Collier, 1962). See especially Chapter 10, "Force of Woman in Medieval Economic and Social Life," pp. 229-54. Beard's thesis is that Blackstone's expositon of Common Law established the fiction of female subjection as an age-old and immutable condition. In the course of her argument, she contrasts the actual condition of women in the Middle Ages with the far more restricted early modern situation that Blackstone codified in the eighteenth century.

of essentially private issues and problems.[42] The very word "family" came eventually to signify those private relations, instead of referring to the household as a social or economic entity. Certain characteristics of mercantilism--the capitalization of the dowry market, the separation of the household sphere from the cash economy, the premium on female leisure, the privatization of family life--gave rise to a situation in which women's status was increasingly marginal to social and political experience but increasingly central to cultural and intellectual life.

In short, when the family was an acknowledged economic unit and a focus for material life, it was, by definition, "an institution for the passing on of life, name and property," and "it was not until the early seventeenth century that it began to be regarded as an instrument of religious and moral improvement."[43] Although Stone attributes this shift in emphasis to Puritan ideology, rather than to the common origins of both phenomena, his evidence confirms the change itself. The religious factor placed greater emphasis on the personal qualities of the individuals to be married--an emphasis that lays the necessary groundwork for respecting their feelings about one another. A wife, moreover, was seen as a helpmeet, a companion, and the authenticity of the needs satisfied in such a relation was increasingly recognized. As Puritanism actively discouraged the double standard of sexual morality, greater latitude had to be allowed for the probability of sexual compatibility within marriage, which provided another incentive for allowing some freedom

---

[42] On these questions, see Alice Clark, *Working Life of Women in the Seventeenth Century* (London: Routledge; New York: Dutton, 1919). Many of Clark's points are presented most clearly in her introductory and concluding chapters.

[43] Stone, *Crisis of the Aristocracy*, p. 591.

of choice. Amiable, supportive company and gratification of lust were adduced, however, as some of the reasons why _men_ should marry, and there is little to suggest that women, who had always functioned under stricter sexual limitations, were being ascribed similar motives or allowed similar liberty. Indeed, Stone's observation that the double standard is essential to arranged marriage takes no account whatever of the experience of women, either while that standard is in force or after it is eliminated.[44] As these principles evolved into a theory of marriage, moreover, there was no declaration that equality between the sexes, in either attributes or achievement, was a desirable--not to say necessary--prerequisite for love or companionship. The vision of sex equality seems to have been confined to the stanzas of heroic poetry.

Throughout the sixteenth century, however, woman was a frequent subject of intellectual debate. In the ecclesiastical realm, discussion centered principally on the sacramentality of marriage and admissibility of divorce.[45] Politically, the appearance or threat of female sovereigns revived the question of women's fitness to rule. John Knox's _First Blast of the Trumpet Against the Monstrous Regiment of Women_ is probably the best known of these. Although it does little more than rehash the arguments of Sir John Fortescue and a number of his medieval predecessors, Knox's work inspired a series of rebuttals from political

---

[44] _Ibid._, p. 612. For contemporary arguments in favor of marriage and discussions of the politics of that institution, see also Judith Kegan Gardiner, "The Renaissance Marriage Debate," paper at the Third Berkshire Conference on the History of Women, Bryn Mawr College, June 1976.

[45] On these issues, see, for example, Chilton Latham Powell, _English Domestic Relations, 1487-1653_ (New York: Columbia University Press, 1917).

hacks on the other side.[46] And, among literary people, the woman question was the topic of formal debate in the humanist academies, as well as the subject of learned lectures and instructional treatises, all of which shared certain assumptions about the nature of the female character, whatever moral judgments they made about it.[47]

Some writers were conscious exponents of the process of re-evaluataion, turning female qualities that had been regarded as defects into acknowledged strengths. Thus, for instance, although both sexes were believed to have all four humours represented in them, the female temperament was supposedly dominated by the cold and humid ones. Granting the greater disposition of heat towards energetic activity and achievements, the defenders of women nonetheless point out that "the dominating heat and dryness of men's temperament, which drives them on to great exploits, also breeds more ardent passions, the enemies of reason."[48] This sort of physiological argument was advanced to refute misogynist arguments based on an identical understanding of the humours and their influence; now, however, the flexibility and accessibility of female nature was perceived as a desirable adjunct to rational behavior, rather than a pernicious obstacle to it.

---

[46] John Knox, The First Blast of the Trumpet Against the Monstrous Regiment of Women, ed. Edward Arber (1558; rpt. London: Arber, 1878). Fortescue's arguments against the right of women to succeed to the throne are summarized in Chrimes, pp. 62-63. The Arber edition also lists the pamphlets written as responses to Knox's work in the two decades following its publication.

[47] E. Fabry, "Three Early Renaissance Treatises on Women," Italian Studies, 11 (1956), 30-55.

[48] Ruth Kelso, Doctrine for the Lady of the Renaissance (Urbana: University of Illinois Press, 1956), p. 16.

The moral virtues that were praised in women included many of the same ones that men possessed, but the <u>social</u> virtues of a lady, which were assumed to be the expression of her inner character, have no precise analogue in the profile of the ideal gentleman. The chief of these virtues is what Kelso trenchantly calls humanity, a quality that people in the Renaissance period might have denominated "love, the desire to please, kindness, pity, or helpfulness."[49] Once more, the emphasis is on a quality that implies both flexibility and a balance between public and private demands. This was the human element that the new priorities of the state demanded. And this was where the lady knights came in.

---

[49] <u>Ibid</u>., p. 26.

CHAPTER THREE

ARIOSTO: THE DOUBLE STANDARD

The first stanza of the Orlando furioso echoes the opening lines of the Aeneid. This imitation serves principally to bring differences between the two poems into immediate and striking relief. The subject is no longer arms and the man, but ladies, knights, arms, love, courtesies, and feats of daring. Instead of a single epic hero and a linear narrative, Ariosto presents us with the multiple heroes and fragmented structure of medieval Italian romance. Nor will he speak only of warfare and public issues, but also of desire and its place in human experience. His first lines are a graceful acknowledgement of Virgil's influence and a statement of epic intention. At the same time, they reflect Ariosto's ironic awareness that in order to create a poem as appropriate to Renaissance conditions as the Aeneid was to its own circumstances, he would have to invert most of Virgil's moral and social categories.[1]

---

[1] Ariosto's opening lines are often described as a parody of Virgil, in which the political concerns that constituted the Aeneid's focus are engulfed and annulled by erotic themes. I think my summary of the problem comes somewhat closer to the truth, recognizing the contradiction, but also respecting Ariosto's fundamental seriousness. For the opposing point of view, see, for instance, Donald Cheney, Spenser's Image of Nature: Wild Man and Shepherd in The Faerie Queene (New Haven: Yale University Press, 1966), pp. 78-79.

Ariosto

It is not simply that Ariosto views sexuality with greater tolerance than Virgil did, but rather that he integrates it into his entire social vision. Ladies, knights, love, arms, courtesy, and daring are not discrete bases that the poet will touch in his narrative; they are organic parts of the same imaginative construct. The sexual themes constitute the poem's motive force, operating within a loose context provided by the military narrative. Almost every canto begins with a fresh reminder of this fact. Ariosto may break off in the middle of an incident or at a natural point of transition, ending, in either case, with conventional encouragement to proceed to the next canto. But he rarely continues the narrative without a stanza or more of general observations about such essential issues as love and reason, constancy, or the female character.

Women, le donne, sound the opening note of the Furioso and represent a constant point of poetic and ideological reference. But woman's character, as it emerges from these references, is not subject to ready generalization, embracing as it does the devotion of Olimpia, Isabella, and Fiordiligi, the fickleness of Doralice, the selfish abandon of Angelica, and the wantonness of countless unnamed wives in the ribald anecdotes. For Ariosto, the range of female possibility exactly corresponds to the moral spectrum afforded by sexuality itself. Since he apparently believed that people experience much of their ethical life through love and sex, it is not a severe limitation for his women to be defined chiefly as sexual beings, whose virtue is a function of their chastity.

Yet it is undeniable that his male characters are allowed a wider sphere of action. Although much of their behavior is also determined by the effects of passion and they, too, may be defined by their constancy as lovers, they have the whole world upon which to express the character of their love. Nor are they invariably judged by the same standards as are applied to women. For instance, the faithless Bireno and the faithless Gabrina are both led by their initial sexual errors into crimes far more vicious than adultery, and both are considered equally evil. Dalinda and Ricciardetto inadvertently endanger others by succumbing to illicit passion, and both are similarly absolved. But there can be no female counterpart of a man like Rinaldo, who is able to remain a paladin worthy of respect, pursuing heroic deeds as well as his desperate love for Angelica, while leaving his wife behind at Montalbano. And although, on one level, Ricciardetto's moral status is comparable to Dalinda's, the reader is also meant to accept his crude deception of Fiordispina and still take his chivalric claims at face value.

Ariosto is far from dogmatic about sexual morality. It is not lust alone that degrades villains, but the graver sins into which it impels them. He condemns the high expectations society imposes on female sexual behavior and the harsh penalties inflicted upon women who fail to live up to those expectations. Nonetheless, he falls into habits of thought and language that restrict the moral stage for most women to their sexuality. The boundaries are not as narrow as they might be only because Ariosto does perceive the sexual realm as an appropriate <u>locus</u> for the development of psychological and political constructs.

As I have indicated, however, there is another realm in which men operate and within which the male characters can prove themselves, removed from the world of love that constitutes most women's whole experience. This sphere is the military setting of the romance-epic. Although the political and sexual areas intersect in Ariosto, certain public questions belong entirely to the chivalric aspect of the Furioso. The state, for example, is most effectively suggested in the military camps and tribunals that are the only formal institutions presented and hence constitute the poem's chief social markers. Moreover, since Ariosto's political views, like all his ideas, are conceived on a human rather than an institutional scale, his social attitudes are frequently expressed in and through the relationships established among warriors.

It is particularly significant, therefore, that Ariosto introduces two women into the ranks of knighthood, using them to impart to the political sector some of the lessons learned in the realm of private life. Two sorts of double standard are at work in the poem: the traditional one that demands sexual purity of women but is able to make allowances for the susceptibility of men, and another that requires men to adhere inflexibly to the chivalric ethic, while permitting women a greater degree of moral innovation. Camouflaged in the medieval metaphor of the romance-epic, the female knights become the exemplars of that innovation, and hence of the political concepts and values of the Renaissance period.

The complexity and the occasional uncertainty of those ideas raise problems that Ariosto attempts to handle by creating two military women, instead of only one. Bradamante is usually cited as the literary novelty, since she is not only an accomplished soldier, but also a woman thoroughly absorbed in her love for the man she is to marry. But Marfisa does not fully belong to the Amazon tradition, either, and is an equally characteristic Renaissance invention. Ariosto's dual image of the lady knight, corresponding to the ethical double standard that functions in the poem, makes it possible for a wide range of (sometimes inconsistent) ideas to be communicated through it. It is important, therefore, to understand the ways in which the two figures function as a conceptual pair, as well as those in which they differ.[2]

It should be stressed that, unlike Pulci and Boiardo, his predecessors in the heroic genre, Ariosto did not regard the world of chivalry as an attractive, if ludicrously outmoded, way of life, but rather as a literary device through which to convey certain values,[3] an apt vehicle for the celebration of the Cinquecento consciousness that was the poem's real subject. The chivalric mode, as Piromalli points out, affords a pretext for the expression of ideas belonging to a civilization that was struggling against the theological and moral concepts of feudalism and creating norms opposed to medieval stringency.[4] Ariosto gives new life to the old forms by infusing them with the Renaissance sensibility--though strictly on his own terms.

In a sense, the Orlando furioso accomplished on the level of art the same ideological feat that Ariosto's Este patrons had achieved in their practical use of the chivalric tradition. They made it concrete, adapting it to their own perception of reality in such a way as simultaneously to endow the archaic legends with some of their own real power and to legitimate that power by reference to the myths of chivalry. Ferrara under Este rule bore more of the outward

---

[2] Both women are also part of another sort of pair, for each has a twin brother who appears in the epic, Marfisa being, in fact, the twin of Bradamante's betrothed, Ruggiero.

[3] Cesare Segre, Esperienze ariostesche (Pisa: Nistri-Lischi, 1966), p. 17.

[4] Antonio Piromalli, Motive e forme della poesia di Ludovico Ariosto (Florence: G. D'Anna, 1954), p. 105.

hallmarks of feudalism than any other city on the Italian peninsula. Culturally, it was the scene of jousts and tournaments inspired by the literature of chivalry, but marking the festivals of the Renaissance; it was a place where the children of the ruling house were given Carolingian names almost as often as those out of classical mythology. At the same time, it was one of the first cities in Europe to assume a modern form, reflected in its urban environment and its highly influential bourgeoisie. Still, the chivalric posturing was no game, any more than the revival of antiquity, which also attracted the enthusiastic patronage of the Estensi. The family's whole approach is a classic illustration of the dictum that at the moment when people

> seem engaged in revolutionizing themselves and things, in creating something that had never existed, precisely in such periods of revolutionary crises they anxiously conjure up the spirits of the past to their service and borrow from them names, battle cries, and costumes in order to present the new scene of world history in this time-honored disguise and this borrowed language.[5]

Like the Estensi, "Ariosto does not come to the epic via or in search of history: He comes to it as he finds it and transforms it by the operation of his own standards and the ideas and ideals of his time."[6] Yet he relies upon it to provide a stable foundation of assumptions and values upon

---

[5] Karl Marx, The Eighteenth Brumaire of Louis Bonaparte (1852; rpt. New York: International, 1963), p. 15.

[6] J.H. Whitfield, A Short History of Italian Literature (London: Penguin, 1969), p. 132.

--and often against--which to act. The chivalric framework is thus, strictly speaking, neither historical nor allegorical.

Participation of female knights in the epic events reflects the extent to which Ariosto's allegory is, throughout, "a tendency and not a system."[7] Bradamante and Marfisa are not models to be taken literally. When, for example, Melissa replies to Bradamante's inquiry about her female descendants, she expatiates for seventeen stanzas about the ladies of Casa d'Este (Canto XIII, 56-73). Bradamante asks whether they will be <u>belle</u> <u>e</u> <u>virtuose</u>, and Melissa speaks of their chastity, their loveliness, their wisdom, their scholarship. Military heroism and political glory are attributed to the brothers, sons, and husbands of these women. Neither the prophetess nor the warrior maiden herself sees this as any diminution of the line so adventurously founded or considers the latter-day women unworthy of their heroic ancestress. But this does not mean that the military role assumed by Bradamante and Marfisa is purely emblematic, just another way of representing the virtues that Este ladies will display in milder historical form. Rather, their chivalric guise enables them to exemplify new ideas entering an old system, just as they are, in their own persons, new "forms" wearing traditional armour. By similar extension of the body-symbolism, their knightly role makes it possible to bring a complex of principles that were understood to be female into the strictly masculine realm of politics.

---

[7] <u>Ibid</u>., p. 136.

Dynasty and Destiny

The chivalric theme, the role of the female knights within it, and the more general political thrust of the <u>Furioso</u> must be understood, first of all, in terms of the poem's dynastic function. For not only are Bradamante and Ruggiero portrayed as the founders of Casa d'Este, but their entire chivalric environment is also incorporated into the heritage of Ferrara. Three distinct stages of that heritage are delineated in the romance-epic: the Trojan past, the Carolingian present, and the Estense future. Each of these serves the limited purpose of legitimating the Este claim to authority as well as the more general one of historically validating the ideas identified with that authority.

Among the traditional sources of mythic legitimacy, imperial Rome is the one to which Ariosto has the least recourse in the <u>Furioso</u>. Universal empire and the universal church are themes that appear in medieval and modern references, rather than through direct allusion to the original Roman empire. But it is because of the Roman experience that the Trojan ancestry has so much rhetorical influence. Descent from the tragically defeated Hector and from his ravished city would be a very weak political symbol in the Renaissance, if Roman glory had not already rehabilitated the Trojan legend for its own purposes. Ariosto's use of the legend repeats the Virgilian assumption that, if descent can be demonstrated, the new civilization bears with it the divine mandate once bestowed upon the fallen city. It places strong emphasis not only on the genealogical facts, but also on the revival of Troy's greatness by her Carolingian posterity.

From this perspective, it is important for the poet to show that Ferrara was founded by a race of Trojans, a notion for which history and tradition provide very little support. In Canto XLI, Ariosto reiterates the accepted "facts" about Antenor's settlement of Padua, in an attempt to lend authority to his later assertion that Ferrara, in turn, was founded by refugees from that settlement:

>Signor, qui presso una città difende
>Il Po fra minacciose e fiere corna;
>La cui iuridizion di qui si stende
>Fin dove il mar fugge dal lito e torna:
>Cede d'antiquità, ma ben contende
>Con le vicine in esser ricca e adorna;
>Le reliquie Troiane la fondaro,
>Che dal flagello d'Attila camparo.
>   (Canto XLIII, 32)[8]

Ruggiero's posthumous child will be elected to lead these Trojan descendants, reinforcing the inheritance of the city and ruling house:

>E del sangue troian riconosciuto
>Da quei Troiani, in lor signor fia eletto
>   (Canto XLI, 64)

The first "Este" prince, moreover, is doubly Trojan, being descended from Hector through parents who combine "li due miglior rivi" [the best strains] of that race. The origins of the Chiaramonte family, to which Bradamante belongs, are well known throughout the epic, but the paternal line is announced more dramatically. Atlante's ghostly voice inter-

---

[8] Citations of the Italian text are from Ludovico Ariosto, <u>Orlando furioso</u>, a cura di Nicola Zingarelli, 6th edition (Milan: Hoepli, 1959).

cedes in the struggle between Marfisa and Ruggiero, telling them that they are brother and sister. They stop their fight, and Ruggiero describes their noble descent to his new-found twin, incidentally explaining to all of us how Hector came to have descendants at all:

> Ruggiero incominciò, che da Troiani
> Per la linea d'Ettorre erano scesi;
> Che poi che Astianatte de le mani
> Campò d'Ulisse, e da li aguati tesi,
> Avendo un de fanciulli coetani
> Per lui lasciato, uscí di quei paesi;
> E dopo un lungo errar per la marina,
> Venne in Sicilia, e dominò Messina.
>
> "I descendenti suoi di qua dal Faro
> Signoreggiar de la Calabria parte;
> E dope più successioni andaro
> Ad abitar ne la città di Marte:
> Più d'uno imperatore, e re preclaro
> Fu di quel sangue in Roma e in altra parte,
> Cominciando a Costante, e a Costantino,
> Sino a Re Carlo figlio di Pipino..."
> (Canto XXXVI, 70-71)

Strengthening pride in Trojan forebears, the poem repeatedly expresses suspicion of Greeks and their descendants, most notably in the passages concerning the (literally) homicidal women in Canto XX and the incidents involving Ruggiero's exploits after his beloved is promised to the Greek emperor's son.

It is not just Trojan blood that Ariosto stresses, but actual relics of the Trojan heroes, their new use signalling the mythic rebirth of national glory. The arms of Hector are especially important from this point of view. At first, Mandricardo has all of Hector's equipment except the sword. A bully and libertine, the Tartar king is also a heroic fighter and, in strictly military terms, he deserves the armor:

> ...lo facea più d'altro glorioso,
> Ch'al castel de la fata di Soria
> L'usbergo avea acquistato luminoso
> Ch'Ettor troian portò mille anni pria,
> Per strana e formidabile aventura,
> Che 'l ragionarne pur mette paura.
> (Canto XIV, 31)

Mandricardo desperately wants the sword that was missing from this panoply when he obtained it, but despite his chivalrous resolve to use no sword at all until he has won that one for himself, there is a strong sense that the weapon is already in the proper hands, for this is

> Durindana ch'Almonte ebbe in gran stima,
> E Orlando or porta, Ettor portava prima.
> (Canto XIV, 43)

The Tartar attempts to obtain the blade by fair means, which are not successful (Canto XXIII, 79ff), and foul ones, which are (Canto XXIV, 58). Mandricardo apparently believes the enchanted sword to be even more powerful than it is, perhaps because it is the weapon with which his father was killed. When Mandricardo himself is killed in a duel over Ruggiero's right to wear the Trojan eagle as his insignia, the arms pass to the more deserving knight. Subsequently, there is an impressive picture of Ruggiero riding to battle beside the leader of the entire pagan host:

> A par a par con lui venia Ruggiero,
> A cui servir non è Marsilio altiero.
>
> L'elmo che dianzi con travaglio tanto
> Trasse di testa al Re di Tartaria,
> L'elmo che celebrato in maggior canto
> Portò il troiano Ettor mill'anni pria,
> Gli porta il Re Marsilio a canto a canto:
> Altri principi et altra baronia
> S'hanno partite l'altr'arme fra loro,
> Ricche di gioie e ben fregiate d'oro.
> (Canto XXXVIII, 77-78)

After his shipwreck and conversion to Christianity, Ruggiero is admitted into the fraternity of paladins. To seal their new friendship, Orlando restores his horse, Frontino, lost in the wreck, and also places the celebrated sword in the hands of the Este patriarch. Within the narrative, Orlando's readiness to abandon his superior claim to the sword is attributed to his good nature, but it is clearly important for the dynastic element of the epic that Hector's arms end up with the Estensi.

Even more directly dynastic is the other Trojan souvenir, the bridal pavilion that Melissa spirits away from the Greek emperor to shelter Bradamante and Ruggiero. Cassandra had embroidered this tent for her heroic brother and

> L'ebbe mentre che visse Ettorre in pregio
> Per chi lo fece, e pel lavoro egregio.
> (Canto XLVI, 81)

MONSTROUS REGIMENT

The far-seeing prophetess had chosen for the decorative theme of this tent in which the dynasty was actually to be founded, the life and career of

> Il più cortese cavallier che mai
> Dovea del ceppo uscir del suo germano
> 					(Canto XLVI, 81)

That is, Cardinal Ippolito d'Este, Ariosto's employer.

In this context, even the most casual references to things Trojan acquire significance. Thus, for example, the comparison of Ruggiero to Ganymede (Canto IV, 47) or of Grifone to Hector (Canto XVIII, 64) and the conventional image of Troy in flames used to describe Ariodante's passion (Canto V, 18) are also reminders of the historical background of the Este heritage.

The Carolingian knights are not merely vehicles for the transmission of Trojan blood to the Estensi; they are very worthy ancestors in their own right. What the Trojans had to recommend them is the glamour of a vanished civilization and the even more attractive history of its "revival" in Rome. Since the Roman empire that was Troy's heir had, in its turn, disappeared, the idea of becoming its successor through mythic birthright had strong appeal for a number of Renaissance powers. Demonstrated descent from Charlemagne's empire made a family both Trojan and Roman, and also established its ties with an unequivocally Christian regime. Charles is the <u>Holy</u> Roman Emperor. His paladins have a spiritual mission, when they remember it, and the enemy is pagan.[9] Charlemagne, crowned by the Pope in Rome, repre-

---

[9] Although he does not make a great point of the enemy's religion, Ariosto invariably identifies Islam with pagan
(Footnote continued)

sents the resurgence of the Empire under auspices that unite church and state.

Ariosto fills his epic with prophecies about his heroes' descendants and their destiny. Like Virgil, he establishes this central theme very early in the poem. Addressing his patron, he announces:

> Voi sentirete fra i piu degni eroi,
> Che nominar con laude m'apparecchio,
> Ricordar quel Ruggier, che fu di voi
> E de vostri avi illustri il ceppo vecchio:
> L'alto valore e chiari gesti suoi
> Vi faro udir...
>   (Canto I, 4)

Virgil's entire epic is pregnant with the future destiny of Rome, but the latter-day gentes, specific Trojan descendants, even Augustus himself, are mentioned only in a few discrete passages. By contrast, the whole fabric of the Furioso is interwoven with direct and indirect allusions to the Estensi. Far from being an intended topic that somehow gets lost in the immense scope of the endeavor, the dynastic theme is continually before the reader. Viewed statistically, more of the poem's 38,736 stanzas are devoted to the

---

[9](continued)
idolatry. The "pagans" possess much the same moral code as the Christians, a code of chivalry, loyalty, and love to which the best of them adhere, at least as long as Discord stays out of their camp. Yet the poem defines them all as "worshippers" of the heathen god Mohammed. It is not clear if Ariosto, who was, after all, a cultivated humanist, was really that confused about the nature of Moslem belief, if he is ironically following the rhetoric of his medieval sources, or if that characterization of the enemy is a convention on the order of, say, "godless communism."

Este family and its progenitors than to any other subject--
certainly more than to the furibond passion of Orlando that
supplies its title.[10] Conceptually, ramifications of the
theme pervade the entire structure, beginning with the
poet's decision to assign a considerably more important
place to the Bradamante-Ruggiero story than Boiardo had
done. And Ariosto, whose sprezzatura remains unshaken when
he describes the most sacred personalities and the highest
reaches of heaven, is apparently sincere when he despairs of
his ability to rise to the "si nobil suggetto" of the Este
origins.

The copious material concerning Casa d'Este has both a
courtly and a more directly political aspect. That is, much
of it deals with personalities and events in the Este history, linking them to the narrative about the founders of
the family. Other references concentrate on the ideology
that Ariosto chooses to associate with his patrons, roughly,
the emerging Renaissance vision of political possibility.
Even the "courtly" passages are not devoid of interest,
however, since they are often closely related to the action
of the Furioso, and to its underlying ideas.

Prophecies about the descendants of Ruggiero and Bradamante occur at moments when they can enrich the epic's
dynastic significance without eliminating tension on the
narrative level about whether and when the couple will eventually be able to marry. In the first episode of this type,
Bradamante encounters the spirit of Merlin and its inter-
preter, Melissa, through the unconscious agency of Pinabello. The "frame-story" within which this first Este history
unfolds parallels the place of that theme in the epic as a

---

[10] K.H. Hartley, "Robert Garnier and Ariosto," Modern Language Review, 56 (1961), 389.

whole, reflecting the double tension between the characters' autonomy of action and the implacable workings of Fortune, and between notions of sexual and political destiny. While searching for Ruggiero, Bradamante meets Pinabello, who tells her of her lover's imprisonment. They are overtaken by the courier from Marseilles, whose urgent message Bradamante rejects:

> Quinci l'onore e il debito le pesa,
> Quindi l'incalza l'amoroso foco:
> Fermasi al fin di sequitar l'impresa
> E trar Ruggier de l'incantato loco
> (Canto II, 65)

For Bradamante, there is a conflict between love and immediate duty, and she chooses to neglect her responsibility to the beleagured town. At first, it seems that she will suffer for her unchivalrous decision, since Pinabello, inferring from the messenger's words that his companion is a Chiarmonte and hence a hereditary enemy, entices her to explore a deep cavern, into which he makes her fall. Not only is the warrior maiden saved by her own resourcefulness, however, but the subterranean passage turns out to be precisely the one in which Melissa and Merlin's ghost are waiting to tell her what fate has in store for her.

The prophecy is thus communicated against a background where the demands of love take precedence over the exigencies of political duty, and individual decisions are contained by a benevolent fortune that is ultimately in charge of how things work out. Within this context, the Este future is described in considerable (and often inaccurate or imaginary) detail. The solemnity of the occasion and the evident approval with which Merlin and Melissa regard

Bradamante make it clear that her dereliction of military duty is actually fulfillment of a higher historical duty, one that requires sexual means for its accomplishment.

At several other crucial points in the epic, the vision of the House of Este points up the current action. In Canto XIII, Melissa tells Bradamante about the enchanted dome and its bewitched prisoners; as the prophetess leads the lady knight to where she will encounter the disguised Atlante, she recapitulates the dynastic theme:

> Quella or per terren culto, or per foresta,
> A gran giornate e in gran fretta la guida,
> Cercando alleviarle tuttavia
> Con parlar grato la noiosa via.
>
> E piu di tutti i bei ragionamenti
> Spesso le repetea, ch'uscir di lei
> E di Ruggier doveano gli eccellenti
> Principi e gloriosi semidei...
>
> Canto XIII, 54-55

This recital and the further illumination about Bradamante's female descendants do more than beguile the time on a difficult journey. By reminding the young warrior that her relationship to Ruggiero has a historical dimension, Melissa is attempting to steel her for the immediate task: to liberate her beloved and his fellow prisoners by killing the wizard disguised as Ruggiero.

The dynastic argument is employed in a more openly rhetorical fashion when Melissa woos Ruggiero away from the enchantments of Alcina. Appearing to him in the form of Atlante, she chides him:

Ariosto

> Se non ti muovon le tue proprie laudi,
> E l'opre escelse, a chi t'ha il cielo eletto,
> La tua succession perché defraudi
> Del ben che mille volte io t'ho predetto?
> Deh perché il ventre eternamente claudi,
> Dove il ciel vuol che sia per te concetto
> La gloriosa e soprumana prole
> Ch'esser de'al mondo piu chiara che'l sole?
> (Canto VII, 60)[11]

This time, her argument is effective and Ruggiero is so ashamed and so eager to redeem himself that Melissa can resume her own form as she continues advising him.

Through Atlante, Ruggiero has apparently learned of his

---

[11] These lines also bring out some ambiguities in the representation of Atlante. He is apparently able to foretell Ruggiero's dynastic destiny, but is afraid that his protégé will not survive to fulfill the prophecy unless he is forcibly restrained from taking part in the war. If Atlante can predict one part of the future so accurately, why can he not also see that Ruggiero is fated to come through the war intact and hence has no need of supernatural goldbricking? Such literal-mindedness in interpreting the doings of a wizard may seem rather misplaced. But Ariosto's use of magic encourages a realistic reading. He is at pains to lend the events that depend on magic as much verisimilitude as possible. Moreover, although some of the most memorable moments in the plot turn on such devices as the ring of Angelica or the Hippogriff, Ariosto does not rely on magic to <u>replace</u> the poetic rationality on which the poem is based. There are considerably fewer mystical occurrences in the <u>Furioso</u> than in other romance-epics, many of these are taken over from Ariosto's sources, and most of them are benevolent. Even those supernatural events that have bad consequences are all part of Atlante's well-intentioned, if confused, plans to keep Ruggiero out of danger. Ariosto's infusion of a modern consciousness into his magician's spells, moreover, resides in the fact that they are not parlor-tricks, but are based on a precise and sensitive understanding of human psychology.

destiny; Melissa has only to remind him. But, within the <u>Orlando</u> <u>furioso</u> itself, it is not until after his conversion to Christianity that Ruggiero hears of his fate:

> Di molte cose intanto ragionava
> Con lui sovente, or al regno di Dio,
> Or agli proprii casi appertinenti,
> Or del suo sangue alle future genti.
>
> (Canto XLI, 60)

In short, Ruggiero is told about how he will die and be avenged at the same time that he learns about the foundation of the Este line and the nature of the Christian God. The good friar's presentation serenely conflates the City of God and the City of Ferrara as he preaches to the greater glory of both.

The prophecies that are well integrated into the narrative are those that concentrate on the Estensi in general. When Ariosto narrows his sights to living individuals in the family, the dominant note becomes one of courtly sycophancy. The arguments Melissa uses to extricate Ruggiero from Alcina's toils are a striking example of this phenomenon, because her discourse moves from the general mission of Ruggiero's descendants to the two particular Estensi who employed Ariosto. Ruggiero, she says, is standing in the way of history, preventing the foundation of an Este line destined for such greatness. How could he nip so brilliant a promise in the bud? And, especially, how could he bear to keep Alfonso and Ippolito d'Este from being born? Although the knight is convinced to break away from the enchantress, the drop in tone turns the scene from one influenced by Mercury's visitation in the <u>Aeneid</u> into a mere parody of Virgil's scene.

Still more bathetic is the point in Canto XXIX, after Isabella's heroic martyrdom, when a genuinely moving moment is destroyed by the fulsome panegyric on all future bearers of that hallowed name, a passage clearly intended as a compliment to Isabella d'Este.[12] The career of Ippolito, as depicted in Cassandra's embroidery, is matched in fatuity only by the fleece representing the noble Cardinal's fate that the reader already encountered in Canto XXXV. And both are almost equalled by the statues of good women displayed by Rinaldo in Canto XLII, where only Ariosto's virtuosity in describing visual art affords any relief.

Reasons of State

Those commentators who are most enthusiastic about the purely "poetic" elements in the epic tend to reject Ariosto's courtier role as a legitimate part of his endeavor. One such commentator goes so far as to maintain that praising the exploits and character of future Estensi spoils the pristine love story of their ancestors, placing it in the deadening category of courtly flattery.[13] This judgment not only reverses the importance of the poem's sexual and dynastic themes, but fails to recognize that, for Ariosto, the

---

[12] In this regard, it is interesting to observe the mutual influence between literature and Este family nomenclature. A great many of the Estensi before Ariosto's time bore names inspired by the Arthurian romances. Ariosto borrowed a number of these names for the ancestral background he invents in the Furioso. And, subsequently, Francesco d'Este, son of Duke Alfonso I and Lucrezia Borgia, named his two illegitimate daughters Marfisa and Bradamante, after Ariosto's lady knights.

[13] Franco Pool, Interpretazione dell'Orlando furioso (Florence: La Nuova Italia, 1968), p. 184.

two are inextricably connected.

Similarly, Croce's preoccupation with his dual formula of harmony and irony forces him to dismiss the Furioso's claims to epic status, insisting that it lacks both the substance and sentiments of such poetry.[14] In fact, the principal characteristic of secondary epic is its involvement with historicial and genealogical myth. The Virgilian model represents the most notable achievement in this direction and, unless one either rejects the Aeneid as an epic, too, or assumes that Ariosto's use of it is wholly ironic, it seems to me difficult to deny that the Orlando furioso is in the same vein. The influence of Virgil and the logic of romance both contribute to Ariosto's treatment of the Estensi in the context of his broader political intention.

As Segre points out, Ariosto had a diplomatic and material obligation to celebrate the Este family, but his handling of that subject is an important element in shifting the poem's essential balance from the fanciful to the realistic.[15] The glorification of a noble family in literary epic had import on one level, simply because "nothing could be more serious than patronly approval."[16] Yet Ariosto really took the Estensi seriously and, in an idealized sense, he took them on their own terms. That is, he apparently shared the family's convictions about the clan's immediate historic mission while, at the same time, systematically attributing to them a wider vision of their political potential than their actual history would appear to

---

[14] Benedetto Croce, Ludovico Ariosto, Part I of Ariosto, Shakespeare e Corneille (1920; rpt. Bari: Laterza, 1963), p. 75.

[15] Segre, p. 18.

[16] Greene, p. 133.

justify. This is quite different from saying, as Croce does, that Ariosto's attitude towards the Estensi was not political, that he admired their power and their patronage of the arts, but used the entire dynastic subject as an imaginative plaything.[17] Rather, the poet establishes a complex dialogue between the Este family as he knew them and the most advanced political philosophy of Renaissance Europe.

Melissa's initial revelations to Bradamante about her descendants touch on this general political picture, stressing the family's far-ranging patrimony, its imperial connections, its divine ordination, and its service to the Church, relating all these elements to the desperate plight of Italy and her cry for liberation. The themes suggested by this introduction to the Estensi recur throughout the epic, along with observations about the human qualities Ariosto considers essential to his political vision. Thus, in Canto III, the personal virtues of the various Este scions parallel their prodigious military and political accomplishments. The generations that are to follow Ruggierino's settlement in Italy will spread Este rule throughout much of Europe. Heirs of Bradamante and Ruggiero will reign in Verona and Spoleto, conquer Urbino and Milan, hold Pesaro, Ancona, Reggio, Modena, Faenza, Rovigo, Commacchio, as well as "mille/Altre castella e populose ville." And their Italian heritage will be increased by matrimonial as well as military triumphs:

> De l'altro [Albertazzo d'Este] la Contessa
> gloriosa,

---

[17] Croce, p. 58.

MONSTROUS REGIMENT

> Saggia e casta Matilde, sarà sposa.
>
> Virtù il farà di tal connubio degno;
> Ch'a quella età non poca laude estimo
> Quasi di meza Italia in dote il regno,
> E la nipote aver d'Enrico primo.
> (Canto III, 29-30)

Nor are they limited to Italy, for the web of relationships spreads northward, as well:

> E sarà degno a cui [Alberto Azzo II] Cesare Otone
> Alda, sua figlia, in matrimonio aggiunga...
>
> Vedi Folco, che par ch'al suo germano
> Ciò che in Italia avea tutto abbi dato,
> E vada a possedere indi lontano
> In mezo agli Alamanni un gran ducato;
> E dia alla casa di Sansogna mano,
> Che caduta sarà tutta da un lato;
> E per la linea de la madre, erede,
> Con la progenie sua la terrà in piede.
> (Canto III, 27-28)

An initial impression of the extent of Este holdings is broadened in the course of the poem by reminders of the family's French origins and connections, Ruggiero's Bulgarian title, and Marfisa's Indian reign. Ariosto is not making a crude (and clearly unenforceable) territorial claim on behalf of his patrons. The wide range of their hereditary realm is, rather, a concrete expression of their Trojan birthright and the idea of Troy-novant.

As this range implies, the poet's imperial preoccupations assume spatial, as well as political dimensions. Ariosto's explicit goal is not an empire for the Estensi. Instead, he develops two distinct ideas--the family's imperial heritage and universal rule--connecting them only by implication. Although his references to contemporary exploration in the New World include some adulatory remarks about the Emperor Charles V, direct beneficiary of the discoveries, he is more enthusiastic about the enterprise itself. Andronica tells Astolfo about the imperial ventures:

> Ma volgendosi gli anni, io veggio uscire
> Da l'estreme contrade di Ponente
> Nuovi Argonauti, e nuovi Tifi, e aprire
> La strada ignota infin al dí presente:
> Altri volteggiar l'Africa e seguire
> Tanto la costa de la negra gente,
> Che passino quel segno onde ritorno
> Fa il sole a noi, lasciando il Capricorno;
>
> E ritrovar del lungo tratto il fine
> Che questo fa parer dui mar diversi;
> E scorrer tutti i liti, e le vicine
> Isole d'Indi, d'Arabi e di Persi:
> Altri lasciar le destre e le mancine
> Rive, che due per opra Erculea fersi;
> E del sole imitando il camin tondo,
> Ritrovar nuove terre e nuovo mondo.
> (Canto XV, 21-22)

It was the will of God that this activity take place under the scepter of His chosen emperor. As Andronica explains it, God will keep men ignorant that the world is round for some seven centuries after the Carolingian Age,

> E serba a farla al tempo manifesta,
> Che vorrà porre il mondo a monarchia,
> Sotto il più saggio Imperatore e giusto,
> Che sia stato o sarà mai, dopo Augusto...
> ....
> Per questi merti la bontà suprema
> Non solamente di quel grande impero
> Ha disegnato ch'abbia diadema
> Ch'ebbe Augusto, Traian, Marco e Severo;
> Ma d'ogni terra e quinci e quindi estrema
> Che mai né al sol né all'anno apre il sentiero:
> E vuol che sotto a questo Imperatore
> Solo un ovile sia, solo un pastore.
>
> (Canto XV, 24, 26)

Considering the (literally) global impact of this idea, Charles V is hardly central to Ariosto's thinking. The passages about the emperor were probably added while the _Furioso_ was in progress. In any event, the concept of universal empire seems to have interested the poet far more than his own extremely contingent candidate for its leader. Even the physical extent of that empire, the geographical panorama itself, appears, as I have indicated, to hold greater fascination for him; the view Astolfo has from the back of the Hippogriff is quite as fresh and exciting as Ariosto's description of the new-found lands paying tribute to the emperor.

Ariosto's geographical enthusiasm has a two-fold ideological basis: It is founded on the idea of a single Christian commonwealth and that of a liberated Italy. Rinaldo's speech to the troops who have come with him to the relief of Paris epitomizes the first of these motives:

Ariosto

> Se donavan gli antiqui una corona
> A chi salvasse a un cittadin la vita,
> Or che degna mercede a voi si dona,
> Salvando multitudine infinita?
> Ma se da invidia, o da viltà, si buona
> E si santa opra rimarrá impedita
> Credetemi che prese quelle mura,
> Né Italia né Lamagna anco è sicura;
>
> Né qualunque altra parte ove s'adori
> Quel che volse per noi pender sul legno...
> ....
> Ma quando ancor nessuno onor, nessuno
> Util v'inanimasse a questa impresa,
> Commun debito è ben, soccorrer l'uno
> L'altro, che militian sotto una Chiesa...
>   (Canto XVI, 36-38)

The military and the spiritual aspects of mutual dependence fuse, here, into a single political vision. But the driving faith that could solidify such unity is missing from Ariosto's intellectual make-up. Even when the poet, speaking in his own voice, calls for a crusade, his reasons are practical as well as pious. To be sure, the holy places ought to be rescued from the infidels, but there is also rich territory out there for Europeans to exploit. ("Out there" rapidly ceases to be Palestine alone and includes everywhere the inhabitants are non-Christian or have dark skins.) At least, the cynical harangue continues, such a mission would get the foreigners out of Italy and set them onto more suitable victims:

> Non hai tu Spagna l'Africa vicina,

Che t'ha via più di questa Italia offesa?
E pur per dar travaglio alla meschina
Lasci la prima tua si bella impresa...

Se 'l dubbio di morir ne le tue tane,
Svizer, di fame, in Lombardia ti guida,
E tra noi cerchi, o chi ti dia del pane,
O per uscir d'inopia chi t'uccida;
Le ricchezze del Turco hai non lontane:
Caccial d'Europa, o almen di Grecia snida;
Cosí potrai o del digiuno trarti,
O cader con piu merto in quelle parti.

Quel ch'a te dico, io dico al tuo vicino
Tedesco ancor: là le ricchezze sono,
Che vi porto da Roma Constantino;
Portonne il meglio, e fe' del resto dono...
                              (Canto XVII, 76-78)

Ariosto's introduction of the Estensi portrays them as loyal soldiers of the Church, and he relates this stance to his idea of world-wide Christian empire. But rescue of Italy from foreign oppressors had far more reality to Ariosto as a working political construct. Again, the theme is adumbrated in Melissa's first prophecy about the Estensi, where the family's repeated role is that of the hero who turns "fair Italy's long grief to joy."[18] Further on in the poem, the famous invective against firearms describes the contemporary conflict between Francis I and Charles V as a

---

[18] Canto III, 32. This phrase is from the translation of William Stewart Rose: Ludovico Ariosto, Orlando furioso, ed. Stewart A. Baker and A. Bartlett Giamatti (Trans. 1823-31; rpt. Indianapolis: Bobbs-Merrill, 1968).

war "che 'l mondo, ma più Italia ha meso in pianti." (Canto XI, 27) At the Rocca di Tristano, Bradamante is shown Merlin's prophetic paintings representing "le guerre ch'i Franceschi da far hano/Di là da l'Alpe," a lengthy history, one of whose recurrent motives is the suffering of the land beyond the Alps. But no circumstantial list is as striking as the more allegorical reference to those depradations that appears as a digression in the tale of Astolfo and King Fineo:

> Oh famelice, inique e fiere Arpie
> Ch'all'accecata Italia e d'error piena,
> Per punir forse antique colpe rie,
> In ogni mensa alto giudicio mena:
> Innocenti fanciulli e madri pie
> Cascan di fame, e veggon ch'una cena
> De questi mostri rei tutto divora
> Ciò che del viver lor sostegno fora.
>
> Troppo fallò chi le spelonche aperse,
> Che già molt'anni erano state chiuse;
> Onde il fetore e l'ingordigia emerse,
> Ch'ad ammorbare Italia si diffuse:
> Il bel vivere allora si summerse;
> E la quiete in tal modo s'escluse,
> Ch'in guerre, in poverta sempre, e in affanni
> E dopo stata, et è per star molt'anni.
>   (Canto XXXIV, 1-2)

Both passages refer to a potential redemption, the historical one placing its trust in the heroic Alofonso d'Avalos, Marchese of Vasto, the other speaking of the time when Italy's own sons awaken to her plight.

The two themes, universal Christian empire and the liberation of Italy, are familiar strains in Italian literature. Ariosto makes them modern by linking them, at every stage, to the present condition of Italy as he perceives it and to the remedies that must arise out of that situation. It is his understanding of the history in which he was living that brings his treatment closer to the realism of a Machiavelli than the evangelism of Dante. There is some controversy among students of Ariosto as to whether or not the poet "believed in" the advent of a Dantesque redeemer of Italy. As the use of inverted commas implies, I think part of the difficulty rests in framing the problem in these terms, which suggest not only the content of an idea, but the way in which it is held. Moreover, despite allusions to several contemporary figures (his Este patrons, the Marchese del Vasto, Andrea Doria) who had served Italy well, Ariosto's concern is never with an individual redeemer. Unlike Virgil, who portrays the Golden Age as being ushered in by the birth of a wondrous child, Ariosto treats that topos as a collective phenomenon, although inspired by the Estensi who:

> ...come il savio Augusto e Numa fenno,
> Sotto il benigno e buon governo loro
> Ritorneran la prima età de l'oro.
> (Canto III, 18)

More often in the Furioso, Italy's redemption is not a personal matter at all, but rather depends on a combination of political method and human attributes. Although Machiavelli uses many illustrations of the princely temperament, they, too, are examples drawn from an individual's strategy and tactics. And, although the final section of The Prince couches its call for the rescue of Italy in terms of a single person, Machiavelli, too, is speaking more of the human dimension than of any particular person.

Although Croce explicitly dismisses all but the most remote comparisons between these two close contemporaries, he admits that for Ariosto, as for Machiavelli, politics is morality.[19] This certainly cannot mean that the poet expects public life to be carried out on the same level of conscience at which an individual Christian is required to live. It must, rather, be interpreted as implying that Ariosto assimilates politics to morality, placing it, at the same time, under the control of the best aspects of the human character as he understood it.[20]

Ariosto's status as a political thinker is enhanced by two passages that also reflect his poetic range. The first of these occurs in Canto XXVI, where Ruggiero and his companions encounter Merlin's sculpted fountain, which Malagigi interprets for them. Merlin's work is both literally and allegorically prophetic, portraying the rulers of Cinquecento Europe beside the horrible beast they have slain. Here, the combination of symbolic and historical techniques functions to place the Este family, with whom the catalogue of monarchs ends, in an appropriate--if highly exaggerated--world-historic context, reflecting Ariosto's comprehension of that broader background.

The other scene takes place on the moon, where Astolfo

---

[19] See Croce, p. 73, for the dismissal and p. 57 for the admission.

[20] It is worth noting that Ariosto also employs the concept of "the state" as Machiavelli does. The case could be made philologically, at least, through reference to such passages as the one wherein Olimpia, reunited with Bireno, "de lo Stato e di se dona il governo" (Canto IX, 86).

has gone to retrieve Orlando's wits. In a rich progression of stanzas, Ariosto betrays a more general sort of political wisdom, compounded almost equally of bitterness and humor:

> Vide un monte di tumide vesiche,
> Che dentro parea aver tumulti e grida:
> E seppe ch'eran le corone antiche,
> E degli Assirii, e de la terra Lida,
> E de Persi e de Greci, che gia furo
> Incliti, et or n'è quasi il nome oscuro.
>
> Ami d'oro e d'argento appresso vede
> In una massa, ch'erano quei doni
> Che si fan con speranza di mercede
> Ai re, agli avari principi, ai patroni...
> ....
> Ruine di cittadi e di castella
> Stavan con gran tesor quivi sozopra;
> Domanda, e sa che son trattati, e quella
> Congiura che sí mal par che si cuopra:
> Vide serpi con faccia di donzella,
> Di monetieri e di ladroni l'opra;
> Poi vide boccie rotte di più sorti,
> Ch'era il servir de le misere corti.
>
> (Canto XXXIV, 76-79)

Although adhering to established literary conventions about the court, these observations are important because they are not used to rationalize a rejection of public life, but to advance the particular kind of politics that Ariosto was to profess.

The realistic attitude that underlies these stanzas is reflected in other elements of the poem, most notably in views expressed about tyranny and justice. Canto XVII begins with a discussion of why tyrants are inflicted on society:

> Il giusto Dio, quando i peccati nostri
> Hanno di remission passato il segno,
> Acciò che la giustizia sua dimostri
> Uguale alla pietà, spesso dá regno
> A tiranni atrocissimi et a mostri,
> E da lor forza, e di mal fare ingegno...
> (Canto XVII, 1)

Ariosto does not infer from this that people should remain passive, nor does he suggest a political remedy beyond the limits of the poem itself. A similar observation may be made about Ariostan justice. Because the military milieu and its chivalric ethos are the epic's analogues to the state, the poet does not trouble to make the kingdoms that appear in his casual anecdotes microcosms of either justice or injustice. (The chief exception, which I shall discuss in greater detail below, is the _sexual_ politics prevailing in those realms.) Thus, Bradamante may point out to her host at the Rocca di Tristano that his decision to eject Ullania is wrong on the merits and also that

> Né che ben giusto alcun giudicio cada,
> Ove prima non s'oda quanto nieghi
> La parte o affermi, e sue ragioni alleghi
> (Canto, XXXII, 101)

But earlier in the same Canto, Brunello is hanged without a hearing, and we learn that this kind of summary justice contains a further inequity, for, if Ruggiero had not been prostrated by his wounds, his influence would have served as protection. When Zerbino is sentenced to be quartered,

> Altra esamina in ciò non si facea,
> Bastava che 'l Signor cosí credea.
> (Canto XXIII, 51)

The point is not that Ariosto can countenance Bradamante's position and its diametrical opposite at the same time, but rather that his response to the question, "What is Justice?" has nothing to do with the incidents in which civil justice is enacted. It resides in qualities that he believes must exist within men before they can be imparted to the state.

When Croce says of Ariosto that "kindness and generosity were the essence of his politics," his intention is to deprecate the political element, representing the poet as nothing more than the universal Man of Good Will, whose real concerns are far from matters and theories of state.[21] This approach fails to take into account the political dimensions of Ariosto's views as the _Furioso_ reveals them. The salient feature of the position, applied to government, is its combination of virtue and flexibility; the Renaissance prince, in Ariosto's definition, practices the highest degree of Christian and chivalric virtue compatible with the need for balance in government. The greatest military victory, therefore, is the one that accomplishes its goal with the smallest damage to one's own army, not the bloody triumph that earns belated "glory":

---

21 See Croce, pp. 56-57.

Ariosto

> Fu il vincer sempremai laudabil cosa,
> Vincasi o per fortuna o per ingegno;
> Gli è ver che la vittoria sanguinosa
> Spesso far suole il capitan men degno;
> E quella eternamente è gloriosa,
> E dei divini onori arriva al segno,
> Quando, servando i suoi senza alcun danno,
> Si fa che gl'inimici in rotta vanno.
> (Canto XV, 1)

Similarly, relations between the prince and his subjects must be based on the kind of trust that comes from a balanced situation. Loyalty is not engendered and supported by feudal oaths, but by such equitable treatment as Rinaldo dispenses to his followers:

> Ciascun d'essi al bisogno era sí saldo,
> Che cento insieme non fuggian per mille;
> E se ne potean molti sceglier fuori,
> Che d'alcun dei famosi eran migliori.
>
> E se Rinaldo ben non era molto
> Ricco né di città né di tesoro,
> Facea sí con parole e con buon volto,
> E ciò ch'avea partendo ognor con loro,
> Ch'un di quel numer mai non gli fu tolto
> Per offerire altrui più somma d'oro:
> Questi da Montalban mai non rimuove,
> Se non lo stringe un gran bisogno altrove.
> (Canto XXXI, 56-57)

On the moral plane, the case is both more fundamental and more complex. A key issue in the narrative, for example, is whether Bradamante and Ruggiero are already married when Amone attempts to betroth his daughter to Leone. In a passage that I shall explore more fully later on, Marfisa, so much a paragon of knightly qualities that she seems almost a parody of them, nonetheless tells the expedient lie without compunction, because it is politically and humanly necessary.

Although chivalry, as Ariosto displays it to us, is always tempered by the poet's ironic stance, he is still able to recruit chivalric values to the service of a modern ideology. It is in this light that Ruggiero's persistent refusal to make use of supernatural powers should be viewed. Magic performs a generally positive function in the <u>Furioso</u>, but Ruggiero's action in not taking unfair advantage of it simultaneously enhances his chivalrous character and disassociates him from a medieval ethos that relied on such devices. Moreover, his eventual submerging of the brilliant enchanted shield parallels Orlando's burial of the firearms, striking a balance between external aids from both past and future cultures in favor of a human norm between the two.

On a somewhat less direct level, Ariosto takes pains to remind us that his heroes fight for principle, not for material gain, and will not even accept certain kinds of spoils. Orlando, for instance,

> ...sempre atto stimò d'animo molle
> Gir con vantaggio in qualsivoglia impresa.
> (Canto IX, 89)

For this reason, also, the paladins are depicted as military men who do not have to go berserk in order to accomplish great feats of daring. In fact, Orlando in his lovesick frenzy and Rodomonte in his perpetually magnificent madness are set up in contrast to a more balanced conduct of war. When the battle is over, the Christian knight can show mercy:

> ...dopo il fatto nulla di maligno
> In sé tenea, ma tutto era clemente
> (Canto XLII, 19)

The internal balance reflected in this sort of courtesy informs the values that the <u>Orlando</u> <u>furioso</u> seeks to communicate. It motivates, for example, the dignity and self-control evinced by Bradamante when she challenges her supposed betrayer to armed combat.

Although the values of love and moderation are themselves traditional, Ariosto makes them new by investing them with a kind of suppleness, in contrast to the rigid standards of the <u>chansons</u> <u>de</u> <u>geste</u>. Moreover, in making "providential love" his central principle, Ariosto effects a drastic shift in values from those Christian and classical sources that wholly separated the realm of earthly love from that of the cardinal virtues. In the <u>Orlando</u> <u>furioso</u>, that love becomes, in fact, the touchstone against which the other values are measured.

<u>Ruggiero's Coming of Age</u>

In order to make sense of the <u>Furioso</u>, it is necessary to read it with a double perspective, shifting continually from the details of a single part to the design of the whole and from narrative discontinuities to thematic unities. The matters I have discussed so far are not simply "background" to the sexual and political questions that are my chief focus. They are part of the same cluster of ideas, essential preliminaries to understanding the main problems, yet not fully apprehended in themselves until the central issue is resolved. In this way, some of the generalizations I have made derive from my interpretation of the Ruggiero-Bradamante-Marfisa axis in the epic, but they also provide fresh insights when reapplied to that narrative strain and undergo, themselves, a deepening and modification in the process.

Many of the conflicting forces in the <u>Furioso</u> are at work in the character and experience of Ruggiero. Although the poem claims no single hero, he is its real protagonist, bringing the narrative and ideological dynamics together. He comes close to being a true character, in that he is the only one in the epic whose internal development is manifest and consistent, the only one who really changes. Of course, Orlando <u>undergoes</u> changes, but their whole point is that they are abrupt, incoherent, and entirely outside his control; Orlando does not learn anything in the course of the poem even after his wits are restored to him. Ruggiero, by contrast, is subjected to a series of lessons that systematically confront him with moral choices and their consequences. <u>Il buono Ruggiero</u> is the closest Ariosto comes in either language or concept to <u>pius Aeneas</u>, the Virgilian hero who bears within himself the fundamental contradiction on which the poem is constructed. By the time Ariosto introduces him, the Ruggiero of the <u>Innamorato</u> has already outgrown some of the youthful high spirits that marked Boiardo's character. But it is in the course of the <u>Furioso</u> that he really grows up, his dignity increasing with his understanding of himself and his world.

The military setting of the poem, governed by its chivalric values, stands for public life in general, controlled by human morality. In much the same way, Ruggiero's military prowess reflects his consciousness at each stage of his development. Ruggiero is always a magnificent fighter; he does not achieve heroic stature in the poem by turning into a good soldier, but by coming increasingly to understand what he has to fight for. He and his twin, Marfisa, are mirror images of knightly skill and mutual admiration:

> Ma di Ruggier pur il valor stupendo
> E senza pari al mondo le sembrava;
> E talor si credea che fosse Marte
> Sceso dal quinto cielo in quella parte...
> ....
> Il buon Turpin, che sa che dice il vero
> E lascia creder poi quel ch'a l'uom piace
> Narra mirabil cose di Ruggiero,
> Ch'udendolo il direste voi mendace:
> Cosí parea di ghiaccio ogni guerriero
> Contra Marfisa, et ella ardente face;
> E non men di Ruggier gli occhi a sé trasse,
> Ch'ella di lui l'alto valor mirasse.
> (Canto XXVI, 20, 23)

His technical performance would be difficult to improve upon, and Ariosto makes no effort to do so. Although seriously wounded in his duel with the savage Mandricardo, he is the victor and goes on to other triumphs. The difference is that his opponents are increasingly worth fighting, and his battles are increasingly tied to the major themes of the poem. Thus, when he joins with the Bulgars against the Greek empire, saving the day for his new allies, he is no longer motivated by the simple love of sport and honor that, for Ariosto, defines medieval knighthood. Rather, he is fighting against those who would claim Bradamante, thus usurping both his love and his historical role, and he is asserting his heritage as the avenging descendant of Hector. The final battle of the *Furioso* is reserved for him as well, and his slaying of Rodomonte is not an anti-climax, but a resolution of major strains that Ariosto has developed in the poem and that Ruggiero, himself, has increasingly assimilated.

The way Ruggiero comes to this position is through the personal conflicts that the narrative forces him to resolve. Reduced to their simplest terms, the first of these conflicts may be defined as taking place between love and lust, the second between love and duty. But this simplification obscures the real point, which is the ambiguity of both sets of contradictions, the resultant double standard, and a resolution that necessarily involves the new principles represented by the two female knights, his sister and his betrothed.

The tension between Ruggiero's honest love for Bradamante and his wayward sexual impulses occurs in the first half of the poem. Each side of this conflict is somewhat vague, yet the narrative handles the issue as if it were a conventional Education of the Hero. The second half of the *Furioso* explores the conflict between lawful fulfillment of Ruggiero's love and accomplishment of his chivalric duty. The definitions are unclear once again, but this time the struggle between the two forces is enacted in terms of Ruggiero's own psychology. In addition to the deliberate duality of "lust," "love," and "duty," Ariosto also constructs a dialectical situation <u>between</u> the two pairs of concepts, in which the reduplicated double standard--sexual permissiveness and chivalric discipline for the male, sexual rigidity and moral flexibility for the female--comes into its own.

152

Ariosto

In creating the terms of Ruggiero's love conflict, Ariosto had to work within the limits established by his predecessor. Boiardo had already "covered" the meeting and enamorment of Bradamante and Ruggiero, providing the *Furioso* with a *fait accompli* as regards one of the most common cruxes of literary love affairs. The separation of the two lovers, their search for each other and the changing reasons for their unconsummated relationship, are Ariosto's substitute for the tensions normally engendered by a couple's passing through adventures on the way to falling in love. They are in love, then, from the beginning, but the first thematic conflict that arises is in their disparate degrees of steadfastness. Bradamante is unwavering in her love and her quest, but Ruggiero repeatedly falls prey to his baser instincts.

His love begins as a fixed point. Thus, when the myrtle tree he unthinkingly injures turns out to have human feelings, indeed to be Astolfo himself, the vow of recompense he takes is by the love of Bradamante. But he is already on Alcina's island, and reparataions to Astolfo are slow in coming.[22] For despite his love and his noble intentions, Ruggiero is the next victim of Alcina's lust, such that

> La bella donna, che cotanto amava,
> Novellamente gli è dal cor partita;
> Che per incanto Alcina gli lo lava
> D'ogni antica amorosa sua ferita
>
> (Canto VII, 18)

---

[22] For the garden as the locus of fundamental and conflicting forces, see A. Bartlett Giamatti, *The Earthly Paradise and the Renaissance Epic* (Princeton: Princeton University Press, 1966), p. 6.

Atlante, with his ambiguous good intentions, was responsible for the precipitate flight that got Ruggiero into this situation, and there is further magic involved in the knight's new thralldom to the enchantress. Its effects are undeniably evil, and the false paradise has to be destroyed by Ruggiero's becoming conscious of what it really is. Ariosto takes pains to present the case for governance by reason clearly and undogmatically, but he is also remarkably tolerant of Ruggiero's lapse. The stanza quoted just above concludes:

> E di sé sola, e del suo amor lo grava,
> E in quello essa riman sola sculpita;
> Sí che scusar il buon Ruggier si deve,
> Se si mostrò quivi incostante, e lieve.
> (Canto VII, 18)

Melissa's arguments about his duty to Bradamante and to history combine with revelation of Alcina's essential ugliness to free Ruggiero from the toils of spurious love and enable him to liberate his fellow-victims. The guidance of Logistilla drives the lesson home to him. But, finally, tolerance for sexual susceptibility remains the dominant note.

It is no surprise, therefore, that Ruggiero's very next adventure recapitulates the same elements, endowing them with even greater moral ambiguity. Although eager to join Bradamante, he decides to tour the world on the Hippogriff. Catching sight of Angelica naked, chained to a rock, waiting to be devoured by the dread Orca, his wish to aid her is initially inspired by thoughts of his own lady:

Ariosto

> E come ne begli occhi gli occhi affisse,
> De la sua Bradamante gli sovenne;
> Pietade e amore a un tempo lo traffisse,
> E di piangere a pena si ritenne...
> (Canto X, 97)

His motives do not remain this pure, however, and by the time he has stunned the monster, he wants Angelica for himself. As Ariosto comments,

> Raro è però che di ragione il morso
> Libidinosa furia a dietro volga.
> (Canto XI, 1)

And the poet's worldly tolerance for a passionate affair has expanded to libertine cynicism towards the projected rape:

> Qual ragion fia che 'l buon Ruggier raffrene;
> Sí che non voglia ora pigliar diletto
> D'Angelica gentil, che nuda tiene
> Nel solitario e commodo boschetto?
> Di Bradamante più non gli soviene,
> Che tanto aver solea fissa nel petto:
> E se gli ne sovien, pur come prima,
> Pazzo è se questa ancor non prezza e stima.
> (Canto XI, 2)

Ariosto's sense of irony turns the scene into farce, as Ruggiero fumbles with heavy armor in his haste to undress, while Angelica realizes just what ring he has placed in her charge and promptly uses it to disappear. The ambiguities in the situation are summarized in the curious stanza describing Ruggiero's reaction:

MONSTROUS REGIMENT

> Fu grave e mala aggiunta all'altro danno
> Vedersi anco restar senza l'augello;
> Questo, non men che 'l feminile inganno,
> Gli preme al cor; ma più che questo e quello,
> Gli preme e fa sentir noioso affanno
> L'aver perduto il prezioso annello;
> Per le virtù non tanto ch'in lui sono,
> Quanto che fu de la sua donna dono.
>
> (Canto XI, 14)

Angelica has escaped an off-hand ravishment by putting the ring into her mouth and disappearing, and Ruggiero's lament is a mixture of disappointed lust and regret for the ring that his own lady had sent him! Ruggiero then climbs up on the Hippogriff and flies away to where he fortuitously saves Bradamante from a giant. The last-minute rescue is not very different from his service to Angelica, but this time he pursues the monster, instead of being left with the lady--towards whom, in any event, his conduct is always irreproachably chaste. The problems raised in the Angelica incident are not satisfactorily solved anywhere in the poem. Ruggiero's subsequent behavior implies that Logistilla's teaching is effective in the long run. Yet, in following it by the interlude with Angelica, Ariosto has taken pains to show us what becomes of such teaching in a flesh and blood situation.

The exigencies of the narrative force a more definite conclusion in the conflict between love and duty, but equivocation long remains Ruggiero's characteristic approach to the problem. His response is so uneasy because the definitions themselves are equivocal. Like Aeneas, he is divided between the demands of love and those of immediate duty, but unlike the Roman hero, he is caught in a situation where that duty is increasingly estranged from his ultimate fate and purpose. It is not love that makes wild and unreasonable demands on him, but the course of action he conceives to be his duty. Ruggiero's troubles begin when, hurrying to rescue Ricciardetto from the stake, he encounters one of Agramante's messengers, who announces that their cause is in desperate straits and that all the pagan forces are being mustered. His present mission is of the utmost urgency, but

> Fu da molti pensier ridutto in forse
> Ruggier, che tutti l'assaliro a un tratto;
> Ma qual per lo miglior dovesse torse,
> Né luogo avea né tempo a pensar atto.
> (Canto XXV, 6)

Nor are Ruggiero's mental processes much more effective after Ricciardetto is freed and he has leisure to consider his decision. He has already agreed to be baptized before asking Bradamante's father for her hand in marriage, and his conversion has little to do with religious zeal. A mild filial feeling and his overwhelming love for Bradamante are the compelling motives:

> Ruggier, che tolto avria non solamente
> Viver cristiano per amor di questa [Bradamante],
> Com'era stato il padre, e antiquamente
> L'avolo e tutta la sua stirpe onesta;
> Ma per farle piacere, immantinente
> Data le avria la vita che gli resta:
> "Non che ne l'acqua (disse) ma nel fuoco
> Per tuo amor porre il capo mi fia poco."
> (Canto XXII, 35)

At the moment when he meets the courier, therefore, the argument for becoming a Christian is informed by love. The duty that calls is his responsibility as a knight, his personal loyalty to King Agramante, whom he is reluctant to desert in time of need. Yet he is aware that marriage with Bradamante also involves duty, for Atlante has often told him about the illustrious line he is destined to beget. His first decision thus pits the obsolete standards of chivalry against the needs of an enlightened future.

Initially, Ruggiero seems to see no disparity between the forces pulling him in different directions, but only conflicting demands on his time. He decides to serve his lord as long as he is needed and then proceed with the baptism and marriage. It is not clear whether he anticipates a Christian or pagan victory and how he thinks the outcome of the war will affect his knightly service or his future plans, for he apparently does not consider the <u>social</u> consequences of his decision. (Will he fight well for Agramante, while hoping Charlemagne wins out? Or do his best and forget that his love may be at stake? Or dishonor himself by a half-hearted performance in battle?) He sees the question in absurdly individual terms: his own private loyalties and public reputation are the only factors to consider. His main concern is lest conversion at this juncture be interpreted as cowardice:

> Quanta gli sarà infamia, quanto scorno,
> Se coi nemici va del suo Signore;
> Oh come a gran viltade, a gran delitto,
> Battezandosi allor gli sarà ascritto.
>
> Potria in ogn'altro tempo esser creduto
> Che vera religion l'avesse mosso;

Ariosto

> Ma ora che bisogna col suo aiuto
> Agramante d'assedio esser riscosso,
> Più tosto da ciascun sarà tenuto,
> Che timore e viltà l'abbia percosso,
> Ch'alcuna opinion di miglior fede.
> (Canto XXV, 81-82)

By the time he writes to Bradamante to explain his postponed baptism, Ruggiero is convinced that his feudal definitions of honor will also weigh with her; his letter argues that preservation of his honor is for her sake, as well,

> Che non si convenia con lei, che tutta
> Era sincera, alcuna cosa brutta.
> (Canto XXV, 87)

Needless to say, Bradamante does not see it that way. She passionately laments his resolve to serve her enemies, and those of her God and sovereign. They should be Ruggiero's enemies, too, not merely because they are hers, but because of his duty to avenge his father. Ruggiero knows that Agramante's father murdered his own, but he is determined to remain loyal to his emperor. By contrast, Marfisa's allegiance alters immediately upon hearing the tale of her father's death. Abandoning the shallow desire to test her skill against the famed paladins of France, she becomes their ally, because her determination to avenge her father and embrace his religion exercises a higher moral force. Ruggiero, however, is still restricted by the code of pagan chivalry. He explains that he did not know the whole story, at first, and now his duty as Agramante's knight overrides his own feelings:

> Ora essendo Agramante che gli pose
> La spada al fianco, farebbe opra rea
> Dandogli morte, e saria traditore;
> Che già tolto l'avea per suo Signore.
> (Canto XXXVI, 80)

He will stay with the pagan side, he maintains, until there is an honorable reason to leave. In the duel with Rinaldo, it is agreed that should either sovereign break the truce, his knight will go over to the other side. Yet when Ruggiero learns that it was Agramante who broke faith, he does not seize upon this breach of honor to redeem his own. His knightly duty has become increasingly discredited as a moral force, yet, although

> Gli pon l'amor de la sua donna un morso
> Per non lasciarlo in Africa più gire
> (Canto XL, 66)

his devotion to Agramante is even stronger, and he resurrects his fear of being called a coward if he "deserts":

> ...s'Agramante in quel caso abbandona,
> A viltà gli sia ascritto et a paura:
> Se del restar la causa parra buona
> A molti, a molti ad accettar fia dura;
> Molti diran che non si de' osservare
> Quel ch'era ingiusto e illicito a giurare.
> (Canto XL, 67)

To the impatient reader, Ruggiero's dilemma begins to appear insoluble. Once again, his specifically military experience provides a metaphor for his whole condition as, on three related occasions, he engages in duels that he can afford neither to win nor to lose. In his struggle with Rinaldo, each champions his own king and cause, and Ruggiero's sense of honor joins with his instinct for self-preservation in insisting that he fight well. But Rinaldo is also Bradamante's brother, and Ruggiero knows he must not achieve the ultimate success:

> L'affanno di Ruggier ben veramente
> E sopra ogn'altro duro, acerbo e forte
> Di cui travaglia il corpo, e più la mente,
> Poi che di due fuggir non può una morte:
> O da Rinaldo, se di lui possente
> Fia meno, o se fia più, da la consorte;
> Che se 'l fratel le uccide, sa ch'incorre
> Ne l'odio suo, che piu che morte aborre.
> ....
> Volteggiando con l'asta il buon Ruggiero
> Ribatte il colpo, e quinci e quindi gira;
> E se percuote pur, disegna loco
> Ove possa a Rinaldo nuocer poco.
> 						(Canto XXXIX, 1-2)

The same hesitation assails him when Dudone is his antagonist, for now he faces a cousin of Bradamante:

> ...perché in mente ogniora avea, di meno
> Offender la sua donna che potea;
> Et era certo se spargea il terreno
> Del sangue di costui, che la offendea
> ....
> Per questo mai di punta non gli trasse,
> E di taglio rarissimo feria;

> Schermiasi, ovunque la mazza calasse,
> Or ribattendo, or dandole la via...
>
> (Canto XL, 80-81)

Those two scenes adumbrate the climactic moment when Ruggiero, standing in for Leone, is forced to duel with Bradamante herself. The irony is particularly heavy, here, since Bradamante petitioned for the trial of her suitors by combat in order to eliminate Leone and allow Ruggiero his rightful chance. But Ruggiero owes his life to the Greek prince and cannot reveal his identity to Bradamante, who does her best because she despises the man whose armour her lover wears. Ruggiero can hardly kill Bradamante to preserve her from an unwanted marriage, and his newly-acquired religion as well as his debt to Leone forbid the suicide that would also protect her. Moreover, to maintain a state of equilibrium in the battle, which is the best he can hope for, means that he "wins" and Leone gets the bride. (Bradamante bears enchanted weapons and is so skilled in the martial arts that a man who can hold out against her until sundown is considered the winner. Moreover, she is presumably fighting very seriously, while any suitor she encounters will certainly try to avoid the Pyrrhic victory entailed in mortally wounding her.) Ruggiero's technique recalls the duels with Rinaldo and Dudone:

> Or si ferma, or volteggia, or si ritira,
> E con la man spesso accompagna il piede;
> Porge or lo scudo, et or la spada gira
> Ove girar la man nimica vede:
> O lei non fere, o se la fere, mira
> Ferirla in parte ove men nuocer crede...
>
> (Canto XLV, 77)

Ruggiero's original conflict between love and duty was resolved by <u>force majeure</u>, as he was shipwrecked by a sudden storm. At first, he is inclined to regard the catastrophe with superstition, thinking it a penalty for his failure to convert as promised. But the good hermit who takes his spiritual education in hand soon teaches him better doctrine, and there is little doubt that by the time he is baptized he is a sincere Christian. However mistaken (and solipsistic) Ruggiero may have been about the reasons for the tempest, the situation clearly requires an event that dramatic to shake him from his devotion to the wrong "duty".

In the duel with Bradamante, the situation is somewhat more complicated. Unlike his continued attachment to Agramante, Ruggiero's devotion to Leone is not mere stubborn adherence to an outdated code of masculinity. The young Greek has saved him from a prolonged and horrible death, and loyalty to him is a debt of honor. But Renaissance thinking, liberated from the absolute categories of medieval morality, does provide a way out. The problem is rapidly translated into a bureaucratic one: Are Bradamante and Ruggiero actually married or just informally betrothed? Until the Council of Trent, the Church accepted clandestine marriages as legitimate, on the principle that it was the contracting parties, not the officiating priest, who were ministers of the sacrament. Thus, under common law, mutual consent plus consummation came to constitute marriage between baptized persons.[23] The twofold problem, therefore, is a legalistic one: Were vows in fact exchanged and consummated and, if so, was Ruggiero a Christian at the time?

It would appear, on the face of it, that the couple

---

[23] See Hartley, p. 389. In practice, where large properties and kingdoms were at stake, procedures were far more thorough.

could not possibly be married. Their vows were private and contingent upon parental approval, reinforced only by Rinaldo's (legally useless) consent. Consummation certainly has not occurred--unless Bradamante has changed her mind since the time when she was

> ...disposta di far tutti
> I piaceri che far vergine saggia
> Debbia ad un suo amator, sí che di lutti,
> Senza il suo onore offendere, il sottraggia
> (Canto XXII, 34)

and unless Ariosto has since used the words "virgin" and "maiden" with unpardonable freedom. The unlikely event cannot have taken place after Ruggiero's conversion, moreover, because the two lovers have not seen each other since then. Bradamante's lamentations when she learns of the obstacles to her marriage say nothing about her being already married to the man she loves. Yet Ruggiero, who is unaware that the issue is being debated in Charlemagne's court, makes the claim to Leone, (Canto XLVI, 37). Marfisa has made the same assertion, with Bradamante's approval, but she

> ...o 'l vero o 'l falso che dicesse,
> Pur lo dicea, ben credo con pensiero,
> Perché Leon più tosto interrompesse
> A dritto e a torto, che per dire il vero;
> E che di volontade lo facesse
> Di Bradamante, che a riaver Ruggiero
> Et escluder Leon, ne la più onesta
> Né la più breve via vedea di questa.
> (Canto XLV, 105)

Her allegation and her offer to prove it in battle, as her brother's champion, sway most of the court. But it is Ruggiero's statement of the same fact, made with no apparent intention of forcing Leone to withdraw his suit, that settles the case. Ruggiero says he has to die so Bradamante will be a widow and free to marry Leone, as the results of the duel have determined that she must. He <u>cannot</u> be telling the truth--yet there would seem to be no point in lying. Leone is a coward, or at least a man who knows his own military limitations and who does not scorn to employ a substitute against a female opponent. (In fact against two different women, because he has come looking for Ruggiero to take up Marfisa's challenge on his behalf.) But, for all his defects, the young Greek is magnanimous. The same spirit that made him free Ruggiero from prison leads him, in the end, to relinquish his claim to Bradamante.

In the matter of Ruggiero's conversion and in the final drama over the marriage, the dominant principle has been one of reconciliation. The line-up of Christians and Moors facing each other like black and white chessmen, which is the position at the beginning of the epic, is an immature situation. Ruggiero's conversion must be represented as a principled act, but it is a matter of growth and development, not a black chess piece suddenly defecting to the white side of the board. Resolution of the love story calls upon a more explicit spirit of compromise. The elements that participate in it are bureaucracy, expediency, diplomacy, and, at length, common humanity.

Many commentators are disturbed by Ariosto's use of the parental-opposition motif at the end of his heroic tale. Despite the chivalric machinery of the duel between the two lovers, they consider that the poem becomes, at this point, essentially a bourgeois domestic drama with a happy ending.

Setting aside the contempt with which the words are imbued and the value judgment that contempt implies, such observations do reveal a fundamental truth. The romance-epic can arrive at an ending uncharacteristic of either romance or epic precisely because it adopts and fosters values alien to those aristocratic media, the same values that were transforming public life and building the bourgeois state.

Bradamante: A Modern Knight

The Orlando furioso sets the discredited old world of the medieval romance against the suggestion of new possibilities. Ariosto's modern sensibility, the consciousness he projects in the poem, is one in which opposites are brought together and reconciled. Paralleling the contrast between medieval and modern in the poem is the tension between madness and sanity. The exaggerations and distortions of chivalric life are identified with insanity, the ethical balance of the modern system with internal, psychological balance:

> In the Orlando furioso...the exalted capabilities of heroes, their supernatural strength, their enchanted weapons, their emotions larger than life, are associated with the blindness of romantic love, while the demands of the social order, the claims of a religious and military conflict, and the dynastic destiny of Bradamante, are symbols of control and subordination to the larger pattern of things, of coming to one's senses.[24]

---

[24] Cheney, p. 88.

Sexual love is not eliminated from the more progressive processes of existence, but integrated into them. The progressive spirit, in fact, is identified as feminine, and it is the female warriors who introduce it into the military and political organization of society.

As I have intimated, Bradamante and Marfisa serve to bring these ideas to the poem's social order. They do not personify them, in a strict allegorical sense, nor, on the other hand, are they true literary characters whose poetic life realistically conveys the new way of thinking. In their persons and in what happens to them, the two lady knights <u>express</u> a certain constellation of attitudes and sentiments. As with all the major figures in the <u>Furioso</u> we do not believe in them, but rather "we accept their expressive felicity--as we accept the expressive felicity of a poetic symbol or image."[25] For example, Bradamante is placed in situations that play upon many of the same themes as occur in Ruggiero's story. Although her decisions are far more impressive and consistent than his, she does not "represent" an opposing position. But, despite the emotional reality she comes to possess, she does not come across as a fully rounded character, either. What is extraordinary about Bradamante, indeed, is that the reader manages to see glimpses of her personality through the often mechanical ramifications of the plot in which she is involved.

Like Ruggiero, Bradamante experiences the conflict between love and duty in a very personal way. She not only confronts it more directly, but she resolves it with greater

---

[25] D. S. Carne-Ross, "The One and the Many: A Reading of <u>Orlando Furioso</u>, Cantos 1 and 8," <u>Arion</u>, 5 (1966), 225. On the question of characterization, see also Caretti, p. 34 and, with particular reference to Bradamante, Walter Binni, <u>Metodo e poesie di Ludovico Ariosto</u>, 2nd ed. (Messina: G. d'Anna, 1961), p. 162.

integrity. Moreover, her function in the poem's moral system _embodies_ the correct resolution for the rest of her world. At several important points, her chivalric role comes into direct conflict with her love for Ruggiero, and in each case she follows her emotions. The first such moment is the instance I have already cited, when the courier from Marseilles catches up with her just as she is setting out to rescue Ruggiero from imprisonment. The subsequent prophecy drives home the message that Bradamante has a higher duty than that of knighthood, yet her duty is not unrelated to the knightly responsibility she never entirely abandons. In fact, at a time when her relationship with Ruggiero is most ambiguous, she does go to the aid of Marseilles:

> La bella donna, disiando invano
> Ch'a lei facesse il suo Ruggier ritorno,
> Stava a Marsilia, ove allo stuol pagano
> Dava da travagliar quasi ogni giorno;
> Il qual scorrea rubando in monte e in piano,
> Per Linguadoca, e per Provenza intorno:
> Et ella ben facea l'ufficio vero
> Di savio duca e d'ottimo guerriero.
> (Canto XIII, 45)

Somewhat later, she is awaiting Ruggiero at Montalbano and she feigns illness as an excuse for not joining her brothers and cousins in relieving Charlemagne:

> Bradamante aspettando che s'appressi
> Il tempo, ch'al disio suo ne vien tardo,
> Inferma disse agli fratelli ch'era,
> E non volse con lor venire in schiera.
> (Canto XXX, 94)

When she does set out at last, her immediate goal is revenge for Ruggiero's supposed infidelity with Marfisa. But it is on this expedition that she accomplishes some of her most noteworthy feats as a warrior. In both cases, Ariosto indicates that Bradamante makes the decision she does because she is a woman, opting for the conventional female choice of private over public concerns. But Ariosto also makes it very clear that he believes hers to be the correct choice --not because "woman's place" is somewhere outside the realm of social existence, but because the two areas must be brought together.

On the one occasion when Bradamante lets her military zeal overcome her constant passion, she very soon has reason to regret it:

> Spesso di cor profondo ella sospira,
> Di pentimento e di dolor compunta,
> Ch'abbia in lei, più ch'amor, potuto l'ira
> "L'ira (dicea) m'ha dal mio amor disgiunta:
> Almen ci avessi io posta alcuna mira,
> Poi ch'avea pur la mala impresa assunta,
> Di saper ritornar donde io veniva;
> Che ben fui d'occhi e di memoria priva."
>
> (Canto XXIII, 7)

The anger that Bradamante so bitterly repents was aroused by her catching sight of Pinabello. She pursues this ancient enemy and, after she has killed him, discovers that she has lost Ruggiero and their guide. It is not just parting company with her beloved that she laments, but the sin that occasioned it, her failure of restraint and temperance. Certainly, the slaying of Pinabello has nothing in it of moderation:

MONSTROUS REGIMENT

> L'ardita Bradamante in questo mezo
> Giunto avea Pinabello a un passo stretto;
> E cento volte gli avea fin a mezo
> Messo il brando pei fianchi e per lo petto
>
> (Canto XXII, 97)

Such a loss of control is quite unusual for Bradamante, and it is significant that it provokes an act that has far-reaching consequences, for Ruggiero will be killed a few years after their marriage by members of the Maganzese family avenging Bradamante's victim. Pinabello's murder is exceptional for another reason, as well, since it is the only clearly-documented case in the poem where Bradamante actually kills her opponent.

In fact, her achievement as a soldier is remarkable in two respects: She is an excellent fighter and she does not usually kill. Both of these qualities are intimately bound up with the political prinicples she represents within the poem. The Pinabello episode shows that Bradamante is not incapable of killing and also indicates what kind of behavior arouses her to murderous fury. (Pinabello's intentions towards her had certainly been homicidal, but since his trick failed, what he is actually punished for is making a fool of the warrior maiden. The rage she feels towards Marfisa, when she thinks that lady has alienated Ruggiero's affections, is of the same order, the common element being Bradamante's profound sense of betrayal.) Ariosto also reminds us that, prior to the point at which he took up the story, Bradamante slew Martasino. As the infidel forces gather and pass in review before Agramante, the Garamanti are still mourning their lost leader:

Ariosto

> L'altra che vien per Martasin si lagna,
> Il qual morto le fu da Bradamante;
> E si duol ch'una femina si vanti
> D'aver ucciso il re de Garamanti.
>
> (Canto XIV, 17)

In general, although her skill at arms is unquestioned, her most memorable victories involve unseating an opponent, perhaps stunning him, without moving in for the <u>coup de grace</u>. At her first appearance in the poem, she unhorses Sacripante almost casually; his chagrin for the defeat and the ease with which it was accomplished are enhanced when he learns that it was a woman who did it. This becomes the standard pattern for Bradamante's military encounters. The three Scandinavian kings are unhorsed with even greater nonchalance, since she meets them when she is severely dejected about Ruggiero's supposed breach of faith and is not particularly interested in fighting. Not only does she knock them over easily at the first attempt, but she does it again when she next meets them. She is in a hurry, and not eager for battle this time, either, but she reluctantly agrees, and her victory is achieved with comic rapidity:

> Bradamante ricusa, come quella
> Ch'in fretta gia, né soggiornar volea:
> Pur tanto e tanto fur molesti, ch'ella
> Che negar senza biasmo non potea,
> Abbassò l'asta, et a tre colpi in terra
> Li mandò tutti; e qui finí la guerra.
>
> (Canto XXXIII, 69)

This time, Ullania knows the maiden's identity, for the sojourn at the Rocca di Tristano has intervened between the two encounters. The three kings evince more shame than Sacripante, for they throw away their weapons, vow to wear no arms for the period of a year, and then only those they can win in combat. In this scene, Ariosto anticipates Bradamante's encounter with Rodomonte, where her sex is an explicit part of the struggle, and where once again her humiliated adversary goes to earth, like a wounded animal, for the space of a year, a month, and a day.

A number of familiar elements are present in the duels that result from her general challenge to the Saracen forces. She has no special animus towards the particular knights she faces, but her purpose in coming is to seek redress for Ruggiero's crime against her womanhood. Some of her emotion infuses each of these encounters, but they are also marked by her usual restraint. She may taunt her fallen antagonists, asking why they don't send out a better man, but she does not harm them physically. In this way, Serpentino, Gardonio, and Ferrau are easily defeated and Bradamante shows them unexampled courtesy:

> Bradamante non sol non era ria
> A quei ch'avea, toccando lor gli scudi,
> Loro i cavalli, e rimontar facea.
> (Canto XXXVI, 10)

Ferrau is embarassed to be unhorsed so readily, but it is he who works it out that the stranger knight must be Bradamante; that realization does not seem to increase his shame. When the struggle with Ruggiero himself proves less fruitful, she turns with relief to victims she does not love:

> ...e vi fa cose
> Che saran fin che giri il ciel famose.

Ariosto

> In poco spazio ne gittò per terra
> Trecento e più con quella lancia d'oro;
> Ella sola quel dí vinse la guerra,
> Messe ella sola in fuga il popul Moro
> (Canto XXXVI, 38-39)

As Ariosto describes her prowess elsewhere, "cio che incontra spezza e getta a terra."

In a great many instances, Ariosto notes explicitly that Bradamante forbears to kill her opponent. The reasons vary, but the poet leaves no doubt of her capacity to do so. For example, she must overpower Brunello in order to obtain the enchanted ring, which is essential to her plans for rescuing Ruggiero. Brunello was Marfisa's particular bete noire in the Orlando innamorato, and his record in that poem bears out Ariosto's observation in the Argument that "la similazione...e necessaria trattando con falsi e perfidi." For Bradamante, trickery is necessary because she rejects the idea of doing away with him:

> ...le par atto vile a insanguinarsi
> D'un uom senza arme, e di sí ignobil sorte
> (Canto IV, 14)

A few stanzas later, she defeats Atlante. It would hardly enhance her chivalric reputation to slay this weak old man and, in any case, she needs him to release Ruggiero and the other prisoners. But Bradamante's chief reason for ignoring his pleas to put him out of his misery is her curiosity about his identity and motives:

> "Tommi la vita, giovene, per Dio,"
> Dicea il vecchio pien d'ira e di dispetto;

> Ma quella a torla avea sí il cor restio,
> Come quel di lasciarla avria diletto.
> La donna di sapere ebbe disio
> Chi fosse il negromante, e a che effetto
> Edificasse in quel luogo selvaggio
> La rocca, e faccia a tutto il mondo oltraggio.
>   (Canto IV, 28)

The next time she meets the magician, she is unable to kill him because he has disguised himself as her beloved. Although Melissa has warned her that this will happen, Bradamante is not prepared for such verisimilitude, and realizes that she has no assurance that Melissa's advice is trustworthy. The nearer she approaches to the apparition, the more she is determined to rely on the evidence of her senses. Her heart

> Seco dicea: "Non è Ruggier costui,
> Che col cor sempre, et or con gli occhi veggio?
> E s'or non veggio e non conosco lui,
> Che mai veder o mai conoscer deggio?
> Perché voglio io de la credenza altrui
> Che la veduta mia giudichi peggio?
> Che senza gli occhi ancor, sol per se stesso
> Può il cor sentir se gli è lontano o appresso."
>   (Canto XIII, 77)

This decision leads to Bradamante's imprisonment in Atlante's dome, and the forces of Reason have to find a new agent to liberate her, along with the other victims of Atlante's magic.

As with many other aspects of Bradamante's character, Marfisa's presence in the poem guards against a facile definition of clemency as the female contribution to warfare. Ruggiero's betrothed does not kill her opponents, but his sister does so with gusto:

> Marfisa cacciò l'asta per lo petto
> Al primo che scontrò, due braccia dietro;
> Poi trasse il brando, e in men che non l'ho detto
> Spezzò quattro elmi, che sembrar di vetro:
> Bradamante no fe' minore effetto,
> Ma l'asta d'or tenne diverso metro;
> Tutti quei che toccò, per terra mise;
> Duo tanti fur, né però alcuno uccise.
> ....
> Chi potrà conto aver d'ogni guerriero
> Ch'a terra mandi quella lancia d'oro?
> O d'ogni testa che tronca o divisa
> Sia da la orribil spada di Marfisa?
> (Canto XXXIX, 12-13)

Although Bradamante's extraordinary display of mercy cannot be attributed to her sex alone, it is nonetheless important that a female character introduces that element into the value structure of the poem. As a warrior, she is chivalrous almost to a fault, but she will have no part of a system that demands life-and-death struggles for their own sake. She always wins, but by the easiest means compatible with honor. In this sense even her military victories are diplomatic, expressing, as they do, the most unmedieval quality of <u>sprezzatura</u>.

Bradamante is at her most magnificent when a military situation calls upon her two most prominent characteristics: her steadfastness as a lover and her skill as a warrior. The first incident to do so is the duel with Rodomonte. Her melancholy mood has been established in the preceding cantos, as she goes forth to avenge her love. At the Rocca di Tristano, her sorrow is somewhat relieved by the entertainment she is offered and by a dream in which Ruggiero assures her that he is still faithful. It is there, also, that she makes it clear that if she is to be judged as a knight, she cannot also be judged as a woman. She will not compete in both a beauty contest and a combat at arms. Defending Ullania's right to remain at the castle, she argues

> Non venni come donna qui, né voglio
> Che sian di donna ora i progressi miei...
>
> Se come cavallier la stanza, o come
> Donna acquistata m'abbia, è manifesto:
> Perché dunque volete darmi nome
> Di donna, se di maschio è ogni mio gesto?
> (Canto XXXII, 102-103)

Despite this assurance, the confrontation with Rodomonte is impressive precisely because it places her military abilities at the service of her feelings as a woman. Elsewhere in the poem, Bradamante is chiefly a woman in love or chiefly a warrior, but here she is both at once.[26] Her customary restraint and dignity are enhanced by her suffering as a lover and elevated by the cause in which she is enlisted. For Bradamante, who sees herself as a woman betrayed, will defend the love and the honor of Fiordiligi and avenge the memory of Isabella, love's noblest martyr. Moreover, her antagonist, who has been successful against so many formida-

---

[26] Attilio Momigliano, Saggio su l'Orlando furioso (1928; rpt. Bari: Laterza, 1959), p. 112.

ble adversaries, treats her with contempt, threatening her with the rape he considers more appropriate to her sex than the trappings of chivalry. To vanquish Rodomonte is thus to strike out at someone who has betrayed love through both violence and grossness. It is also a victory over a most impressive opponent, since Rodomonte is not only a remarkable fighter, but represents a moral force that runs precisely counter to the spirit of the Orlando furioso.

The battle with Rodomonte attains so high a level because its purpose coincides with Bradamante's ethical function in the poem, as well as with her immediate mood. But victory does not satisfy the need to avenge herself against the betrayer of her own love, and Bradamante continues her interrupted pursuit of the "false" Ruggiero. Her experiences at the Saracen camp are the reverse of the triumph over Rodomonte, because they originate in groundless sexual jealousy. The pagan champions she defeats before Ruggiero comes onto the field arouse no special feeling, so her behavior with them is controlled and courteous. When Ruggiero is her antagonist, however, conflicting emotions render her powerless. Love and the anger evoked by an affront to love contend for mastery of Bradamante's lance, while Ruggiero, informed of her identity and puzzled about her attack, tries only to protect himself without injuring her. After the brief respite in which she unhorses three hundred or more of the enemy, she faces Marfisa, and the emotion arising from her misapprehension makes her both more ardent and more awkward than usual. As Ariosto so vividly demonstrates in the struggle over Angelica, jealousy is invariably a destructive emotion--and its first victim is reason.

The contrast between the éclat of her performance against Rodomonte and her comparative clumsiness when

Ruggiero is her opponent points up a striking aspect of Bradamante's character: She is the only one of Ariosto's knights whose prowess is always related to the rightness of her cause. Thus, she can never defeat Ruggiero, because she should not be fighting him in the first place. In one of their armed encounters, she is laboring under a misapprehension about his guilt, in the other, about his identity. With Rodomonte, on the other hand, her military skill is supported by correct and deeply-held convictions. Most of her other battles, although occurring within the general context of Christian versus Saracen, are morally neutral, serving mainly as vehicles for her martial skill and exquisite chivalry. In this light, the defeat of Sacripante assumes greater significance, since it interrupts his proposed ravishment of Angelica. Bradamante, though unquestionably chaste, is not, like Spenser's Britomart, the knight-exemplar of chastity. But Ariosto underscores her moral identity by introducing her, for her first appearance in the poem, as the Nemesis of would-be seducers.

The God to whom Charlemagne prays is on the Christian side, but only in the long run. Short-run battles throughout the poem are settled by skill or, more rarely, by luck and magic. Generally speaking, a knight's success has nothing to do with the morality of his actions. Ruggiero's prowess is identical whether his motive be frivolous, serious, or absolutely wrong-headed. Rodomonte's military magnificence is all the more striking because it serves his evil ends. And Orlando's unselective madness seems only to enhance his might. It is worth noting, therefore, that for <u>one</u> paladin there is an invariable connection between success and virtue and that that one is a female knight.

Ariosto

Marfisa: The New Woman

In this, as in other matters, the character of Marfisa provides a counter-weight to that of Bradamante, forestalling crude generalizations about Ariosto's use of the lady knight. Marfisa's ability with sword and lance does not vary with the cause she serves, any more than it does for the male knights. What is impressive about Ruggiero's redoubtable twin is that her cause <u>does</u> vary and that, unlike the static Amazons upon whom she is modelled, she herself changes and develops in the course of the poem. Ariosto's treatment of Marfisa imparts new life to a stock figure and, in so doing, enriches his vision of female—and chivalric—possibility.

The presence of Marfisa, herself an original in many aspects, also frees Ariosto from literary tradition in the creation of Bradamante. For when she stands beside her stalwart sister-in-arms as she does through the last quarter of the poem, Bradamante appears to have little in common with the warrior women of antiquity.[27] Bradamante is chaste, but looks forward to a fruitful marriage with her beloved Ruggiero. Marfisa is pledged to chastity and neither wants nor needs the love of men. In fact, Marfisa appears to have little need for any human support or com-

---

[27] The only motif associated with Bradamante that is reminiscent of an antique woman warrior is the moment, repeated several times, in which her sex is revealed when visor and helmet are removed and her hair tumbles down. This recalls Achilles' discovery of Penthesilea's sex as he loosens the headgear of the slain Amazon queen. Although the classical legend was probably Ariosto's source, the idea is one that might well be suggested by narrative necessity. And in no case does instant enamorment follow upon the unveiling of Bradamante's femininity, as it does in the Penthesilea legend.

panionship, whereas Bradamante, although often alone, has friends and family, comrades, confederates and allies and even, in Melissa, a kind of fairy-godmother. Marfisa and Bradamante are equally matched in valor and martial ability, but it is Marfisa who is the professional soldier, lacking Bradamante's scruples about killing her opponents and deriving a certain relish from any fight.

Like the Amazons, Marfisa has no desire for sexual relationships or for traditional female roles. She is as invulnerable to the darts of love as she is to the weapons of men. She appears as a sexual object only in Bradamante's jealous fantasies and in the lubricious schemes of Mandricardo who, meeting her in feminine garb, plans to win her in combat and trade her off as a sop to Rodomonte. Ariosto expresses his contempt for such an arrangement:

> Sí come Amor si regga a questa guisa
> Che vender la sua donna, o permutarla
> Possa l'amante, né a ragion s'attrista,
> Se quando una ne perde, una n'acquista.
> (Canto XXVI, 70)

But it is up to Marfisa to defend herself, after her champions have fallen. Her challenge to Mandricardo declares her independence of their protection and of all sexual ties. Because she is a cavalier in her own right, Mandricardo's triumph is premature:

> Io ti concedo che diresti il vero
> Ch'io sarei tua per la ragion di guerra,
> Quando mio Signor fosse o cavalliero
> Alcun di questi c'hai gittato in terra:
> Io sua non son, né d'altri son che mia:

Ariosto

> Dunque me tolga a me chi mi desia.
>
> So scudo e lancia adoperare anch'io
> E piu d'un cavalliero in terra ho posto.
> Datemi l'arme (disse) e il destrier mio...
>   (Canto XXVI, 79-80)

After this ringing defiance, it is most appropriate that she should be compared to an Amazon when she appears in the lists to continue her interrupted duel with the Tartar. No longer clad in the womanly robes her comrades had urged upon her, clothing that had attracted Mandricardo and forced her into temporary dependency, this time she has chosen her own dress:

> In abito succinta era Marfisa,
> Qual si convenne a donna et a guerriera;
> Termoodonte forse a quella guisa
> Vide Ippolita ornarsi e la sua schiera.
>   (Canto XXVII, 52)

Marfisa's Amazonian qualities are emphasized by her deliberate isolation. The phoenix is her emblem, and Ariosto explains that it symbolizes both her unique achievement and her solitary sexual condition. She is the only knight, moreover, for whom standing alone is a matter of chivalric pride. After their arrival in Marseilles, she urges her companions to separate and not continue travelling in a group:

> Dicendo che lodevole non era
> Ch'andasser tanti cavallieri insieme;
> Che gli storni e i colombi vanno in schiera,
> I daini e i cervi e ogn'animal che teme;

> Ma l'audace falcon, l'aquila altiera,
> Che ne l'aiuto altrui non metton speme,
> Orsi, tigri, leon, soli ne vanno,
> Che di più forza alcun timor non hanno.
>
> Nessun degli altri fu di quel pensiero,
> Si ch'a lei sola toccò a far partita...
> (Canto XX, 103-104)

The exponent and supreme exemplar of knight errantry, Marfisa is a strong and ruthless soldier. Fighting beside her brother and Bradamante's kin against the combined Saracen and Maganzese forces, she and Ruggiero are "la scelta e 'l fior d'ogni guerriero." The outcome is left in doubt when she and Bradamante duel, but elsewhere it is clear that she shows less compassion for her victims, more enjoyment of the combat itself. After a successful bout, her sex is (often dramatically) revealed. But her conduct is so straightforward and her heroism so impressive that the revelation almost never evokes the special shame at being bested by a female that Bradamante's victories inspire. Only Zerbino, who has proved uncourteous as well as unsuccessful, is further humiliated to learn that a woman has outdone him in both aspects of chivalry. Marfisa is magnificent whether her cause is Christian or pagan, but her first battle after conversion is a particularly striking example of her style in combat. (See Canto XXIX, 1-15.) Here, Bradamante is her equal in conviction and rage, but as they both storm through the Moorish horde, it is Marfisa who breaks helmets as if they were glass and then proceeds to deal quite as thoroughly with their wearers.

In Boiardo's *Orlando innamorato*, Marfisa's most salient feature is her fiery temper, frequently aroused by the clever trickery of Brunello. The comic passages in which her ire is aroused make her appear huge and clumsily stupid beside the subtle dwarf. Ariosto retains the theme of Marfisa's enmity towards Brunello, but, since his Marfisa is no longer an apt foil for the conjurer's wiles, he does not seem to know what to do with the borrowed material, and the result is rather grim. In the <u>Furioso</u>, Marfisa is still hot-tempered and hasty, but these qualities are seen as extensions of her admirable candor and directness. Her only blunder worthy of the old Boiardan Marfisa is in the first incident in which she appears, when she recognizes that the prize on display is her own armor and takes the most direct and disastrous steps towards retrieving it.

More often, however, her temper shows up in combat and in her Hotspur-like eagerness to get into action or settle matters with a good, bloody fight. When she encounters Astolfo and his companions, she has adopted the life of a knight errant, seeking immortal fame through her chivalric feats. She decides to accompany the knights on their return to France, not because she is committed to either side in the Holy War then in progress, but simply because

> Marfisa avuto avea lungo disire
> Al paragon dei paladin venire;
>
> E far esperienza se l'effetto
> Si pareggiava a tanta nominanza...
> (Canto XVIII, 133-134)

Her eagerness never flags, and she is always ready to back up a statement or a belief with arms. Even after she has accepted the demands of diplomacy in the matter of Ruggiero's marriage to Bradamante, she feels that her protestations are inadequate unless she becomes her brother's military champion as well:

> Poi che non c'è Ruggier, che la contesa
> De la moglier fra sé e costui discioglia;
> Acciò per mancamento di difesa
> Così senza rumor non se gli toglia,
> Io che gli son sorella, questa impresa
> Piglio contra a ciascun, sia chi si voglia,
> Che dica aver ragione in Bradamante,
> O di merto a Ruggiero andare inante.
> (Canto XLVI, 57)

This readiness to explode into combat is the opposite of Bradamante's courteous restraint. It serves, once more, to counteract hasty generalizations about the female character, and, at the same time, to enrich Ariosto's already varied image of women. Marfisa also contributes to Ariosto's burlesque of the chivalric ideal. Just as Orlando's wild singleness of vision represents one aspect of a system that will insanely destroy itself rather than change, Marfisa's knightly temperament is another view of the exaggerations of chivalry. Marfisa is not mad. On the contrary, she is the epitome of what a knight should be--and so perfect a model serves to point up the absurdity of the ideal. That the model is a woman only makes the absurdity more apparent, for the standards of knighthood are supposed to correspond exactly to an image of _manly_ nobility.

If Marfisa's entire being ranged between the stalwart Amazon and the clownish knight, she would be a simple character to discuss, but the poem's vision of what women have to contribute to public life would be greatly distorted. In fact, those poles are only Ariosto's rendering of Boiardo's creation; they are modifications of a stereotype. Ariosto's imagining goes further, however, and he makes Marfisa into as genuine a character as his literary mode permits. Ultimately, her contribution to the politics of the epic is encompassed by two other qualities with which Ariosto endows her: a profound sense of justice and extraordinary loyalty.

Probably the most striking way in which Marfisa differs from the archetypal Amazon is that she is neither a man-hater nor a partisan of her own sex. Rather, she possesses a notion of a balanced commonwealth that overrides the intemperate demands of gender. The island of man-killers evokes the same horrified response from her as from her male companions, and she assumes the role of challenger, although she knows she can fulfill only the military, not the sexual requirements of the job. Thus it is clear from the beginning that Marfisa has no intention of accepting the island's rules as given and that she thinks she can fight her way out of any situation, bringing her opponents down in the process. She will not take the high position such a gynocracy would grant to her while her equally meritorious friends languish in prison because they are of the wrong sex:

> S'io ci fossi per donna conosciuta,
> So ch'avrei da le donne onore e pregio;
> E volentieri io ci sarei tenuta
> E tra le prime forse del collegio:
> Ma con costoro essendoci venuta,
> Non ci vo d'essi aver più privilegio;
> Troppo error fora, ch'io mi stessi o andassi
> Libera, e gli altri in servitù lasciassi.
> (Canto XX, 78)

Her summary treatment of Marganore's misogynist stronghold makes it clear that it is _injustice_, not female power, that she considers inimical to the balance of nature. The homicidal women at least began with just cause for complaint. They were victims of what Ariosto considers man's major sin against love: fickleness and abandonment. The women's crime is to make all members of the male sex who wander into their power suffer for the actions of their own particular betrayers. Marganore is also punishing all females because of the actions of one woman, but, in this case, the original "offense" was really an act of the greatest heroism, reminiscent of Isabella's martyrdom of love and vengeance. Here, Marfisa identifies with the victims of sexist tyranny, blushing to behold the humiliation of Ullania and her waiting-women. She fights nobly alongside her brother and his betrothed for the defeat of Marganore, and when he is overthrown it is she who binds him up and turns him over to Drusilla, she who establishes the law that in this place, as a corrective to previous evil, women shall rule henceforth. She is the one who has the new law inscribed on a column and she is the one who will return before the year's end to make sure it is being enforced.

In these parallel incidents, Ariosto is not debating the merits of the two sexes as governors or their respective propensities for tyranny, much less the question of sex equality. Skilfully weaving certain facts about sexual life into his arguments, he is nonetheless talking about something larger than sex--the balance of human forces he considers essential to the psychology of an individual or to the proper conduct of the state. It is important for our perception of Marfisa and her function in the poem that she unhesitatingly chooses that equilibrium, whether her own sex is the oppressor or the oppressed.

Marfisa's fierce loyalty is the abiding feature of her

personality, and it usually motivates her to act in the most impulsive and direct fashion. Once her services are enlisted on the Saracen side, for instance, her feelings are only strengthened upon learning of Agramante's massive defeat:

> Già non volse Marfisa imitar l'atto
> Di Rodomonte: anzi com'ella intese
> Ch'Agramante da Carlo era disfatto,
> Sue genti morte, saccheggiate e prese,
> E che con pochi in Arli era ritratto,
> Senza aspettare invito il camin prese:
> Venne in aiuto de la sua corona,
> E l'aver gli proferse e la persona.
> (Canto XXXII, 6)

Her devotion is comparable only to that of Ruggiero, but her motives are purer. Thus, when she learns that a higher loyalty, to her murdered father, decrees that Agramante should be her enemy, not her leader, she adopts the Christian cause and faith immediately. Her lack of hesitation is not a sign that the decision is lightly taken, but rather that her principles are so deeply-rooted as to admit no other choice. Hereafter, she is a brave and worthy follower of Charlemagne.

Her loyalty to a person or a cause is most often reflected in prompt action, her characteristic mode of expression. But that loyalty eventually becomes the means of teaching her politic behavior, as her feeling for her brother induces her to lie about his prior marriage to Bradamante. Marfisa, the soul of honesty and direct action, comes to recognize that more than one kind of truth, more than one kind of action, are required to effect a social reconciliation and, in her recognition, she embodies that idea in the polity of the poem.

Ladies Present

Female characters in the *Furioso* range from the most depraved to the most saintly spirits. With the exception of the two lady knights, however, their moral arena is defined by the world of sexuality. The entrance of Bradamante and Marfisa onto the military scene introduces a transforming feminine value-structure into public life, not by rejecting sexuality, but by acknowledging its centrality. The real force of this development is unfortunately diluted for those readers who see the female warriors as something other than women. Pio Rajna's classic guide to the poem cautions us that the two ought not to be confused with the giantesses of popular legend, for these latter are a race apart, something between man and beast.[28] Although their humanity is thus scrupulously granted, many commentators call their femininity into question. After discussing the peculiarities of Angelica, as well as Bradamante and Marfisa, Grilli turns with evident relief from these strong women to "figure veramente donne."[29] I have made reference to Momigliano's observation that only in her duel with Rodomonte do Bradamante's womanly and military aspects work together. His formula did reinforce my particular argument, but it also contains the potentially dangerous notion that to Ariosto, also, "woman" and "warrior" were distinct and rarely compatible categories. Croce takes this assumption a

---

[28] Quoted in Alfredo Grilli, <u>Figure muliebre nell'Orlando furioso</u> (Ferrara: Stabilmento tipografico Estense, 1933), p. 18.

[29] <u>Ibid.</u>, p. 19.

step further, speaking of the epic's containing "e donne-guerriere e donne realmente donne."[30]

At its most grotesque, such a reading attributes all the noblest human qualities of the female warriors to the admixture of masculinity in their character. Thus, Bradamante is said to stand "di mezzo tra il femmineo e il virile," and to possess a nature that is "simpatica e virile."[31] She combines a great (and allegedly feminine) capacity to love with "una risolutezza ed una dignitate virile."[32] This interpretation misses the point, making it as impossible to understand the lady knights as Croce's peculiar observation that the <u>Furioso</u> itself should be appreciated like a beautiful woman makes it to read the poem itself.[33]

In fact, from its opening line, Ariosto's epic contains "a streak of civilizing feminism."[34] Women are basic to the development of the crucial ideas of the poem, as well as to the organization of the plot. What is important about Bradamante and Marfisa is precisely that they do not differ in essentials from other women characters. Bradamante's military role enhances, rather than negating her love for Ruggiero, and as a lover she shares in the mainstream of female feeling in the poem. Marfisa's loyalty is another manifes-

---

[30] Croce, p. 60. I am assuming that "regalmente," which this edition actually says, is a misprint. My assumption is borne out in the English translation of Douglas Ainslie (New York: Holt, 1920) which makes reference to "warrior women and women who were women," (page 63).

[31] Grilli, pp. 17-18 and 16.

[32] Momigliano, p. 118.

[33] Croce, p. 7.

[34] Whitfield, p. 135.

tation of feminine emotion, since it originates in and is directed by love. (Of course, not all women in the *Furioso* are equally steadfast in their emotions. But the only characters in the poem who partake of the quality in a positive sense are women.) They bring the emotion that Ariosto associates with the female principle out of the private sphere reserved for women and into the public domain of men. From the sixteenth-century perspective, the transformation they effect is indeed a civilizing action. It is ironic that so many subsequent readers have rejected Ariosto's own definition of Marfisa and Bradamante and thus resisted the poem's most vital Renaissance current.

CHAPTER FOUR
TASSO: THE SOCIAL SACRAMENT

To move from the world of the <u>Orlando furioso</u> to the world of the <u>Gerusalemme liberata</u> is to pass from dream into nightmare. Ariosto's lavishly crowded scene has been swept almost bare, leaving a stark landscape in which a smaller number of characters and incidents stand out more sharply, and the energy that informs particular events is exaggerated by their isolation against the austere background. Like a nightmare, moreover, the <u>Gerusalemme liberata</u> focuses inward, to the point where the characters, the poet, and the audience are joined in a highly subjective universe. Tasso peoples his narrative with characters who are restless and unresolved, who translate objective experience into the categories that define their own psychology.

At the same time, the poem's allegorical structure mediates a similar process for the reader. The allegory is not an inert appendage to the epic, but participates in its most dynamic and direct communication. Thus, for example, the enchanted wood is really haunted, but it takes on a different aspect for each man who approaches it, corresponding to his personal fears and preoccupations. On the literal level, Tasso describes the ghostly occupation of the forest, but the language in which he conveys its effects is veiled and imprecise, communicating, as well, some of the menace it holds for the Crusaders who project their own terrors onto it. Yet the wood also possesses an allegorical significance in Tasso's overall vision, a significance that is reinforced, rather than dissipated, by the private interpretations to which it is subjected within the poem.

This constant reference inward, rare in the modes of epic and romance, has directed a disproportionate amount of critical attention to Tasso's own subjective experience. At one time, such commentary focused on an often crudely biographical reading of his poems. The present critical trend, dominated by Italian scholars, takes a somewhat more sophisticated approach to the facts that are known about Tasso's life and the use that can be made of them. It stresses his inner history, his intellectual and psychological development, usually relating it to a perceived conflict between the <u>Liberata</u> as a heroic poem and the love passages that constitute its most striking moments. The spiritual struggles that wracked Tasso's life are rediscovered in his poetic work, and the insights this knowledge provides are then applied to a reading of the poem.

It seems to me that such a method fails to do justice to Tasso's own awareness of the problem and thus ignores his attempts to solve it within the confines of the <u>Gerusalemme liberata</u>. For, unlike many other issues in the interpretation of literature, the central contradiction in Tasso's work is one that the poet fully recognized and with which he tried to grapple. The conflict, as he understood it, was not between the high public themes of epic and the private exigencies of love, but rather between the objective world of historical events and the subjective world of inner experience. Far from identifying sexuality with the purely personal, he attempts to use it as an integrative force that resolves the tension between the two poles. It is in this effort that Christian allegory comes into its own.

Tasso

Man's World, Woman's World, God's World

In the next few pages, I outline a theory about Tasso's view of sex as a social and spiritual force; the rest of this chapter is intended to develop and substantiate these initial observations. It should be recognized, first of all, that the setting of the <u>Liberata</u>, like that of the <u>Furioso</u>, is the masculine environment of a military campaign. In contrast to Ariosto, however, Tasso does not often depart from his basic narrative, and, when he does, the digression is an enrichment of his major themes, rather than a divergence from them. Thus, the female characters, embodying emotional qualities that Tasso wishes to assimilate into his army, are not kept away from the military sphere, but play out their parts within it. Erminia, Sofronia, and Armida bring their traditional femininity to bear on the Holy War, just as the women warriors, Clorinda and Gildippe, assume their less conventional roles in that context. Tenderness and passion are identified primarily with the female in the poem, and Tasso makes every effort to bend these emotions to the requirements of the epic's public world.

The three heroines, moreover, are all Saracens, and the expression of furious emotion is identified with the pagan, as well as the feminine character. A similar motif occurs in Virgil's portrayal of Turnus who, like Argante and Solimano, represents the heroic demise of an old dispensation. In his self-destructive passion, Turnus is directly related to the furibond goddesses and hence to the female principle. But, whereas Virgil, associating emotional displays with female nature and female sexuality, has to purge both from his ultimate social vision, Tasso tries to salvage the potentially good elements in passionate feeling. In so doing, he rejects Virgil's solution. It is, in fact, the female temperament that he sees as the repository of positive emotion. Unhealthy passion, as reflected in Saracen heroes like Argante and Solimano, has its moment of tragic splendor, but it is not susceptible of redemption. Erminia, Clorinda, and Armida possess the same pagan energy, but, as women, prove themselves more open to salvation. All three eventually embrace Christianity, thereby contributing their capacity for deep feeling to the rather ascetic culture of the Crusades.

Although female characters and the sexual emotions are an integrative force in the epic, resolution does not take place through the union of lovers. Tasso's treatment of the issues involved is too tortuous, and his conception of the final good too qualified for so forthright a conclusion. Ariosto rewards one pair of lovers, at least, with matrimony and a fruitful dynasty. But Tasso, whose vision of the integral life is more thoroughly sacramental, is not able to offer his couples the sacrament of marriage. On the personal level, no set of lovers in the Gerusalemme liberata fully consummates a relationship; their coming together is always illusory, frustrated, partial, or curtailed. Indeed, the principle Tasso defines as female can be integrated into the poet's ideal scheme at all only because he views relations between the sexes as the means to an end, not the end itself.

The women's assimilation is also made possible by the fact that the realm into which they are absorbed is a social as well as an existential phenomenon. They do not simply become Christians; they enter into the Christian world. Just as the Saracen forces have both a moral and a political identity, the Crusaders' camp represents the Christian state, as well as the Christian faith. Their conversion brings the women into the complex of ideas and institutions that constitute Christianity, much as the Holy Land itself is integrated into Christendom. Only Clorinda, who is baptized at the moment of her death, experiences the religious dimension of Christianity in the abstract, whereas Armida and Erminia are also absorbed into the social relations that make up the Christian world. Each of them does so through her involvement with the man she loves, but her acceptance into the orbit of Christian society is far less ambiguous than her eventual union with her beloved.

Since the Christian sphere is not, itself, a static phenomenon, their admission into it has some impact on the process of that society. Tasso is attempting throughout the epic to define the ideal commonwealth. His Christians and Saracens are fundamentally different from one another, a fact that is in no way blurred by the sympathy the pagan heroes evoke in their final hours. Nor does Tasso evince a Virgilian nostalgia for the old world that is being swept away by the onslaught of the new dispensation, for such ambivalence would be inconsistent with Christian convictions. But, although the Crusaders are always portrayed as representing the "right side" in the global struggle, their values are also in transition. The Saracen women are not expected to alter their own essential nature when they convert. On the one hand, Christianity is seen as enabling them to realize their true selves, while, on the other, their inclusion in the Christian ranks brings to Goffredo's army the emotionality, the warmth, the gentleness, and the passion it lacked and that are associated with the female principle.

Tasso's vision has no place for a character like Ariosto's Ruggiero, the Saracen knight who already exemplifies the chivalric ideal and whose conversion does not force us to reexamine the Christian society he enters. In the *Gerusalemme liberata*, the Christian state reflects a conventionally masculine ideal, and the integration of the pagan women forces it to confront and accept qualities identified as female and embodied in particular women characters. In this regard, it is important to consider Tasso's own hesitations in dealing with the "feminine" emotions. He tends, for example, to separate those responses from female participation in military action. Moreover, the inclusion of the qualities and the women themselves invariably requires their subordination to masculine forces. And the failure to consummate sexual relationships on the sexual plane seriously distorts the kind of rhetorical and ideological contribution they can make.

The Dynastic Didact

The intersection of sexual forces and social issues is reflected in Tasso's handling of the dynastic theme. Although it lacks the scope and the synthetic force of Ariosto's treatment, Tasso's approach to the Este myth is neither grudging nor casual. Because the sexual situations in the *Gerusalemme liberata* are resolved only allegorically, his patrons' historical mission has to be understood in the larger didactic context of the epic, rather than through the story of a heroic couple and their charismatic offspring. Those passages of the epic that deal specifically with the Este family and its future do not represent an end in themselves, as they would for Ariosto, but only the beginning of a more complex and systematic vision.

On the most immediate level, the *Gerusalemme liberata* is concerned with several heroic ancestors of Ferrara's ruling family. They are very clearly identified as members of Casa d'Este, forebears of the House's future greatness, but Tasso does not discuss the line in any genealogical detail--exact or mythical. The significant fact about this descent is that it cannot be explicitly traced to any of the lovers in the poem. Rinaldo, the most important Este "ancestor" on the scene, is spiritually and politically reunited with Armida in the epic's final battle, but he is now a consecrated being, and a resumption of their former sexual relationship, this time under Christian auspices, is morally impossible. Despite the lack of clarity about their biological role, both Rinaldo and his uncle Guelfo are accepted in the canon of Este ancestors, with their virtues and triumphs redounding to the glory of their sixteenth-century heirs. Thus, the survey of the Christian troops in Canto I dwells on Guelfo's right to two domains, through his Italian and his German heritage. The stanzas in which he is introduced emphasize the extent of his lands and the justice of his reign. By contrast, the brief passages devoted to the other military chiefs and _their_ territories are little more than a fast-moving travelogue.

Rinaldo's dynastic function in the epic is that of a moral, not a natural progenitor of the Estensi. His name belongs to the favorite knight in Italian versions of romance, but _that_ Rinaldo had never been cited as a direct Este ancestor and Tasso's character has little in comon with his more familiar Carolingian namesake. Wilkins argues that the invention of a heroic ancestor serves primarily as a vehicle for praising the poet's ducal patrons.[1] This was conventional practice, of course, but the case is weakened, here, by the absence of emphasis on the blood tie between

---

[1] Ernest Hatch Wilkins, <u>A History of Italian Literature</u> (Cambridge, Massachusetts: Harvard University Press, 1954), p. 273.

Rinaldo and the Estensi. Wilkins' position reflects, in any case, a gross oversimplification of Tasso's historical sense, and misses the significance of his political myth.

Much of that richer significance is suggested in the prophecies of Pietro l'Eremita. The venerable seer shows Rinaldo a shield on which are carved the noble deeds of the Crusader's Este forebears. Both the shield-device and the recital are familiar conventions in epic and romance. The unique aspect of this version is the context in which it occurs and the kind of future to which it points. Pietro is addressing Rinaldo just after the young man's return from his entanglement with Armida; the speech begins as an exhortation to Rinaldo to make use of the fine qualities with which he has been endowed. In a magnificent simile, the seer asks Rinaldo if he will live up to his better self or

> ...vorrai tu lunge da l'alte cime
> Giacer, quasi tra valli augel sublime?
> (Canto XVII, 61)[2]

Nor is Rinaldo's personal salvation Pietro's only goal, for it is as a leader of men that the young hero is to exercise his gifts. Nature, the holy man declares,

> ...ti diè l'ire ancor veloci e pronte,
> Non perché l'usi ne' civili assalti,
> Ne perché sian di desidèri ingordi
> Elle ministre, e da ragion discordi;

---

[2] Citations of the Italian text are from Francesco Flora's edition of the *Poesie* of Tasso, prepared for the series "I Classici Rizzoli" (Milan-Rome, 1934). The particular reprint referred to is the 1950 edition in the "Biblioteca Universale Rizzoli," with annotation by Lodovico Magugliani.

Tasso

> Ma perché il tuo valore, armato d'esse,
> Più fèro assalga gli aversari esterni;
> E sian con maggior forza indi ripresse
> Le cupidigie, empi nemici interni.
> Dunque ne l'uso, per cui fûr concesse,
> L'impieghi il saggio duce, e le governi;
> Ed a suo senno or tepide, or ardenti
> Le faccia, ed or le affretti, ed or le allenti.
> (Canto XVII, 62-63)

It is after this appeal to Rinaldo that Pietro reinforces his argument by graphically reminding him of his ancestors' accomplishments.

Then, as they continue their nocturnal ride to the Christian camp, Pietro goes on to praise the descendants who will arise from Rinaldo's seed. The tone in which he delivers this panegyric is enraptured, beyond even his hortatory excesses in interpreting the shield. For one thing, there is no more shield, nor can he refer to any of the other visual representations of the future common to the epic mode. Where Virgil paraded Aeneas' Roman descendants before him and Ariosto confronted his heroes with a virtual museum-full of paintings, statues, bas-reliefs, and tapestries about future generations, Tasso relies on a strictly internal vision of what is to come. He describes Pietro as unfolding the future from a state of trance, his Christian mysticism serving the ends of a secular dynasty. Unlike Ariosto's Merlin, who apparently coexists with Christianity but is not a part of it, Pietro claims that God is the source of his revelations. Thus, what he has to say about the Estensi assumes the character of sacred history.

C. P. Brand describes Pietro's rapture as "strangely un-Christian," a view that I think is a misreading of the

Messianic vision that enabled Tasso to fuse the sacred and the profane as he does.[3] Failure to apprehend that vision in its full complexity would make the passage not merely un-Christian, but downright blasphemous--or bathetic. For, after Pietro expatiates briefly on the supremacy of the Este family as a source of heroes, he narrows his discourse to Duke Alfonso II and the historical role Tasso envisaged for his own patron,

> Che nascer dée, quando, corrotto e veglio,
> Povero fia d'uomini illustri il mondo
>
> (Canto XVII, 90)

Although Pietro's divine inspiration has provided him with very accurate information about the part of Alfonso's career that preceded composition of the Gerusalemme liberata, the Duke's eventual role is one about which he offers only fervent speculation. Thus, he describes Alfonso functioning as the ideal Renaissance prince:

> De la matura età pregi men degni
> Non fiano stabilir pace e quïete;
> Mantener sue città, fra l'arme e i regni
> Di possenti vicin, tranquille e chete;
> Nutrire e fecondar l'arti e gl'ignegni,
> Celebrar giochi illustri e pompe liete;
> Librar con giusta lance e pene e premi,
> Mirar da lunge e preveder gli estremi.
>
> (Canto XVII, 92)

---

[3] C. P. Brand, Torquato Tasso: A Study of the Poet and his Contribution to English Literature (Cambridge: Cambridge University Press, 1965), p. 86.

When he turns to what was still the future in Tasso's day, however, the mood becomes conditional, Pietro's wishes merge with those of the poet, and his advice assumes the authority of the First Crusade addressing its spiritual heir:

> Oh s'avvenisse mai che contra gli empi
> Che tutte infesteran le terre e i mari,
> E de la pace in quei miseri tempi
> Daran le leggi a i popoli più chiari,
> Duce sen gisse a vendicare i tempî
> Da lor distrutti, e i violati altari:
> Qual ei giusta farìa grave vendetta
> Su 'l gran tiranno e su l'iniqua setta!
>
> Indarno a lui con mille schiere armate
> Quinci il Turco opporrìasi, e quindi il Mauro;
> Ch'egli portar potrebbe oltre l'Eufrate,
> Ed oltre i gioghi del nevoso Tauro,
> Ed oltre i regni ov'è perpetua state,
> La Croce e'l bianco augello e i gigli d'auro;
> E per battesmo de le nere fronti
> Del gran Nilo scoprir le ignote fonti.
> (Canto XVII, 93-94)

In Tasso's view, the most enlightened secular leadership is inseparable from the terrestrial--and imperial--claims of God and the Church. Pietro l'Eremita hopes that the unborn Alfonso, whose image has been confided to him in a vision, will apply his unquestioned princely gifts to the reconquest of the Holy Land and what it represents.

When the poet speaks in his own voice, it is apparent that the sentiments expressed by Pietro are those of Torquato Tasso. Very early in the epic, the "magnanimo Alfonso" is addressed directly:

> Forse un dì fia che la presàga penna
> Osi scriver di te ch'or n'accenna.
>
> E ben ragion, s'egli avverrà ch'in pace
> Il buon popol di Cristo unqua si veda,
> E con navi e cavalli al fèro trace
> Cerchi ritôr la grande ingiusta preda,
> Ch'a te lo scettro in terra, o, se ti piace,
> L'alto imperio de' mari a te conceda.
> Emulo di Goffredo, i nostri carmi
> In tanto ascolta, e t'apparecchia a l'armi.
> (Canto I, 4-5)

Alfonso is called "emulo di Goffredo," although il pio Goffredo sets an even less attainable example than pius Aeneas. Tasso makes the rhetorical comparison here because he is trying to steel the Duke to a task as monumental as the First Crusade. But he realizes that there is an imperfection in the very frigidity of Goffredo's perfection. What is needed to complete the heroic image are the qualities of a Rinaldo:

> A te le prime parti, a lui concesse
> Son le seconde: tu sei capo, ei mano
> Di questo campo; e sostener sua vece
> Altri non pote, e farlo a te non lece.
> (Canto XIV, 13)

As a member of Casa d'Este, Alfonso could be both head and hand of the new Crusade, especially since the poem's most directly dynastic prophecy, occurring in the same address to Goffredo, foretells precisely that mingling of the two lines:

> Sarà il tuo sangue a suo commisto, e deve
> Progenie uscirne gloriosa e chiara.
> (Canto XIV, 19)

It is important to emphasize, however, that passages like this one, reflecting on actual descent and heredity, are very rare in the Liberata, and that where they occur, they are invariably related to the full historical scheme.

The tone of Tasso's advice to his patron differs markedly from that employed by his predecessors. In both the Aeneid and the Orlando furioso, the poet sets himself up as advisor to the princely patron, often sweetening the moral pill by writing as if the practice he recommends were already being followed by the prince and that therefore the lines were descriptive, rather than prescriptive. Similarly, tales of ancestral virtue often point to proper behavior for the contemporary prince. This use of history coincides with the larger mythology the epics are elaborating, for Virgil and Ariosto both seek to reinforce the idea of their patrons' inherited legitimacy by allusion to their individual merits. Although the two sorts of claim, birthright and personal worth, work neatly together, neither poet has many illusions about the limits of the claim. Both speak of the dynasty they serve as fulfilling the will of God, but this means that Virgil's gens Iulia and Ariosto's Casa d'Este play a part in the divine plan for human life, not that they become instruments in a larger cosmic scheme. God is on the side of Ippolito d'Este and, theological cavils apart, He was on the side of Augustus Caesar; only Tasso would take the further step of urging his patron to take action confirming that <u>he</u> is on <u>God's</u> side.

Moreover, Virgil and Ariosto might not be heeded as moral preceptors, but the political advice and support their epics afforded was never unwelcome. Tasso, on the other hand, uses his epic to call for a mission Alfonso was by no means ready to embrace. And the poet makes it quite clear that his praise of the Duke's virtues will remain a series of empty formulae unless those virtues are placed in the service of Christ and the salvation of Christianity. Although Charlemagne's beleagured armies face the same challenge in the <u>Furioso</u>, Ariosto leaves any analogy with the contemporary situation deliberately vague; the mission he does wish on the Estensi is patriotic, imperial, and bourgeois. Cardinal Ippolito may have taken a Philistine attitude to Ariosto's poem, but the political task it outlines was very much to his taste. By contrast, the <u>Gerusalemme liberata</u> devotes very little direct energy to the dynastic question, none at all to diplomatic flattery. Praise of the Estensi is invariably linked to the world-historic role they are expected to assume. Viewed as a courtly exercise, the story of the First Crusade, even with the Este contribution at its center, offers cold comfort to a Renaissance ruler.

A Political Vision

For Tasso, the theme of the Crusade was not merely "a more authentic historical version" of the material Boiardo and Ariosto employed.[4] His choice of subject was deliberate and, to his mind, entirely relevant to his own time. Graham

---

[4] Graham Hough, <u>A Preface to The Faerie Queene</u> (New York: Norton, 1963), p. 62.

Hough, acknowledging Tasso's conformity to the spirit of his age, nonetheless ascribes the choice to the enforced lack of a "national" theme. In Hough's view, the First Crusade is a timely subject simply because "after 500 years Christendom was still at war with the Saracens; the exploits of the Emperor Charles V against the Moors in Tunis were still fresh in the memory."[5] Those exploits, however, were far more germane to Ariosto's conception of historical allegory than to Tasso's. In the Liberata, the Crusade is not conceived as a simple political task, colorfully evoked in order to inspire the reader and patron to a similar political enterprise. Neither Goffredo's mission nor Alfonso d'Este's is so limited in its intention and its potential effect, for, as I shall demonstrate, Tasso sees a Crusade as the way to unify Christendom around the common goal of restoring holiness to the world.

This task subsumes and gives life to the patriotic and dynastic motives in the poem. It is not merely that Tasso, finding himself in a fragmented Italy at a time of ideological upheaval and division had no immediate national design to give shape to his epic. Rather, he rejects the temporal realm of politics except as a means to the end that lends it significance; the Gerusalemme liberata does not lack a national element, but its overriding theme is intentionally --and passionately--supra-national. In the Orlando furioso, Ariosto appears not to recognize that there is any contradiction between the ideal of a united Christendom and the dynastic or national interest of the Estensi. The Gerusalemme liberata, on the other hand, admits the conflict, but assumes that the only reason for continued Este predominance is to give leadership to the Christian cause, treating that

---

[5] Ibid.

spiritual leadership as its own political reward.

Thus, Tasso's opening lines constitute another variation on the Virgilian formula. As the Aeneid sings of arms and the man, delineating the geographical and imperial destiny the hero is to fulfill within the epic, the Furioso peoples the political canvas with ladies and their knights, its introductory stanza proclaiming that courtesies and feats of arms will share the scene with the cause to which they are dedicated. The Liberata returns to arms and the man, but with a significant difference. If Tasso does not play with the concept, as Ariosto does, neither does he accept its earthbound limits. The arms he celebrates are "pietose" and his captain's principal mission is not territorial, but religious. His destiny is achieved not by founding a worldly kingdom, but asserting a spiritual one; just as Aeneas is the man who brought the Trojan heritage to the shores of Italy, so Goffredo is the one "che 'l gran sepolcro liberò di Cristo." Tasso imitates Virgil, also, in following his first lines with a summary of the vicissitudes his hero faces in pursuit of his goal. Once more, and without directly deprecating the pagan leader, Tasso places Goffredo's experience on a higher plane--in terms of both the inner suffering he undergoes and the cosmic nature of the struggle in which he is engaged.

This impression is reinforced by contrasting the final stanzas of the Liberata with the way the other two epics end. Both Virgil and Ariosto conclude their stories with the slaying of one last adversary. In each case, this death does bring the overall scheme together, but it also serves to remind us that the end of the adventure story means the end of the epic. Tasso, however, takes us beyond the final battle and returns us to the cause itself, so that the last stanza of the Liberata echoes the first:

> Così vince Goffredo; ed a lui tanto
> Avanza ancor de la diurna luce,
> Ch'a la città già liberata, al santo
> Ostel di Cristo i vincitor conduce.
> Né pur deposto il sanguinoso manto,
> Viene al tempio con gli altri il sommo duce;
> E qui l'arme sospende, e qui devoto
> Il gran Sepolcro adora, e scioglie il vóto.
>
> (Canto XX, 144)

It is in the context of this introduction and conclusion that Tasso's exhortations to his patron and the entire dynastic thrust of the poem must be understood. Tasso makes it clear from the beginning that his interpretation of "good government" places equal and serious emphasis on both words.

In this regard, the poet's attitude towards Boemondo is particularly instructive. The newly established ruler of Antioch is the only leader who does not respond to Goffredo's marshalling of forces in Canto One, and his absence from the Christian ranks is observed and lamented at several subsequent points. Yet Boemondo is not a slacker in any conventional sense. He has won Antioch as his lawful prize and stays behind to govern it:

> ...fondar Boemondo al novo regno
> Suo d'Antiochia alti principii mira,
> E leggi imporre, ed introdur costume
> Ed arti, e culto di verace nume...
>
> (Canto I, 9)

But in time of war--holy war--the imposition and implementation of earthly justice is not enough, and Boemondo, by dropping out of the Crusade, is mistaking the form of Christian government for its substance. As if to underscore the inadequacy of Boemondo's choice, Tasso notes his absence during the initial catalogue of Christian forces, a survey that he daringly conducts from the point of view of God Himself. In this perspective, Boemondo's absence cannot fail to evoke disapproval and even disdain. Now, not only is the King of Antioch doing a good job by temporal standards, he is doing precisely the same sort of job that the Dukes of Ferrara are praised for elsewhere in the poem. Combined with the direct address to Alfonso several stanzas earlier, the message is inescapable: The ultimate righteousness and legitimacy of Este rule depends not only on inheritance and statecraft, but on consistently demonstrated spiritual merit.

Still more disquieting are the implications of Goffredo's speech to his men in the first Canto. On one level, this may be interpreted as the conventional exhortation before a last obstacle is attempted, the chief strategic consideration being that present gains cannot be retained, much less consolidated, unless the final goal is also achieved. Divine authority is invoked to strengthen this argument:

> Or se da noi rivolte e torte sono
> Contra quel fin che 'l donator dispose,
> Temo cen privi, e favola a le genti
> Quel sì chiaro rimbombo al fin diventi.
> (Canto I, 26)

But, convention or no, the handwriting is on the wall--should the Estensi choose to read it aright.

The motive force of the <u>Gerusalemme liberata</u> is the drive towards salvation, but it would be both naive and inadequate to interpret this thrust, the spirit of the Counter-Reformation, as an urge above or distinct from class or national politics. In fact, what is missing in the *Orlando furioso* is precisely a sense that Christian ideology was being developed and transformed in response to the same economic and social conflicts that were transforming political life. Tasso, writing out of a consciousness formed by another half-century of religious turmoil, places primary emphasis on the spiritual aspect of the struggle. But this means that religious--and even theological--considerations inform his social vision, not that they take its place.

It is in its concentration on the nature of kingship and the personality of the prince that the *Gerusalemme liberata* is most explicitly related to the politics of the Counter Reformation. The eventual result of the Reformation movement may well have been, as DeSanctis claims, the secularization of religion and of all social life, but its immediate effect, for Catholics as well as Protestants, was quite the reverse.[6] This does not mean that there was a reinstatement of medieval absolutism in principle or in fact. Instead, a new relationship was established among social interests and the ideas that sustained them. On the Counter-Reformation side, this new dialectic led to an intensification of the concern with kingship that character-

---

[6] See Francesco DeSanctis, *History of Italian Literature*, trans. Joan Redfern, II (1876; rpt. New York: Basic Books, 1959), 625. Identifying with the liberal bourgeoisie of his own century, DeSanctis sees movements of resistance to Spanish or papal authority as the only progressive forces at work in Tasso's time. Rhetorically, at least, he identifies the trend of Counter-Reformation Romanism with "divine right, theocracy, Caesarism, the absorption of the individual into the collective," without acknowledging that this trend was also in some measure a consequence of the developing hegemony of the bourgeoisie.

ized contemporary political thinking.

Thus Goffredo, in the poem's opening line, is not simply the man, but the leader of men, the <u>captain</u>, who reclaimed the tomb of Christ. And as the epic progresses, he is invested with the attributes of royal, as well as military leadership, "indosando idealmente il manto di porpora."[7] The figure of Goffredo in particular and the prince in general, is also at the center of the allusions to court life that occur with surprising frequency throughout a poem whose principal milieu is the military encampment. DeSanctis speaks of the latter part of the Cinquecento as a period when "religion became an instrument of politics, and religious despotism became the material auxiliary of political despotism."[8] What Tasso is expressing through the Crusades and the dominant image of Goffredo is something else, however: religious exaltation in the service of political exaltation.

Goffredo is a charismatic medieval leader, endowed and protected by heaven, yet he also reflects the political values of the sixteenth century. When he intervenes in the internecine conflict Alecto has incited within the Christian ranks, he acts under direct divine inspiration, but as a king, not a prophet:

>   Ha la corazza in dosso, e nobil veste
>   Riccamente l'adorna oltra il costume.
>   Nudo e le mani e 'l vólto, e di celeste
>   Maestà vi risplende un novo lume:
>   Scote l'aurato scettro, e sol con queste

---

[7] Giovanni Getto, <u>Interpretazione</u> <u>del</u> <u>Tasso</u> (Naples: Edizioni scientifiche italiane, 1951), p. 323.

[8] DeSanctis, p. 625.

> Arme acquetar quegli impeti presume.
> Tal si mostra a coloro, e tal ragiona;
> Né come d'uom mortal la voce suona
>
> (Canto VIII, 78)

The divine source of Goffredo's splendid authority in this situation is unambiguous:

> E fama che fu visto in vólto crudo
> Ed in atto feroce e minacciante
> Un alato guerrier tener lo scudo
> De la difesa al pio Buglion davante,
> E vibrar fulminando il ferro ignudo
> Che di sangue vedeasi ancor stillante:
> Sangue era forse di città, di regni,
> Che provocâr del Cielo i tardi sdegni.
>
> (Canto VIII, 84)

Moreover, his character as the soldier of God, *il pio* Goffredo, is not in conflict with, but is responsible for the flexible nature of the justice he dispenses, for his *pietà* embraces religious devotion and compassion. It is this quality that enables him to interpret justice in the spirit of the Renaissance:

> E per or la giustizia a la pietate
> Ceda, né sovra i rei la pena scenda.
> A gli altri merti or questo error perdono,
> Ed al vostro Rinaldo anco vi dono.
>
> (Canto VIII, 80)

Tasso reinforces this sense of Goffredo's princely mandate, once the revolt is quelled, by having him turn from his role as saint and judge to his character as military leader:

> ...ritorna Goffredo al padiglione,
> A varie cose, a nove imprese intento;
> Ch'assalir la cittadé egli dispone
> Pria che 'l secondo o 'l terzo dí sia spento:
> E rivedendo va l'incise travi,
> Già in macchine conteste orrende e gravi.
>   (Canto VIII, 85)

Goffredo is a rigid and ascetic leader, but in his ability to perform many roles and in the way he carries them out, he exemplifies a Renaissance, and not a medieval ideal of kingship.

Pietro l'Eremita's prophecies make it clear, however, that Tasso does not believe that the range of gifts with which he endows Goffredo is sufficient for the actual Renaissance prince. Goffredo may be more varied and flexible than he at first appears, but his character lacks balance. He is not capable of compromise, applying diplomatic or bureaucratic solutions to questions of political principle, and he does not possess the human warmth that would motivate such compromise. It is important, therefore, that when Rinaldo is about to be pardoned and restored to his place in the Christian ranks, Pietro states that the ideal leader would combine the qualities of Goffredo and Rinaldo, and that such a mixture would, in times to come, enrich the House of Este. Although Tasso is not explicit about how or when the two lines are to be joined, it is obvious that the resolution will have to involve sexual relationships and female agency; Tasso apparently accepts the further admixture of "feminine" qualities as also contributing to the political balance of both the state and the individual.

In a few other places, Tasso gives evidence of a consciousness that is consistent with the political practice and ideology of his time. The journey to Armida's island, for example, although it is accomplished by magic, is remarkable for its geographical realism and the poet's evident delight in the Mediterranean world through which the "fatal donzella" guides the Crusaders. The same pleasure is reflected in the lady's excursus upon lands yet undiscovered that were not to be conquered and Christianized until Tasso's own time. Her praise of Columbus views with equal enthusiasm the boldness of his enterprise, its "civilizing" function, and its imperial goal:

>   ...la fé di Piero
> Fiavi introdotta, ed ogni civil arte;
> Né già sempre sarà che la via lunga
> Questi da' vostri popoli disgiunga.
>
> Tempo verrà che fian d'Ercolo i segni
> Favola vile a i naviganti industri;
> E i mari riposti, or senza nome, e i regni
> Ignoti ancor, tra voi saranno illustri.
> Fia ch 'l più ardito allor di tutti i legni,
> Quanto circonda il mar, circondi e lustri,
> E la terra misuri, immensa mole,
> Vittorioso, ed emulo del sole.
>
> Un uom de la Liguria avrà ardimento
> A l'incognito corso esporsi in prima:
> ...
> Tu spiegherai, Colombo, a un novo polo
> Lontane sì le fortunate antenne,
> Ch'a pena seguirà con gli occhi il volo

> La fama c'ha mille occhi e mille penne.
> Canti ella Alcide e Bacco, e di te solo
> Basti a i posteri tuoi ch'alquanto accenne;
> Ché quel poco darà lunga memoria
> Di poema dignissima e d'istoria.
>
> (Canto XV, 29-32)

Tasso's evident interest in the discoveries that were leading to the conquest and settlement of the New World should not be underestimated or regarded as an ideological anomaly. In the text, as in his thinking, support for the explorations originates in a desire to share the messsage of Christian salvation with the benighted peoples of the earth. That the opportunity to do so coincided with the Counter Reformation was, of course, a formative influence in that movement's development and direction. In this sense, Tasso's attitude does no more than echo the missionary zeal characteristic of the early Jesuits and their enthusiastic co-religionists. It should be emphasized, however, that the poet does not regard Columbus' adventures as simply securing new terrain for Christ, but appears to glory in them for their own sake, perceiving and approving the social and economic consequences of imperial expansion. This awareness is important, I think, because it offers a corrective to the view that Tasso's spiritual vision of politics was so rarefied as to ignore the realities of contemporary life. It is particularly significant, in the light of Tasso's views about the historical and religious basis of epic, that he considers the exploits of Columbus to be worthy of celebration in heroic poetry.[9] His eyes may be ineffectually fixed

---

[9] As epitomized in his *Discorsi* on the heroic poem, Tasso believed that heroic poetry should be grounded in Christian
(Footnote continued)

on Heaven but, at least in his own mind, his view also comprehended more mundane concerns.

The extent to which Tasso understood a politics more practical than Messianic is also reflected in his invocation to the Muse in Canto XVII. He calls upon her to enlighten him about an issue he obviously considers deserving of the most serious and responsible treatment: the political background of his story, the divisions and alliances within the Saracen party, the strategic considerations and social forces operative in a situation that saw "sotto l'arme/Mezzo il mondo raccolto." Whereas the earlier overview of Christian troops emphasized the unity underlying their diversity, the survey of the enemy stresses a disunity that is not attributed, as in Ariosto, to individual idiosyncracies or to divisive outside influences, but is based in materially different political interests that Tasso himself quite clearly grasps and communicates.

Love and Marriage

It is against this complex of social and ideological values that the sexual dramas are enacted. And it is the often contradictory demands implicit in this vision that give the sexual relationships their eventual form. Tasso's concerns in the poem are dynastic, but his patrons' spiritual heritage was more important to him than their biological descent. He valued the human qualities embodied in women, as well as the sensations and emotions aroused by sexuality. Yet he could find no way for these experiences to enter his

---

[9](continued)
history, with the mystical or magical element focused on demonstrating the role of (divinely-inspired) marvels in that history.

commonwealth without destroying it. There existed no Christian institution that would enable him to combine his vision of heightened Christianity with his idea of sexual love. Marriage had not yet taken on that ideal character and the family was certainly not a material vehicle for its expression. Tasso appears to perceive some of the possibilities, but he is unable to realize them without jeopardizing the structures of spiritual purity he has created.

Yet the sexual themes are just as essential to the development of the Gerusalemme liberata as they are to the Orlando furioso. Graham Hough remarks that the actual love interest in the First Crusade was not very strong, but that in Tasso's version it is the love adventures we remember.[10] This is not simply because the love passages are more colorful than the military, spiritual, or political aspects of the Crusades, but because, in order to possess the symbolic importance it did for him, Tasso's First Crusade had to be infused with the positive values of sexual passion. From one critical perspective, the attempt is so successful that it looks as if the motive force of the poem is not "religion, patriotism, vengeance or hatred, but love, an all-powerful, invincible passion for Torquato's heroes."[11] Another common opinion is that the poetic life of the epic does indeed reside in its sexual themes, but that Tasso's treatment of them is a departure from his "real" subject. The truth is less simple than either of these interpretations would allow. Love is neither the sole subject of the poem nor a life-breathing ornament on some other subject.

---

[10] Hough, p. 62.

[11] Vincent Luciani, A Brief History of Italian Literature (New York: S. F. Vanni, 1967), p. 135.

Rather, the epic's entire sexual content might be summarized in DeSanctis' description of the love affair between Rinaldo and Armida: "This, which the critics called an 'episode,' is the real conception of his poem."[12] The various sexual relationships and the psychology that directs them provided grounds for exploring a rich range of imaginative and expressive possibilities; it is as if the historical subject represented a fixed point in Tasso's vision, while the sexual theme was more flexible and allowed him greater freedom of invention. Hough observes that Tasso's design is so coherent that "even in Armida's garden the siege of Jerusalem is never forgotten for long."[13] I would go further and say that, for Tasso, the only way to reach Jerusalem leads through Armida's garden.

The elements of sexual experience that are most vivid in the love affairs Tasso depicts are sensuality and loss. Precisely because he is less direct and lusty in the telling than Ariosto is, his descriptions of sexual acts and feelings are more prolonged, more lyrical. Ariosto shows us men driven mad with desire, but he does not communicate the actual desire they feel. The Gerusalemme liberata dwells less on the furious results of passion and more on the passion itself. Tasso's is an intrinsically sexier poem, not because repression stirs the imagination more than fulfillment, but because the poet's approach, even when the sequel to fulfillment is going to be renunciation, is apparently free of irony.

In the long run, however, it is not sexual fulfillment that Tasso concentrates on, but frustration, denial, and control. It is not, as Hough states, that a happy love is

---

[12] DeSanctis, p. 641.

[13] Hough, p. 63.

outside Tasso's imaginative range, but rather that, as he also admits, the erotic element "has to be redeemed before it can be fully admitted," and, in the process, becomes something other than sexual love.[14] Brand claims that all the loves the poem describes are finally "legalized or spiritualized."[15] It is significant that the great loves in the epic are limited further: They can end only by being "spiritualized" or left unresolved. The option of legitimization through marriage is not open to Tasso's heroes, as it is to Gildippe and Odoardo or to Sofronia and Olindo, couples who are not unheroic, themselves, but whose stories are nonetheless peripheral to the true epic action.

All this suggests that Tasso's attitude towards marriage and his treatment of it in the poem deserve further scrutiny. It is not simply a twentieth-century bias, informed by idealization of monogamous love-matches, that dictates this approach. Familiarity with the developing heroic tradition evokes the same questions about a vision of marriage that would serve to sanctify the adulterous love celebrated by medieval poets and, at the same time, inject the energies of sexual passion into the domestic and dynastic institutions of family life.

Although illicit relations abound in the Orlando furioso, Ariosto also represents marriage as the logical outcome of several love affairs in the poem, including that of the epic's principal couple, Bradamante and Ruggiero. Nor does he explicitly admit that in so doing he is taking part in a radical redefinition of both poetic love and ideal marriage. He recognizes that marriage can be motivated by considerations of property, prestige, or policy and, in the parental

---

[14] Hough, pp. 67 and 68.
[15] Brand, p. 182. See also p. 114.

objections to Bradamante's choice, he unmasks venal bourgeois assumptions about the contract and the institution. But it is the young lovers who have God and destiny on their side; Ariosto is almost casual about his declaration that marriage for love is the right way. Although the fact of the marriage is important for both the narrative and ideological structures of his epic, he does not construct a complete theory of marital love around the event.

Spenser works with the raw materials that Ariosto provides, but his view of marriage is not limited to the human scale of the Orlando furioso. In the Amoretti and the Epithalamion, he appears to take for granted that the spiritual and sentimental attitudes developed by the troubadours, the stilnovisti, and the Petrarchists as the expression of ideal or fleshly adultery could be readily translated into terms appropriate for the celebration of lawful love and Christian marriage. He shares the assumptions of Castiglione's Cortegiano that Platonic and courtly love conventions can lend their external form to the new substance of serious courtship and matrimony.[16] The allegory of The Faerie Queene takes the premise much further, building a complex scheme of temporal and transcendent significance upon marriages in Britain and in Faerie-land.

Hough remarks that it is difficult even to imagine a

---

[16] See Baldassare Castiglione, Il libro del cortegiano in Opere di Baldassare Castiglione, Giovanni della Casa, Benvenuto Cellini, a cura di Carlo Cordie (Milan-Naples: Ricciardi, n.d.), Books III and IV. In discussing the loves of a court lady, Castiglione has his spokesman, Giuliano de' Medici, express the opinion that if such a lady is unmarried her love ought to be directed towards someone she can marry. It is interesting to note, in surveying this development of Renaissance thinking about love and marriage, that Torquato's own father, Bernardo Tasso, contributed to it in his Amadigi (See Brand, p. 63).

place in the _Gerusalemme liberata_ for anything like the "happy and untrammelled reunion" of Scudamour and Amoret.[17] This is not simply because Tasso is incapable of creating a happy ending, but because his vision, even when it is most allegorical, does not admit some of the conceptual lacunae that occur in Ariosto and Spenser. _Narrative_ lacunae are quite frequent, of course, so that the reader is left in doubt about such basic issues as what actually happens to Erminia and Armida once they have played their part and their stories have received symbolic resolution. But, on the intellectual level, I do not believe that Tasso could settle for a definition of marriage that encompassed only matrimony, a definition, that is, that stopped at the beginning. Although Ariosto and Spenser are both concerned with dynastic questions, there is little in their poems that shows they are aware of any concrete aspect of the family that creates and constitutes a dynasty. The Garden of Adonis is rich in the promise of fertility, but it contains no hints about the social institutions that nurture and sustain human life beyond conception.

By contrast, Tasso's dialogue, _Il padre di famiglia_, demonstrates a practical grasp of the family as the dominant institution in private life. He is aware, first of all, that the family _is_ an institution, that it posesses a government and a structure of power, and that these are all part of a larger system. In a well regulated household, he maintains, the wife obeys her husband,

> non in quel modo che 'l servo al signore e 'l corpo all'animo ubbedisce, ma civilmente, in quel

---

[17] Hough, p. 69. It is not clear, unfortunately, which reunion is in question here.

modo che nelle città ben ordinate i cittadini ubbediscono alle leggi e a' magistrati, o nell' anima nostra, nella quale, cosí ordinate le potenze come nelle città gli ordini dei cittadini, la parte affetuosa suole alle ragionevole ubbedire.[18]

In this passage, Tasso goes beyond the stereotyped identification of the female with nature and the emotions, the male with culture and rationality. By adding the political simile, he not only deepens his observations about the marital relationship, but also says something about his conception of the state and good government. Indeed, this set of mutually reinforcing analogies epitomizes some of the Renaissance period's basic ideas about politics. Order in the state is a product of balanced elements, a condition that requires the inclusion of the female principle. But the proper balance, in Tasso's opinion, carefully subordinates feminine qualities and participation to masculine attributes and power. It is not a situation that can be attained in the household or symbolized in the state by the marriage of equals that Ariosto and Spenser postulate.

The balance and harmony implicit in his ordered polity is also reflected in Tasso's methodical description of the father's functions: "La cura del padre di famiglia a due

---

[18] Torquato Tasso, Il padre di famiglia, in Dialoghi, ed. Ezio Raimondi (Florence: Sansoni, 1958), Vol. I, Section 73, 356. It is worth noting that, whereas the narrowly private view of the family itself has also served to narrow our definition of the word, Tasso is able to move easily from consideration of the "famigliata" as family, that is as a structure of personal relations, and the "famiglia" as household, a structure of material relations. Although Tasso, like Ariosto and Spenser, concentrates in his poem on the private relationship that brought the family into being, he has not restricted his conception of the "famiglia" to that conveyed in bourgeois mythology.

cose si stende, alle persone e a le facoltà, e...con le persone tre uffici dee essercitare, di marito, di padre e di signore; e nelle facultà [sic] due fini si propone, la conservazione e l'accrescimento."[19] The significance of the commercial images here ought not, perhaps, to be exaggerated, but they do indicate a certain penetration of the marketplace mentality into personal life. Tasso's analysis also extends to the divison of labor between the sexes, which he believes to be founded on something very like the nineteenth-century idea of the separate spheres. Tasso's notion of patriarchal responsibility does not admit even the pretense that those spheres are equal, however:

> la cura delle facoltà...s'impiega nella conservazione e nell'accrescimento ed e divisa tra 'l padre 'e la madre di famiglia, perciochè par così proprio del padre di famiglia l'accrescere come della madre il conservare, nondimeno a chi minutamente considera, la cura del accrescimento è propria del padre di famiglia e l'altra è commune, che che gli antichi in questo proposito s'abbiano detto.[20]

The very prolixity of Tasso's prose, here, serves to remind us how remote is this domestic world from Armida's island. The ideal home depicted in this dialogue is the product of human effort and consciousness, the opposite of the <u>locus amoenus</u> where an apparently natural beauty abounds and sexual love--at least temporarily--has free rein. Indeed, Tasso

---

[19] Ibid., Section 60, 353.
[20] Ibid., Section 119, 371.

is quite aware that uncontrolled sexuality would destroy the harmonious governance of the ideal household. The restrained embraces he recommends as the assurance of conjugal felicity are, he admits, very different from the excesses in which lovers indulge.[21] Far from being a precondition for marriage, love and its open sexual expression represent a threat to it, just as they do to the Virgilian state, and for the same reasons.

The <u>Padre di famiglia</u> belongs, of course, to a genre very different from the romance-epic, and Tasso's contribution to the tradition was little more than a variation on familiar themes from ancient and modern sources, of which Alberti's treatise on the family is probably the best known.[22] The dialogue is not really a reliable touchstone, then, against which to measure the views of sexual matters that are elaborated in the <u>Gerusalemme liberata</u>. It does show that Tasso, unlike the other writers of the romance-epic, gave systematic thought to the politics of family life and that his conclusions were entirely orthodox--indeed, classic. Such austerity in his prose writings need not preclude greater social and emotional freedom in the poetry, but it does mean that if Tasso were to connect marriage with sensuous and spiritual union, he would be forced to consider institutional implications beyond the actual mating of two lovers.

The household Tasso imagines in <u>Il padre di famiglia</u> is

---

[21] <u>Ibid.</u>, Sections 84-87, 360-361.

[22] In Tasso's own time, the writers who took part in the tradition included Speron Speroni, Flaminio dei Noteri, Francesco Patrizi, Lodovico Dolci and Francesco Tomasi. See Bruno Basile, "Fonti culturale e invenzione letteraria nel 'Padre di famiglia' di Torquato Tasso," <u>Convivio</u>, 36 (1968), 277-92.

the serene center of virtuous existence. Yet the poet has no illusions about the material basis of the relations that make up family life, and he would have found it difficult to provide a "Hollywood ending" for any pair of lovers without dealing in some way with the contradiction between spiritual edification and bourgeois institutions. It is not clear how consciously Tasso explored this contradiction himself, but the two marriages he does allow into the <u>Gerusalemme liberata</u> provide at least partial insight into the way he perceived the problem. If anything, Sofronia's marriage to Olindo and Gildippe's to Odoardo indicate that the poet was intensely aware of the love and marriage conventions within which he was working and the ironic consequences of pursuing them to their logical conclusion.

This rather distorted perspective is most evident in the brief episode of Sofronia and Olindo in Canto II. It is one measure of his sensibility, first of all, that he invents this particular story as the vehicle for describing internal tensions in Jerusalem just prior to the final conquest. There is no historical basis for the tale of the stolen painting, the beautiful volunteer for martyrdom, and her self-sacrificing lover; in fact, the incident that occurred at an analagous point in the actual First Crusade involved someone's throwing a dead dog into a mosque. Tasso's version, of course, places all the onus of desecrating a holy object onto the Saracens. This way, the original impiety, as well as the cruelty and injustice, are theirs alone. It also provides him with the opportunity to test poetic love conventions against historical reality.

The initial description of Sofronia endows her with all the traditional virtues of the beloved lady in the sonnets --including a self-effacing modesty almost as extreme as that of Wordsworth's Lucy. Her loveliness is not destined to blush unseen, however, for it has already inspired a passion that is quite familiar to the readers of love poetry:

> Vergine era fra lor di già matura
> Verginità, d'alti pensieri e regi,
> D'alta beltà; ma su beltà non cura,
> O tanto sol quant'onestà sen fregi:
> E il suo pregio maggior, che tra le mura
> D'augusta casa asconde i suoi gran pregi;
> E del vagheggiatori ella s'invola
> A le lodi, a gli sguardi inculta e sola.
>
> Pur guardia esser non può, ch'in tutto celi
> Beltà degna ch'appaia e che s'ammiri;
> Né tu il consenti, Amor, ma la riveli
> D'un giovenetto a i cupidi desiri.
> Amor, ch'or cieco, or Argo, ora ne veli,
> Di benda gli occhi, ora ce li apri e giri,
> Tu per mille custodie entro a i più casti
> Verginei alberghi il guardo altrui portasti.
> (Canto II, 14-15)

There is nothing remarkable about this description except that it occurs at a tense moment in the narrative, when all the Christians have been sentenced to death in reprisal for what was either a pious individual act or the result of divine intervention. It is a most unself-conscious bit of poetry, but Tasso cannot have been equally unaware of the effect created by contrasting the convention with the situation into which he introduces it.

The sense that these lines are an allusion to an inappropriate tradition is enhanced by Sofronia's behavior for the remaining stanzas in which she appears. The almost pathologically retiring heroine of the love passages is replaced by a bold and fearless Christian who is ready to embrace martyrdom for her people and her creed. Nor does her strength at this moment appear to be a new role that necessity has forced on her, as Olindo's volunteering to die in her place reflects love's ennobling influence on him. In fact, there is a significant reversal of values in this episode, since it is the woman who is moved by concern for the whole community and for an abstract principle, the man whose involvement requires a private emotional link to the public event. This reversal has led critics to impose further--and irresponsible--definitions of sexual character upon them, so that Sofronia is often described as a "virile" character, softened and "humanized" by the more "feminine" Olindo.[23]

What I find particularly striking about this episode is the way it caricatures Petrarchan love theatrics and the way the joint martyrdom assumes a para-military guise. Olindo's adolescent passion is full of conventional antithetical feelings, as he "both loves and resents, reveres and desires" his lady.[24] Love makes him a better man, as the tradition suggests that it should, but his proposed martyrdom remains a sexual, not a religious sacrifice, with the threatening flames of the stake a shockingly literal rendering of the accustomed rhetorical heart-burnings. It is usually the case with Tasso that the imminence of death seems to inspire love with a new intensity. But in this

---

[23] DeSanctis, p. 656 and Luciani, p. 126. Both these commentators refer to Sofronia's need for "humanization"--a need that is not so apparent to them in the case of a strong or austere male character.

[24] Brand, pp. 102-3.

instance, the danger merely makes Olindo's emotion appear comic and rather grotesque, for if the lover cries, "I burn," when the flames are lapping at his feet, he is speaking no more than the truth, and it is no longer the fire in his soul that most concerns us. Olindo's own words on the occasion confirm this sense of a reduction of conventions to bizarrely logical absurdity. Fate, he claims, had long kept him and Sofronia apart,

> Ma duramente or ne congiunge in morte.
> Piacemi almen, poi ch'in sì strane guise
> Morir pur déi, del rogo esser consorte,
> Se del letto non fui: duolmi il tuo fato,
> Il mio non gia, poi ch'io ti moro a lato.
>
> Ed oh mia sorte avventurosa a pieno!
> Oh fortunati miei dolci martìri!
> S'impetrerò che giunto seno a seno
> L'anima mia ne la tua bocca spiri:
> E venendo tu meco a un tempo meno
> In me fuor mandi gli ultimi sospiri.
>   (Canto II, 34-35)

From his treatment of Sofronia and from what we know of his religious zeal, it seems unlikely that Tasso is ridiculing the idea of martyrdom for the faith. It is Olindo and his Petrarchan motivations that are being satirized. Tasso's dismissal of the pair after their rescue by Clorinda deepens this impression, since it is one of the few comic remarks in the entire <u>Gerusalemme liberata</u> and the only one attributed to the narrator himself. Olindo, he says,

> Volse con lei morire: ella non schiva.
> Poi che seco non muor, che seco viva.
> (Canto II, 53)

The spiritual setting, the near-martyrdom, and the substituted sacrament of marriage seem not to impress the poet as causes for solemnity. And these lines make it clear that he does not seriously regard matrimony as the means of joining two bodies and souls in the service of God.

An aspect of the Sofronia-Olindo relationship that is less frequently commented upon is their competitiveness in the face of martyrdom and the military language in which the competition is couched. When Olindo attempts to save his beloved by confessing to the theft of the sacred image, he tries to lend credence to his tale by attributing her confession to madness, deprecating a woman's ability to plan and execute such a crime. Sofronia's reply prefigures her attitude when Clorinda finds them actually bound to the stake and "piu vigor mostra il men forte sesso." Her answer to Olindo is gentle and pitying, but not without a certain forceful pride:

> A che ne vieni, o misero innocente?
> Qual consiglio o furor ti guida o tira?
> Non son io dunque senza te possente
> A sostener ciò che d'un uom può l'ira?
> Ho petto anch'io, ch'ad una morte crede
> Di bastar solo, e compagnia non chiede.
> (Canto II, 30)

The scene rapidly degenerates into farce as Olindo accepts the funeral pyre as a replacement for the marriage bed and then the marriage bed itself is granted as a replacement for the intended sacrifice. But at the point of Olindo's confession and Sofronia's rejection of his proffered martyrdom, the poet's tone is devoid of irony and the contest of wills appears magnificent to him:

> Oh spettacolo grande ove a tenzone
> Sono Amore e magnanima virtute!
> (Canto II, 31)

The situation is ironically reminiscent of themes in both Ariosto and Spenser wherein the struggle between two lovers culminates in a hard-won victory and a marriage. But in this version there can be no winner, and the marriage that results has nothing to do with the battle that has been waged.

Gildippe and Odoardo, the married lovers who are also comrades in arms, fill an iconographic, rather than a narrative function. Their inclusion in the Liberata would seem to bring together all the major themes we are considering, but the presentation is sterile and does not greatly enrich our apprehension of the issues. The couple is introduced in the catalogue of Christian warriors:

> Ove voi me, di numerar già lasso,
> Gildippe ed Odoardo, amanti e sposi,
> Rapite? o ne la guerra anco consorti,
> Non sarete disgiunti ancor che morti!
> (Canto I, 56)

Our first view of them thus foreshadows the last, and the essential impression they convey is one of stasis, rather than tension. Tasso follows the initial lines with an explanation of how Gildippe came to be a soldier, and, here again, one has a sense of poetic opportunity lost:

> Ne le scuole d'Amor che non s'apprende?
> Ivi si fe' costei guerriera ardita:
> Va sempre affissa al caro fianco; e pende
> Da un fato solo l'una a l'altra vita:
> Colpo che ad un sol noccia unqua non scende,
> Ma indiviso è il dolor d'ogni ferita:
> E spesso è l'un ferito, e l'altro langue;
> E versa l'alma quel, se questa il sangue.
>
> (Canto I, 57)

Now, the <u>Gerusalemme</u> <u>liberata</u> is a narrative in which each of the principal female characters is involved in a military campaign and in a love affair that is related to that campaign. In such a context, the presence of Gildippe and Odoardo might enrich the poem by serving as a pure and uncomplicated example of love's inspiration in war. Moreover, since their love embraces common dedication to a holy cause, they are bound in a closer intimacy than earthly love alone could achieve--almost literally one spirit and one flesh. Yet, aside from this single stanza, Tasso does not realize the full conceptual potential of their love.

Gildippe and Odoardo appear only a few more times in the body of the poem. They are pointed out, identically dressed in white, in the scene where Erminia identifies all the Christian knights (Canto III, 40). And they volunteer <u>as</u> <u>a</u> <u>couple</u> to meet Argante's challenge to single combat (Canto VII, 7). In one battle scene, Gildippe is used as a Christian counterpart to Clorinda, so that

> Mentre così l'indomita guerriera
> Le squadre d'Occidente apre e flagella,

Tasso

> Non fa d'in contra a lei Gildippe altera
> De' saracini suoi strage men fella.
> Era il sesso il medesmo, e simile era
> L'ardimento e 'l valore in questa e in quella.
> (Canto IX, 71)

It is only at the last, however, that the two warrior-lovers come to the fore and fulfill any of the functions that Tasso suggests elsewhere. The honor of striking the first successful blow in the battle falls to Gildippe and Tasso makes much of her sex in the lines dedicted to her initial charge. Describing her drawing of the first blood, Tasso comments, "Tanto di gloria a la feminea mano/Concesse il Cielo." Yet her achievement is said to be won by "la destra viril" as she proceeds with the massacre. Soon Odoardo joins her and we see how the intimacy of their love serves the pair on the battlefield:

> ...lo sposo fedel, che di lei teme,
> Corre in soccorso a la diletta moglie.
> Così congiunta, la concorde coppia
> Ne la fida union le forze addoppia.
>
> Arte di schermo nova e non più udita
> A i magnanimi amanti usar vedresti:
> Oblia di sé la guardia, e l'altrui vita
> Difende intentamente e quella e questi.
> Ribatte i colpi la guerriera ardita,
> Che vengono al suo caro aspri e molesti;
> Egli a l'arme a lei dritte oppon lo scudo;
> V'opporrìa, s'uopo fosse, il capo ignudo.
>
> Propria l'altrui difesa, e propria face

> L'uno e l'altro di lor l'altrui vendetta.
>
> (Canto XX, 35-37)

Gildippe is the only knight who is not afraid to stand up to Altamoro after he has brutally slain one Christian champion after another. In her bravery, she surpasses the Amazons to whom Tasso compares her:

> Nulla Amazone mai su 'l Termodonte
> Imbracciò scudo, o maneggiò bipenne
> Audace sì, com'ella audace in verso
> Al furor va de formidabil Perso.
>
> (Canto XX, 41)

Gildippe is "better" than the heroines of legend both because she accomplishes her feats in the service of God and because her military career is not an alternative to heterosexual love, but a fulfillment of it. In Ariosto, a female warrior's victim often experiences particular shame at learning he was bested by a woman; although Altamoro believes his opponent to be a man, he evinces the same exaggerated embarrassment, and, even when he gains the upper hand, he skulks away after stunning Gildippe, without delivering the coup de grâce. This final blow is left to Solimano, who does not scorn to fight and kill a woman, choosing, rather, to taunt her for her sex and the couple for their relationship:

> ...Ecco la putta e 'l drudo:
> Meglio per te s'avessi il fuso e l'ago,
> Ch'in tua difesa aver la spada e 'l vago.
>
> (Canto XX, 95)

Solimano's grossness and his cruelty only intensify the poignancy of the couple's joint death. Both fall, unable to utter any last words, but they die in one another's arms, and are consecrated to each other for eternity. At the last, Odoardo mourns only his wife's fate, not his own: "e sol di lei gli dole." The words echo those of Olindo facing his martyrdom with Sofronia, as the scene itself is reminiscent of the fate they thought would be theirs. It is almost as if Tasso had thoughtfully provided a self-parody in advance. What is more likely is that he recognized the artistic integrity of the Gildippe-Odoardo story and did not wish to spoil it, but still retained all his original suspicions of marriage as a resolution. The comic ending of the earlier episode in no way lessens the seriousness and pathos of this scene, but it does provide a corrective for those who feel the need for one.

Both of these pairs are comparatively minor figures in the total scheme of the Gerusalemme liberata and both could be omitted without altering its general direction. Because they are minor characters, Tasso is able to limit his consideration of what marriage means for them to the couple's internal relationship. He does not have to consider any of the social and religious consequences that would be entailed by a marriage involving characters who carry the poem's major ideological weight. It is useful, therefore, to examine how he does handle the principal love affairs of the epic as they relate to the interlocking themes of religion, government, and sexuality.

Clorinda: Neither Man Nor Beast

None of the three heroines of the Gerusalemme liberata falls readily within the rather wide range established by

Ariosto's female characters. As direct participants in the Holy War, Clorinda, Erminia, and Armida assume roles that bear little resemblance to the parts Bradamante, Angelica, and Marfisa play in their struggle. Yet the three heroines of the Liberata apparently subsume in their several characters everything Tasso has to say about the female sex. And their love relationships--Clorinda's with Tancredi, Erminia's with Tancredi, and Armida's with Rinaldo--encompass all his ideas about the effects and implications of incorporating a female element into the traditionally masculine business of war and statecraft. As my initial remarks about marriage suggest, the stories of the three women are often as interesting for what they omit as they are for what they include.

Clorinda, Erminia, and Armida have three significant things in common. First of all, as I have indicated, all of them achieve a state of spiritual reconciliation with their lovers, but none of them ends up married. All of them have a part in the military aspect of the struggle. And all of them begin as infidels, accepting conversion as part of the political and sexual drama they are enacting. Their reception into the Christian life is always through a man--in two cases, through their love for that man--and this reflects the process of subjugation that they and everything they represent must undergo in order to be accepted at all.

Even more significant, perhaps, is the centrality of the conversion drama to what the poem is about, for the repeated fact of conversion is a defining element of the Liberata. The baptism of Ruggiero and Marfisa leaves no evident mark on the Furioso; they can convert with apparent ease because they are entering a world where those who have always been Christians lead equally unexamined spiritual lives. In the Gerusalemme liberata, however, conversion is not limited to those who were brought up as Saracens: The Crusader heroes also experience their religion with a passion that amounts--as in the case of Rinaldo on Monte Oliveto--to a complete spiritual regeneration. Conversion thus serves as a vehicle for asserting the domination of the female principle by the male, yet, at the same time, it is the fundamental Christian experience in the epic. The questions raised by this double function are best explored along with the sexual theme, by considering each lady in turn.

Although all three of Tasso's heroines have a direct part in the military action of the epic, Clorinda is the only one who may be described without qualification as a woman warrior. She resembles the classical prototypes more closely than the lady knights of other romance-epics or the involuntary combatants with whom she shares the scene in the Liberata. Yet Tasso has encompassed the contradictions of her situation so boldly that she remains one of the most misinterpreted characters in the poem. Where the poet presents the complex tensions of her inner life--in their religious and sexual manifestations--critics have tended to simplify what she is, reducing her to one static image or another and ignoring the literary function of the contradictions.

Most commentators recognize, at least, that Clorinda represents a variation on a traditional theme. Thus, she has been described as "the sister--both lesser and greater --of Camilla of the Aeneid,"[25] and also as "a softened version of Ariosto's Marfisa."[26] Working the same vein, though with a certain insensitivity to literary convention, Brand

---

[25] Mario Praz, "Armida's Garden," Comparative Literature Studies, 5 (1968), 5.

[26] Hough, p. 63.

considers her an original creation of Tasso's: "Clorinda, an invented character, is justified by the statement in an anonymous chronicle that the Saracen women fought against the Crusaders."[27] The source of all her departures from literary and historical antecedents lies in something implied in my allusion to the contradictory nature of Clorinda's inner life: That is, she *has* an inner life. She does not function in a purely iconographic fashion, as Camilla does, and she is not all heroic extroversion like Marfisa. Rather, she is a fully developed person in Tasso's terms, which means that she lives most completely in her own subjectivity. Thus, what is sometimes called her inaccessibility is not a sign of the stereotyped Unattainable Woman, but an aspect of her personal remoteness, her isolation, and her pride.

Many of these elements are concentrated in her relation to spiritual questions. When she is first introduced, Clorinda is not only a volunteer in the Saracen cause but a believing and practicing Moslem. Spontaneous pity moves her to stay the execution of Sofronia and Olindo as she arrives in Jerusalem, but this is not rooted in sentimentality because they are lovers, nor is it meant to foreshadow her own eventual openness to conversion. Rather, she has an intuition that what is going on is wrong according to the lights by which she lives, which are the precepts of Islam. When she learns the full story, she realizes she was right. As she asks for the release of the two young Christians in return for services she has yet to render, her quiet confidence in her own worth is most impressive. She is certain the prisoners are innocent because she understands the prin-

---

[27] Brand, p. 87.

ciples of her own religion and how they apply to what has transpired:

> Fu dell nostre leggi irriverenza
> Quell'opra far, che persuase 'l mago;
> Ché non convien ne' nostri tempii a nui
> Gl'idoli avere, e men gl'idoli altrui.
>
> Dunque suso a Macon recar mi giova
> Il miracol de l'opra; ed ei la fece
> Per dimostrar ch'i tempii suoi con nova
> Religon contaminar non lece.
> Faccia Ismeno incantando ogni sua prova,
> Egli a cui le malie son d'arme in vece;
> Trattiamo il ferro pur noi cavalieri;
> Quest'arte è nostra, e 'n questa sol si speri.
> (Canto II, 50-51)

Clorinda is aware that superstitious theft of a sacred image is peculiarly contrary to the precepts of Islam. In expressing her convictions she shows herself to be the only true Moslem in the works of Tasso--to say nothing of those of Ariosto, where the distinction this passage draws between Moslem and pagan infidels is never acknowledged. Clorinda is not only a believing Moslem, she is a soldier of Allah. Both her faith and her commitment to its defense are communicated in the contemptuous dismissal of Ismeno and his mysteries with which she concludes her argument.

According to the view of the truth that pervades the Gerusalemme liberata, however, it is almost a contradiction in terms to speak of someone as a "true Moslem." I do not mean to suggest that Tasso's attitude is informed by an ecumenical spirit, but rather to call attention to what the incident reveals about Clorinda's character and her equivocal role in Saracen society. In this regard, it is important to recall that it is not her cogent reasoning, based on Islamic practice, that prevails, but a personal request for the prisoners' release. Despite this false alarm, the king is still afraid of Jerusalem's Christian population and sends them all into exile. He makes no connection between what Clorinda has said and his own actions or feelings. His approach underscores the warrior maiden's isolation, the strong impression she conveys of never quite belonging or fitting in to her surroundings--even when she is among those she considers her own people. Such progressive moments of psychological isolation are all building towards a powerful narrative climax when the gates of Jerusalem are shut and Clorinda is left alone among the Christian forces.

Another irony involved in referring to Clorinda as a "true Moslem" is that, although she remains unaware of it until just before her death, she was born of Christian parents. This is another way in which Tasso conveys some of the loneliness of Clorinda's situation. A white child with black parents, she represents a dangerous anomaly in her father's court and is not allowed to grow up there. The classic substitution of another child takes place, and the black mother sends her own infant off with a trusted servant. Since Tasso does not enlarge on this motif of black and white and no moral significance is attached to the fact of color, it can only be interpreted as a symbol of Clorinda's status as a perpetual outsider. From the beginning of her association with Islam, therefore, she is an incongruity, since it has always been her destiny to be a Christian. Ruggiero and Marfisa are also the children of Christian parents, but their discovery of this fact and their eventual conversion are part of the Furioso's plot, not examples of their personal search for identity. With Clorinda, however, there is a literal enactment of the notion that to accept Christ as one's saviour means to find one's true self.

Unlike Marfisa, who converts immediately upon learning her own history, or Ruggiero, whose acceptance of baptism has a complex ethical and material background, Clorinda holds fast to the faith in which she was raised. When Arsete tells her about her mother's pleas that the exiled baby be baptized and about his own vision of St. George declaring sponsorship of the child, he is regretful, feeling that the future bodes ill for Clorinda and that he has done wrong in bringing her up as a Moslem. Perhaps a child should never be encouraged to oppose the parents' religion, he speculates, and maybe Christianity really is the true faith, anyway. Despite the personal doubts and premonitions that have begun to assail her, Clorinda expresses her determination to stand by the creed he has taught her even in the face of death:

> Quella fé seguirò che vera or parmi,
> Che tu co 'l latte già de la nutrice
> Sugger mi fêsti, e che vuoi dubbia or farmi:
> Né per temenza lascierò, né lice
> A magnanimo cor, l'impresa e l'armi;
> Non se la morte nel più fier sembiante
> Che sgomenti i mortali avessi inante.
> (Canto XII, 41)

Although the uneasiness she felt was never explicitly spiritual, her conversion is a true one, occurring when she is mortally wounded, facing death with humility and courage:

> Ella, mentre cadea, la voce afflitta
> Movendo, disse le parole estreme;
> Parole ch'a lei novo un spirto ditta,
> Spirto di fé, di carità, di speme;
> Virtù ch'or Dio le infonde, e se rubella
> In vita fu, la vuole in morte ancella.
>
> --Amico, hai vinto: io ti perdòn...perdona
> Tu ancora, al corpo no, che nulla pave,
> A l'alma sì: deh! per lei prega, e dona
> Battesmo a me ch'ogni mia colpa lave.--
> (Canto XII, 65-66)

The actual baptism is a moment fraught with conflicting emotions, for it is when Tancredi removes her helmet to perform the "grande ufficio e pio" that he discovers her identity and realizes that he is responsible for the death of the woman he loves. There may be a sexual poignancy in the removal of the armor and the discovery, but it is all on Tancredi's side. Clorinda, baptized in the pure water of a mountain stream, dies in quiet ecstasy, but there is no indication that this is related to personal feelings for her slayer or that she even knows who he is. In the language of chivalry, she calls him "friend," and, in terms of her new-found faith, he is the instrument of her accession to salvation. Tasso masterfully depicts their parallel emotions without combining or confusing them, so that Tancredi's sword-thrust and his own reaction are felt as sexual acts, while her reception of the wound and her apotheosis occur on an entirely different plane. (This contrast is reminiscent of the difference between the way Sofronia faces her martyrdom and the way Olindo faces his.) The scene meticulously distinguishes between the two, drawing its principal imagery from the central paradoxes of Christian faith:

> Non morì già; che sue virtuti accolse
> Tutte in quel punto, e in guardia al cor le mise,
> E premendo il suo affanno, a dar si volse
> Vita con l'acqua a chi col ferro uccise.
> Mentre egli il suon de' sacri detti sciolse,
> Colei di gioia trasmutossi, e rise;
> E in atto di morir lieto e vivace,
> Dir parea: "S'apre il Cielo; io vado in pace."
>
> D'un bel pallore ha il bianco volto asperso,
> Come a' gigli sarîan miste viole:
> E gli occhi al cielo affissa; e in lei converso
> Sembra per la pietate il cielo e 'l sole:
> E la man nuda e fredda alzando verso
> Il cavaliero, in vece di parole,
> Gli dà pegno di pace. In questa forma
> Passa la bella donna, e par che dorma.
> (Canto XII, 68-69)

At the same time, the grief that Tancredi undergoes has an unequivocally sexual basis:

> Come l'alma gentile uscita ei vede,
> Rallenta quel vigor ch'avea raccolto;
> E l'imperio di sé libero cede
> Al duol già fatto impetüoso e stolto,
> Ch'al cor si stringe, e, chiusa in breve sede
> La vita, empie di morte i sensi e 'l vólto.
> Già simile a l'estinto il vivo langue
> Al colore, al silenzio, a gli atti, al sangue.

E ben la vita sua, sdegnosa e schiva
Spezzanda a forza il suo ritegno frale,
La bella anima sciolta al fin seguiva,
Che poco inanzi a lei spiegava l'ale;
Ma quivi stuol de' Franchi a caso arriva,
Cui trae bisogno d'acqua o d'altre tale;
E con la donna il cavalier ne porta,
In sé mal vivo, e morto in lei ch'è morta.
                                (Canto XII, 70-71)

The tragic elements of this story have attracted a great deal of critical commentary. It is Clorinda who is the tragic hero, in terms of her personal stature and the development of her destiny. Yet Tancredi, who is deeply-- but merely--pathetic, gets most of the attention.[28] Even more disquieting is the way Clorinda's behavior is interpreted when she is the focus of her own death scene. In a tone at once salacious and condescending, critics describe her death as a belated but welcome flowering of womanhood in this hitherto "unfeminine" creature. Pool sees Arsete's recital of his mistress' history as foreshadowing her destiny, in that the defenseless infant Clorinda serves as a precursor of the defenseless warrior she becomes in her final duel. And he observes that her femininity is able to assert itself "solo nell'ora della agonia." It is as if commentators relished this extraordinary display of weakness since it enables them at last to describe Clorinda in terms of femininity and pathos, as a heroine "more human in death

---

[28] See, for instance, Franco Pool, Desiderio e realtà nella poesia del Tasso (Padua: Liviana, 1960), p. 106. Pool speaks with great sensitivity of the scene's unfolding like a Greek tragedy in epic form, from the moment that Clorinda is isolated among the hostile forces. But he proceeds to treat it as if it were Tancredi's tragedy.

than in life." Actually, of course, Clorinda is no weaker than any other dying warrior and, throughout, it is her soldierly courage, which would be noble and accepted in a man, that is represented as inhuman in a woman. The preoccupation with her powerlessness in the face of a mortal wound reflects a certain relief--and rejoicing--that the superwoman is in fact mortal.

The sympathetic reader finds a more sensitive measure of Clorinda's humanity in the exceptional inwardness of her nature. Like Marfisa before her, she embodies the ideals of chivalry, rather than sheer military force. However, in her readiness to settle every issue of principle or honor at swordpoint, Ariosto's blunt young Amazon is often a comic figure. Clorinda is drawn with more restraint and it is appropriate that St. George, the archetype of Christian chivalry, placed her under his protection in her infancy. If there is any Christian saint that this ardent Moslem resembles, in fact, it is the devout, chaste, and courteous St. George, with his full panoply of medieval and primitive associations. In addition to being Clorinda's unacknowledged protector, St. George is also a patron saint of Ferrara, the city whose mythic fate is intimately connected to the politcs of the Liberata. Although it is a relatively weak link, this shared patronage helps establish Clorinda as one of the city's spiritual ancestors--despite the fact that, while an unredeemed warrior on the Saracen side, she is the slayer of Guelfo d'Este. (It is hard to know what to make of this latter fact. Tasso simply indicates in one line that Clorinda's arrow killed Guelfo. He makes no special point of the event, and it clearly is not intended to weaken Christian sympathy for the warrior maiden.)

Although she adheres to the code of knighthood, Clorinda also possesses a more elemental set of values. She personifies chivalric ideals, so that among the Saracens she creates the impression of being a foreign princess come to aid--but not precisely to join--their army. Moreover, from her first appearance, her exotic armor and dress and her tiger emblem set her apart and make her seem like a creature as untamed as those she hunts. For it is as a huntress, not primarily a soldier, that she is presented. Further, unlike the other women warriors we have encountered, she has chosen her lot and has deliberately rejected the trappings and occupations deemed appropriate to the female condition:

> Costei gl'ingegni feminili e gli usi
> Tutti sprezzò sin da l'età più acerba;
> A i lavori d'Aracne, a l'ago, a i fusi
> Inchinar non degnò la man superba;
> Fuggì gli abiti molli e i lochi chiusi,
> Che ne' campi onestate anco si serba:
> Armò d'orgoglio il volto, e si compiacque
> Rigido farlo; e pur rigido piacque.
>
> Tenera ancor con pargoletta destra
> Strinse e lentó d'un corridore il morso;
> Trattò l'asta e la spada, ed in palestra
> Indurò i membri, ed allenògli al corso:
> Poscia o per via montana o per silvestra
> L'orme seguì di fier leone e d'orso;
> Seguì le guerre; e in esse e fra le selve
> Fèra a gli uomini parve, uomo a le belve.
> (Canto II, 39-40)

The passage provides another example of Clorinda's estrangement from any community--human or otherwise.

Even more striking is the sense of freedom it conveys

and the feeling that Tasso has recaptured the spirit of Camilla. But Camilla has only one dimension to her nature, whereas Clorinda's first action in the poem, the rescue of Sofronia and Olindo, shows that she is a complex moral being. In the exercises of war, she is quite as skilled as her Amazon forebears, although her participation is always based on principle. Thus, leading her first military charge of the epic,

> --Ben con alto principio a noi conviene,
> Dicea, far de l'Asia oggi la speme.--
> (Canto III, 13)

And it is she who draws the first blood of the battle. In a subsequent encounter (Canto IX, 68-70), the description of her prowess is particularly vivid, as she hacks her way through the Frankish army, leaving incredible carnage in her wake. Yet the huntress is never entirely lost within the warrior, and that image forms one basis for the impressive description of Clorinda with her bow poised for action:

> ...in su la torre altissima Angolare
> Sovra tutti Clorinda eccelsa appare.
>
> A costei la faretra e 'l grave incarco
> De l'acute quadrella al tergo pende.
> Ella già ne le mani ha preso l'arco
> E già lo stral v'ha su la corda, e 'l tende;
> E desiosa di ferire, al varco
> La bella arciera i suoi nemici attende.
> Tal già credean la vergine di Delo
> Tra l'alte nubi saettar dal cielo.
> (Canto XI, 27-28)

She is not just posing up on that tower, and she proceeds to loose arrow after arrow, killing and wounding Christian leaders in a scene that amounts to a kind of stationary <u>aristeia</u> (Canto XI, 41-46). Finally, one of her arrows strikes Goffredo and saves the day for the defenders of Jerusalem:

> ...a lui venne una saetta a volo,
> E ne la gamba il colse, e la trafisse
> Nel più nervoso, ove è più acuto il duolo.
> Che di tua man, Clorinda, il colpo uscisse,
> La fama il canta, e tuo l'onor n'è solo:
> Se questo dì servaggio e morte schiva
> La tua gente pagana, a te s'ascriva.
>   (Canto XI, 54)

Although their heroism is individual and unique, the Amazon queens of antiquity are always accompanied by a troop of warrior maidens. Clorinda rides alone, in the tradition of knight errantry, but that makes her role as an example for her sex and a leader of women even more impressive:

> E, mirando la vergine gagliarda,
> Vero amor de la patria arma le donne:
> Correr le vedi, e collocarsi in guarda
> Con chiome sparse, e con succinte gonne,
> E lanciar dardi, e non mostrar paura
> D'esporre il petto per l'amate mura.
>   (Canto XI, 58)

This is a real departure from the Virgilian tradition, for the women Clorinda leads are no special breed of warrior-females. They are the Saracen women of Jerusalem, inspired by her example and by their own patriotism. Like the Trojan and Latin matrons of the Aeneid, they act in concert. Uniquely to Tasso's narrative, however, they are not a mob of hysterics, but a body of citizens that love of country and courageous leadership turns into a fighting force.

Some of the differences between Clorinda and the archetypal virgin warrior are apparent in this brief scene. The key is that although she is of heroic stature, Clorinda is portrayed as a human being, not a divinity or an idol. It is this quality that the critics are attempting to identify when, most ironically, they characterize her as "feminine." According to Getto, for example, "il fascino di Clorinda scaturisce dalla sua solitaria e incontaminata e irraggiungabile bellezza, da quella stupenda muliebrità isolata sul campo di battaglia."[29] Nicole De Leval agrees that "Clorinda è guerriera ma anche donna dolcissima nella sua celata bellezza."[30] Pool even claims to find support for the imposition of a sexual stereotype in her proud rejection of the womanly role and life: "anche quest'armatura spirituale --come la corazza da cui sboccia la bella chiome bionde-- lascia spergarli aperti su una segreta dolcezza di sensibilità propria dell'anima femminile." Moreover, he perceives some (presumably feminine) wavering in her character, a response to Tancredi's declarations that persists, despite her attempts to stifle it, and that creates within her a "segreta incertezza."[31] To the extent that it, too, involves a certain weakness, the pathos of Tancredi's unre-

---

[29] Getto, p. 398.

[30] Nicole De Leval, "Le coppie più rappresentative dell' Orlando furioso e della Gerusalemme liberata," Revue des langues vivantes, 30 (1964), 157.

[31] Pool, p. 130.

quited love is also assimilated to Clorinda; Tancredi moves the reader more as a lover than as a military hero and his love thus becomes inseparable from the character of his beloved.

It seems to me that in all this concern with the uncontaminated, the solitary, the secret, and the sealed-up, there is a certain unhealthy fixation on Clorinda's virginity. Or rather, perhaps, a critical confusion about what to make of a female who is warm and ardent and yet independent of that world of sexuality from which women are supposed to derive their primary identity.

For the fact remains that Clorinda is indifferent to love, interested only in the principles to which she is committed and the actions her commitment implies. It becomes a problem for the reader only because the situation does not fit the two existing models. The classic warrior maiden, as represented by Camilla and Marfisa, is not only a virgin, but is also untroubled by the importunities of love, whereas the new heroine of romance-epic, as represented by Bradamante and Britomart, is a woman capable of love and destined to marry. Clorinda's case is more equivocal. Sexual love seems to have no more charm for her than the female destiny she has discarded, yet she is a woman beloved, and the drama of Tancredi's sacred and profane loves in some sense touches our interpretation of its object. Insofar as it is her own, Clorinda's tragic fate follows its own internal dynamic and is implicit in her nature as we come to understand it in the poem. It is also true, however, that her story has a further development--albeit unrelated to <u>her</u> actual character--in the developing consciousness of Tancredi.

The warrior maiden's role in the love affair is at all times either passive, negative, or posthumous. She remains unmoved by Tancredi's Petrarchan posturing--indeed, she seems to brush it aside like an obscene remark addressed to her in passing. This detachment cannot be over-emphasized, particularly since, prior to her death, Tancredi's feeling for her is not only "un suo vano amor," but also faintly comic. In the first duel between the two, Tasso makes use of the exaggerated conventions of love poetry to caricature the tradition and, by implication, the emotions it celebrates. By taking the language of eyes that slay with a single glance, hearts that are captured and wounded, and the rest of the courtly baggage onto the field of battle, Tasso achieves a kind of Baroque bathos. The effect is not unlike what happens when Olindo's theatrical heart-burnings are transferred to a real stake with real flames. And the poet's tone demonstrates an ironic control of both the material and the situation.

The duel occurs, first of all, at a moment when the reader is prepared for irony. In the preceding stanza, Erminia, from the ramparts, has identified Tancredi and, knowing that her words will be safely misinterpreted, expresses her desire to make him her prisoner. Then Clorinda and Tancredi engage, they aim their lances at each other's visors, and her helmet is knocked off. Tasso takes maximum advantage of double entendre in this situation; his way of describing what happens is: "i tronchi in alto/Volaro e parte nuda ella ne resta," (Canto III, 21). It is, of course, only her face that is stark naked, her lovely hair streaming out to reveal both her gender and her identity. But Tasso recognizes the sexual metaphor intrinsic to the lances and the joust on horseback, as well as the way these conceits were extended in the poetry of love, and he uses both for his own ends.

Comparison of this passage with the final duel assures

that one will not project inappropriate sexual content onto the latter. Something is certainly happening there, but Tasso's stance--and Tancredi's--are very different from what they were in the earlier encounter. Nor is it sufficient to say that with the death of the lady the affair has now entered the final stage of the conventional Petrarchan cycle. Tasso's principal departure from Petrarchism is that he has placed the affair, from its inception, in a social and moral context. His consciousness of the limitations and dangers of earth-bound sexual love is not born only after Clorinda's death; it pervades the earlier phases of the relationship. He may treat Tancredi with some humor, as one who insists on taking figures of speech literally, but he views the situation itself quite seriously.

As things stand at the beginning of the Gerusalemme liberata, an honest love is impossible between the two: Clorinda is an infidel fighting on the Saracen side and, in any case, is not interested in Tancredi or in love. The first difficulty may be dealt with easily, since she can always accept the true faith and receive baptism. Her conversion, when it takes place, is certainly sincere, but Hough points out that "in the imaginative economy of the poem...she is saved because she is the worthy object of Tancredi's love."[32] If she had agreed to baptism earlier, she would have been acceptably Christian and a potential bride, but no longer Clorinda. A living Clorinda, Christian or no, could not retain her most admirable qualities while returning Tancredi's love, for those qualities are rooted in her pride, her independence, and her identity as a "pagan." After baptism and death, words of love may be attributed to Clorinda's ghost that would have completely violated the

---

[32] Hough, p. 79.

character and the integrity of the living woman.

Only death, moreover, can remove that love from the sexual sphere, and it is clear that, for Tasso, there can be no compromise between holiness and human sexuality. As Clorinda's apparition assures her dreaming lover, she now loves him, too, as much as she can love a fleshly being. She realizes that she owes her salvation to Tancredi and expects to share eternal bliss with him--if he is able to resist sexual temptation henceforth:

> Tale io son, tua mercé: tu me da i vivi
> Del mortal mondo, per error, togliesti;
> Tu in grembo a Dio fra gl'immortali e divi,
> Per pietà, di salir degna mi fêsti.
> Quivi io beata amando godo, e quivi
> Spero che per te loco anco s'appresti,
> Ove al gran sole e ne l'eterno die
> Vagheggiarai le sue bellezze e mie.
>
> Se tu medesmo non t'invidii il Cielo
> E non travii co'l vaneggiar de' sensi,
> Vivi, e sappi ch'io t'amo, e non te 'l celo,
> Quanto più creatura amar conviensi.
> (Canto XII, 92-93)

It is significant, I think, that Tancredi has this vision just after Pietro l'Eremita has castigated him for the grief he is devoting to a profane love. Neither Clorinda's death nor the spiritual bond created by her baptism at his hands has sufficed to transform the kind of love he feels. It is the dream-vision that makes it clear that Clorinda has been elevated to a point where she can no longer be the object of even frustrated sexual desire. In this sense, Tancredi's duel with Argante is particularly striking, for the Circassian knight considers himself the champion of the dead Clorinda, as well as of the dying city of Jerusalem. He explicitly taunts Tancredi as a slayer of women, and it is only according to the "higher" values of Christianity that his loyalty and love can be viewed as misdirected. In (Christian) fact, "when Tancredi slays him, he repudiates through...[Clorinda's] would-be avenger the earthly, pagan aspect of his ill-placed love."[33] Clorinda must not be "avenged," because it was not wrong to send her to heaven.

Thus hedged about with qualifications, Clorinda is able to enter into the Christian sphere and impart her virtues to the Christian state. Although she herself cannot be assimilated, she remains the heroine whose best qualities--bravery, loyalty, asceticism, piety--may be most readily appropriated by Crusader culture. One reason for this, however, is that those qualities are, by and large, already present in that culture, and the question naturally arises as to whether the integration of Clorinda brings in anything new in the way of female characteristics or sexual relationships.

Erminia: The Cloistered Vagabond

Erminia possesses a precisely opposite set of qualities and she presents, therefore, an entirely different set of poetic problems. Her nature is stereotypically feminine and her defining quality is her obsessive love for Tancredi. To bring Erminia into the Christian world means the admission

---

[33] Beatrice Corrigan, "Erminia and Tancredi: The Happy Ending," *Italica*, 40 (1963), 329.

of unequivocally feminine values that may serve to counterbalance the virile absolutism of that world. But, given the centrality of love to her very being, how can Erminia be assimilated into the Christian realm without a redefinition of the social and spiritual functions of sexual relations? Tasso hints at such redefinition, but the primary resolution he provides is through the formulae of Christian redemption. Although she never ceases to love Tancredi, Erminia does change in the course of the epic, undergoing a process of spiritual self-discovery that becomes the moral equivalent of sexual fulfillment and makes it possible for Tasso to achieve a sense of resolution without explicitly violating the sexual norms he has established.

Her polarity with Clorinda is most explicitly set forth and elaborated, but Erminia actually stands in the middle of a spectrum of female sexuality, whose extremes are occupied, respectively, by Clorinda and Armida. She may be thought to represent a compromise between them in that she is the only heroine of the *Liberata* who "uses neither wiles nor arms against the man."[34] Beatrice Corrigan considers her the female counterpart of Goffredo, since both of them move single-mindedly towards their highest goal. Corrigan goes so far as to compare Erminia's presumed entranced into Tancredi's household with Goffredo's into Jerusalem.[35] In order for this to be true, however, on any but the most abstract level of rhetoric, Tasso would have had to elaborate a theory that integrated private and public life. Such a theory would presumably regard marriage as the chief personal-spiritual institution, much as the state is the chief political-spiritual institution. In the absence of any

---

[34] Corrigan, p. 329.

[35] Ibid., p. 331.

development of this sort in Tasso's thought, Erminia's character remains clearly delineated, but her place in the scale of female heroism is less clear.

As is often the case, critical commentary on Erminia's femininity consists largely in the imposition of (often anachronistic) sexual generalizations. Thus, we are told that she is "feminine" because she is shy, timid, and no Amazon,[36] because she possesses great spiritual simplicity,[37] and because she is pure, modest, ingenuous, and sensitive.[38] In fact, Tasso's ability to create so delicate a creature is taken as evidence of his own "feminine" sensibility--which is to say his elegaic capacity. Tasso would agree that Erminia is feminine and that it was his intention to make her so, but there is no evidence that his views of sexual <u>character</u>, as contrasted with norms of morality, were as rigid as those of some critics or that he believed that the female has less moral autonomy than the male. Thus, Erminia is passive: As Corrigan points out, she uses the characteristic methods of neither sex in pursuit of Tancredi. In fact, she dos not pursue him at all, and merely suffers passively. Tasso makes no claim, however, that her lack of aggressiveness represents the most feminine type of female personality, merely suggesting that it is one type.

The two most striking features of Erminia's character --both of which might contribute to a definition of the feminine that is not bathed in sentimentality--are her commitment to healing and her steadfast love for Tancredi. Although a non-combatant, Erminia does eventually become a

---

[36] Hough, p. 68.

[37] De Leval, p. 159.

[38] Pool, p. 126.

participant in the Holy War, and her involvement is a measure of her shifting political and religious loyalties. But, in her temperament and her actions, she remains the precise opposite of a soldier. Her medical lore and skills reflect a concern for sustaining and preserving life that may well be called "feminine," particularly since Tasso makes a point of the fact that she acquired the relevant information at her mother's knee and that, in her part of the world, such knowledge is the province of royal ladies:

> E però ch'ella de la madre apprese,
> Qual più secreta sia virtù de l'erbe,
> E con quai carmi ne le membra offese
> Sani ogni piaga, e il duol si disacerbe,
> (Arte che per usanza in quel paese
> Ne le figlie de i re par che si serbe),
> Vorrìa di sua man propria a le ferute
> Del suo caro signor recar salute.
>   (Canto VI, 67)

In fact, it is not her beloved she must nurse, but the man who is responsible for his injuries whom he, in turn, has wounded. And despite her feelings, it is not only her general morality, but a sense of religious and "professional" duty that keeps her from helping Argante to his death, rather than restoring him to health:

> Ella l'amato medicar desía,
> E curar il nemico a lei conviene:
> Pensa talor d'erba nocente e ria
> Succo sparger in lui che l'avvelene;
> Ma schiva poi la man vergine e pia
> Trattar l'arti maligne, e se n'astiene.

MONSTROUS REGIMENT

> Brama ella al men ch'in uso tal sia vóta
> Di sua virtude ogn'erba ed ogni nota.
>   (Canto VI, 68)

Since it is through her mastery of medicine that Erminia eventually wins her place in Tancredi's life, it may be useful to consider what other associations the healing arts have in the <u>Gerusalemme liberata</u>. It is worth noting, first of all, that Tasso does not identify these arts with magic or prophecy. The Saracens have Ismeno in their camp, the Crusaders, Pietro l'Eremita, and the character with which Tasso endows the two aptly symbolizes their respective causes. But neither brings his spiritual power to bear on medical questions. There are, moreover, no miraculous cures on the Saracen side, while Goffredo's arrow wound is healed instantly through the agency of an herb that his guardian angel procures. The angel cannot heal the wound by magic or with some heavenly ointment, for that would be contrary to Tasso's view of the relation of terrestrial cause and effect to divine will. His super-human contribution is simply to fly to Mount Ida and bring back the most effective <u>natural</u> medication in existence:

> Or qui l'angiol custode, al duol indegno
> Mosso di lui, colse dittamo in Ida:
> Erba crinita di purpureo fiore,
> C'have in giovani foglie alto valore.
>
> E ben mastra natura a le montane
> Capre n'insegna la virtù celata,
> Qualor vengon percosse, e lor rimane
> Nel fianco affissa la saetta alata.
> Questa, ben che da parti assai lontane,

Tasso

> In un momento l'angelo ha recata;
> E, non veduto, entro le mediche onde
> De gli apprestati bagni il succo infonde;
>
> E del fonte di Lidia i sacri umori,
> E l'odorata panacea vi mesce.
> (Canto XI, 72-74)

The incident reveals other aspects of Tasso's attitude towards practitioners of medicine through the introduction of Eròtimo, the Crusaders' camp physician:

> ...l' antico Eròtimo, che nacque
> In riva al Po, s'adopra in sua salute;
> Il qual de l'erbe e de le nobil acque
> Ben conosceva ogni uso, ogni virtute:
> Caro a le Muse ancor; ma si compiacque
> Ne la gloria minor de l'arti mute;
> Sol curo torre a morte i corpi frali,
> E potea far i nomi anco immortali.
> (Canto XI, 70)

Although we cannot refine too much on a single stanza, and Eròtimo does not appear elsewhere in the poem, it is interesting that, in him, medicine is associated with worthy old age, with origins on the banks of the Po (perhaps in Ferrara itself?), and with the creation of poetry--all of these positive values in Tasso's world-view. For the comparison with Erminia, the last attribute is perhaps the most important, for Tasso explicitly contrasts the immortal hymns Eròtimo might have made with his commitment to the healing of frail mortal flesh, and, although he points out the irony, he does not deplore the old man's choice, particularly since it is carried out in the service of the Crusade, and hence of the most elevated kind of human life.

Thus, when Vafrino and Erminia come upon the fallen Tancredi in Canto XIX, the reader is prepared to regard the curing of the wounded as an act with holy, patriotic, and creative potential. No herbs are available, this time, and there is no guardian angel to obtain them from the sacred heights of Troy. To effect a cure, Erminia must employ her old knowledge of the right charms to recite, but she must also find new remedies. It is her love that teaches her what to do. Tancredi's wounds are not deep, but he is seriously weakened by loss of blood and the first concern of his nurse must be to bind his wounds. For this purpose, she has only two materials: her veil, which is both symbol and protector of virgin modesty, and her hair:

> Vede che 'l mal da la stanchezza nasce,
> E da gli umori in troppa copia sparti.
> Ma non ha, fuor ch'un velo, onde gli fasce
> Le sue ferite, in sì solinghe parti.
> Amor le trova inusitate fasce,
> E di pietà le insegna insolite arti:
> L'asciugò con le chiome, e rilegolle
> Pur con le chiome, che troncar si volle
>
> (Canto XIX, 112)

The cutting of her hair to dry and bandage his wounds is an act that implies the deepest Christian humility and that also has evident erotic implications. Both elements are present, for instance, in the iconological association of hair with St. Mary Magdalene. Erminia's act recalls, as well, the ritual in which newly professed nuns become the brides of Christ. In the poem, it is the ultimate gesture by which Erminia signals that she belongs completely to Tancredi and to the faith for which he is struggling. Her love has brought her to this point, and it is significant in the poem's overall scheme of sexual values that a woman's love serves the same function in the cure of Tancredi that divine intervention accomplished in the cure of Goffredo.

Hough points out that love turns the still-pagan Erminia into a "singularly attractive example of the Christian virtues--humble, docile, charitable--towards her enemies as well as those to whom natural affection draws her."[39] In a very real sense, then, her profane love serves a sacred end. It is impressive to note, in fact, how completely the profile of the devout Christian coincides with that of the "feminine" woman, so that in saying she is "feminine" or in speaking of her abandonment to love, one is also summarizing her whole spiritual being.

Critical discussions of Erminia's love tend to concentrate, nonetheless, on its tender, lyrical moments and its elegaic inspiration, without admitting its ties to the rest of Tasso's moral universe. DeSanctis, in fact, refuses to take seriously any other aspect of her character or its implications, declaring that "when Erminia is heroic, she is only comic and Erminia discoursing on love and honour is cold and academic, but Erminia abandoned to love has exquisite moments of lyricism."[40] To take this position is, of course, to miss Tasso's point, for it is important to her spiritual development that Erminia is not a simple country maiden abandoned to love, but a princess. It is her royal rank that is responsible for her medical skill, as well as for Tancredi's courteous treatment of his prisoner and her

---

[39] Hough, p. 68.

[40] DeSanctis, pp. 657-8.

own presence in Jerusalem. The poet seems to think her status and dignity important enough to mention at the same time he recapitulates the story of her enamorment:

> Ma fulle in guisa allor Tancredi umano,
> Che nulla ingiuria in sua balìa sostenne:
> Ed onorata fu, ne la ruïna
> De l'alta patria sua, come reina.
>
> L'onorò, la servì, di libertate
> Dono le fece il cavaliero egregio;
> E le furo da lui tutte lasciate
> Le gemme e gli ori e cio ch'avea di pregio.
> Ella vedendo in giovanetta etate
> E in leggiadri sembianti animo regio
> Restò presa d'Amor, che mai non strinse
> Laccio di quel più fermo onde lei cinse.
>
> Così se 'l corpo libertà rïebbe,
> Fu l'alma sempre in servitute astretta.
> Ben molto a lei d'abbandonar increbbe
> Il signor caro e la prigion diletta:
> Ma l'onestà regal, che mai non debbe
> Da magnanima donna esser negletta,
> La costrinse a partirsi; e con l'antica
> Madre a ricoverarsi in terra amica.
>   (Canto VI, 56-58)

Again, it is the full experience of the pastoral life that changes her, not being forced to live simply, for the rude garments of her new situation do not alter her royal dignity or hide her regal bearing:

Tasso

> Ma nel moto de gli occhi e de le membra
> Non già di boschi abitatrice sembra.
>
> Non copre abito vil la nobil luce,
> E quanto è in lei d'altero e di gentile;
> E fuor la maestà regia traluce
> Per gli atti ancor de l'esercizio umìle.
>
> (Canto VII, 17-18)

Yet, when she tells Vafrino about her love for Tancredi, she feels that she remains his prisoner and that, through her love, she has lost not only status and dignity, but self-respect, as well. Describing the motives behind her nocturnal flight, she says,

> Al fin, cercando al viver mio soccorso,
> Mi sciolse amor d'ogni rispetto il morso.
>
> (Canto XIX, 97)

And the other changes that have served to mature her character have left that feeling untouched, so that, in returning to Jerusalem her abject and prayerful aspiration remains:

> Oh, pur colui che circondolle intorno
> A l'alma sì che non fia chi le scioglia,
> Non dica: Errante ancella, altro soggiorno
> Cércati pure: e me seco non voglia,
> Ma pietoso gradisca il mio ritorno,
> E ne l'antica mia prigion m'accoglia!
>
> (Canto XIX, 101)

In a sense, her conviction that she is unworthy of Tancredi is heightened by her experience after running away, for she knows she has broken certain taboos imposed on proper young princesses and fears he might--however ironically--reject his "errante ancella" for her "unwomanly" behavior.

It is in this self-abnegating passion, above all, that Erminia's character contrasts most vividly with that of Clorinda. The polarity between them is all the more pronounced in that they are part of a "triangle." The man Erminia loves is in love with Clorinda, while Clorinda is as indifferent to him as to the rest of his sex. It is a triangle without dramatic tension, however, since the three characters involved do not interact with each other and the two women are not rivals in any conventional sense. Rather, the tension that exists in the situation is ironic, in that each woman's condition serves to sharpen and clarify the image of the other.

Although his enamorment takes place before her very eyes, Erminia seems unaware that Tancredi loves Clorinda, and when she feels envy for her friend it is her freedom of movement she envies and--explicitly--her freedom from the narrow restrictions of female life. Finding Clorinda's room empty, she tries on the liberating garments of the warrior maiden as if to try on her personality and her freedom as well. And, most significantly, it is while she is dressed in this clothing that she conceives the idea of using it to effect her flight. But she never envies or wishes for herself the principal kind of freedom that Clorinda enjoys and that is the source of her whole way of life, that is, the freedom of the heart. <u>She</u> would use Clorinda's armor to win Tancredi, and when she decides to make temporary use of it to bring her to where he lies, she feels it is Love that inspires and strengthens her:

> ...tra sé dice sospirando:--O quanto
> Beata è la fortissima donzella!
> Quant'io la invidio! e non la invidio il vanto
> O 'l feminil onor de l'esser bella.
> A lei non tarda i passi il lungo manto,
> Né 'l suo valor rinchiude invida cella;
> Ma veste l'arme, e se d'uscirne agogna
> Vassene, e non la tien téma or vergogna.
>
> Ah perché forti a me natura e 'l cielo
> Altrettanto non fêr le membra e 'l petto,
> Onde potessi anch'io la gonna e 'l velo
> Cangiar ne la corazza e ne l'elmetto?
> Ché sì non riterrebbe arsura o gelo,
> Non turbo o pioggia il mio infiammato affetto,
> Ch'al sol non fossi ed al notturno lampo
> Accompagnata o sola, armata in campo.
>
> (Canto VI, 82-83)

Furthermore, just as the warrior maiden is the object of a love Erminia longs for and that she herself does not want, so Erminia dreams of dying at Tancredi's hand, the fate that actually overtakes Clorinda:

> O vero a me da la sua destra il fianco
> Sendo percosso, e riaperto il core,
> Pur risanata in cotal guisa al manco
> Colpo di ferro avria piaga d'Amore:
> Ed or la mente in pace e 'l corpo stanco
> Riposariansi; e forse il vincitore
> Regnato avrebbe il mio cenere e l'ossa
> D'alcun onor di lagrime e di fossa.
>
> (Canto VI, 85)

More than anything else, this wish of Erminia's reveals the potentially sexual content of Clorinda's death and of the military struggle that precedes it. It reveals, as well, the extent to which Erminia has let go of her sense of proportion and is lost in adolescent fantasies.

In certain important respects, Erminia and Clorinda are quite similar: Both are very solitary and, in their isolation, both go through the evangelical process of losing themselves to find their salvation. Clorinda, as I have indicated, never fits in with her surroundings, never really belongs anywhere. Erminia is literally alone, in that she is apparently the sole surviving member of her family, but she is also isolated because she has to conceal her love for Tancredi. Clorinda's refusal of love serves to set her apart from others, whereas Erminia's immersion in love as effectively isolates her.

At the center of Erminia's story, of course, is her nocturnal escape from Jerusalem and the experiences she passes through as a consequence of her flight. She leaves to join Tancredi, but, before she can do so, she must undergo a process of maturation that will bring her closer to him spiritually, as well. In this sense, it is not the pastoral idyll, but the psychic and political journey, that actually brings her to him. Her growing identification with the Christian cause is the result of this moral development, and its climax is not the cure of Tancredi, which she would gladly have effected in any case, but the saving of Goffredo's life through revelation of the plot to assassinate him.

In her attempt to find herself spiritually, Erminia adopts different garments, along with the roles they entail. (Hence her trying on of Clorinda's armor and her dreams of the more superficial aspects of Clorinda's freedom.) In Arcadia, she wears the rough clothing of the shepherds among whom she lives and works. And, in the scene where she encounters and cures Tancredi, she is wearing a <u>peregrina gonna</u>. Corrigan maintains that, although <u>peregrina</u> may mean foreign or strange, in this context its primary meaning is intended and that it is a pilgrim's gown--and hence a Christian identity--she is wearing when her situation finally arrives at its successful conclusion.[41]

But what measure of felicity does that conclusion really provide? It is hard to tell whether the resolution of Erminia's love story constitutes a happy ending, because it is hard to tell precisely what happens. Tasso himself said that he had ended the story "come ha voluta la musa," and if so it was the muse of allegory, forgetting that Tasso's epic has a social basis and a historical function, who dictated the ending.[42] After Erminia binds up Tancredi's wounds, some of his men come in search of him. He gives orders for the respectful treatment of his enemy's corpse and, still thinking he may die, asks to be brought into Jerusalem, so that he may fulfill his vow. Erminia accompanies them into the Holy City and Vafrino finds her an "albergo assai chiuso e secreto." And that is where the love story ends. Tancredi reappears to take up arms, despite his weakness, at a desperate point in the final battle, but we hear no more of Erminia. Most commentators consider that the real ending occurs in the moments before the arrival of Tancredi's troops, when Erminia orders her patient to rest and sits on the ground with his head in her lap:

---

[41] Corrigan, p. 332.

[42] See Torquato Tasso, <u>Lettere</u>, I, 86, April 1576, quoted in Corrigan, p. 311.

MONSTROUS REGIMENT

>   ...(te 'l comando
> Come medica tua) taci e riposa.
> Salute avrai; prepara il guiderdone--
> Ed al suo capo il grembo indi suppone.
>   (Canto XIX, 114)

This scene has a certain static, pictorial quality that makes it seem more like a conclusion than the real end of Erminia's story, but, as I observed before, it is the conclusion of an allegory, not that of a narrative with historical pretensions. People do not lie happily ever after with their heads in their loving nurses' laps, yet what actually happens beyond this sylvan pietà is extremely unclear.

We do know that Tancredi owes his life to Erminia, and when he first regains consciousness she makes a mild joke about her guiderdone. According to the laws of chivalry, he belongs as much to her now as she did to him when she was his prisoner. Moreover, by her actions and her character, she has a claim on the affection of a man who knows that his beloved Clorinda has gone to a higher sphere. In her loyalties and her convictions, Erminia is now a Christian--and she is the hereditary princess of Antioch. Tancredi cannot simply invite her to become the resident physician in his household. A marriage founded on mature love and mutual respect would seem to provide a harmonious balance of "masculine" and "feminine" qualities and constitute a vehicle for translating the spiritual relationship of Erminia and Tancredi into social terms. Such a marriage would not represent the kind of ideological breakthrough that the marriage of, say, Bradamante and Ruggiero achieves. But, by way of compensation, Tasso would be working with a more profound consciousness of the innovation, a more deliberate rejection of the adulterous tradition of courtly love, and a clearer understanding of the sacramental nature of the social institution he was helping to create.

Or so, at least, it would seem. But Tasso leaves the question entirely open to speculation. In a letter to Scipione Gonzaga, one of the six "revisori" to whom he submitted installments of the <u>Liberata</u>, he says that he would like to make Erminia's conversion more explicit and have her enter a convent at the end, but that certain artistic impediments prevent this:

> Solo l'amor d'Erminia par che, in un certo modo, abbia felice fine. Io vorrei anco a questo dar un fine buono, e farla non sol far cristiana, ma religiosa monaca. So ch'io non potrò parlar più oltre di lei, di quel ch'avea fatto, senza alcun pregiudicio de l'arte...Io vorrei aggiungere nel penultimo dieci stanza ne le quali si contenesse questa conversione.[43]

Corrigan, whose evidence I have been citing throughout, interprets Tasso's failure to make a nun of Erminia as proof that he accepted the "happy ending" of making her a wife. She claims that Erminia has now fulfilled her own fantasies of saving Tancredi's life and thus earning honorable marriage as well as the admiration of Latin matrons.[44] The princess' love dictated her fantasies:

> Deh! ben fôra, a l'in contra, uffizio umano,
> E ben ne avresti tu gioia e diletto,

---

[43] <u>Ibid.</u>, quoted in Corrigan, p. 325.
[44] See Corrigan, pp. 330-332.

> Se la pietosa tua medica mano
> Avicinassi al valoroso petto;
> Ché per te fatto il tuo signor poi sano
> Colorirebbe il suo smarrito aspetto:
> E le bellezze sue, che spente or sono,
> Vagheggiaresti in lui quasi tuo dono.
>
> Parte ancor poi ne le sue lodi avresti,
> E ne l'opre ch'ei fêsse alte e famose;
> Ond'egli te d'abbracciamenti onesti
> Farìa lieta, e di nozze avventurose.
> Poi móstra a dito ed onorata andresti
> Fra le madri latine e fra le spose
> Là ne la bella Italia, ov'è la sede
> Del valor vero e de la vera fede.
>   (Canto VI, 76-77)

Surely we are meant to understand Erminia's desire as being the same kind of adolescent dream as the wish to be killed by Tancredi that appears in this same passage. If so, it is not meant as a foreshadowing of her actual fate. Moreover, if we are to take Erminia's eventual conversion seriously and believe in the spiritual evolution that leads up to it, it is hard to know how to read the line about Italy as the seat of the true faith, for Erminia's love has not yet taught her that this is so. In any case, it is more in keeping with Christian morality for Erminia to get her reward after it has ceased to be her goal and in a form different from that envisaged in her youthful imaginings. On this point, Brand maintains that Tasso leaves the ending of Erminia's story vague so as not to spoil it. He adds that "she may be thought to have won Tancredi's love by her unselfish devotion and to have outlived her childish dream in the brief contact with reality."⁴⁵ But since the essence of her "childish dream" was that she would win Tancredi's love by her unselfish devotion, it is not obvious in which direction this argument tends.

There is some agreement among critics, however, that the ambiguity of the ending allows the reader to imagine a marriage without Tasso's having to commit himself that far. The sense of tragic disappointment that pervades the <u>Liberata</u> is thus felt to be in temporary abeyance for these two. Hough claims that the melancholy vagueness itself is characteristic of Tasso but that we are, at least, "left with the feeling that...(Erminia) will probably succeed" in winning Tancredi.⁴⁶ It seems to me important to recognize that Tasso did understand the different levels of allegory and that if he has created a false sense of resolution, he did not do it out of some irresponsible dreaminess about narrative fact, but because there was no other way to keep the material under control.

I believe, however, that Luciani is right when he says that "Tancredi's love for Clorinda is only reciprocated after her death, whereas Erminia's love is never requited."⁴⁷ Moreover, the resolution of the Clorinda-Tancredi strain in the epic is precisely the reason why a marriage between Tancredi and Erminia cannot be accomplished. Tasso may be willing to let certain narrative details remain unsettled, but his views are always consistent. When, for instance, Armida tries her wiles on the Crusaders, Tancredi remains as unmoved as Goffredo. Of the latter, Tasso says that "sazio

---

[45] Brand, p. 104.
[46] Hough, p. 69.
[47] Luciani, p. 135.

del mondo, i piacer frali/sprezza." The lures she sends out to him are in vain,

> Né impedimento alcun torcer da l'orme
> Puote, che Dio ne segna, i pensier santi.
> (Canto V, 63)

As for Tancredi, his love for Clorinda occupies the same place in his life that his chief's single-minded dedication to Christ has in his. So Tancredi, too, is invulnerable to Armida's charms:

> Però ch'altro desio gli ingombra il seno,
> Né vi può loco aver novello ardore:
> Ché sì come da l'un l'altro veneno
> Guardar ne suol, tal l'un da l'altro amore.
> Questi soli non vinse...
> (Canto V, 65)

And this is while Clorinda is still alive, the unattainable pagan warrior. Once she is dead, it is impossible for Tancredi to become Erminia's faithful and loving husband on earth while awaiting an eventual reunion with his adored Clorinda in heaven. Ariosto might be able to create a character with such delusions, but it would have to be on the level of burlesque. Moreover, if Erminia's love story were to end in a marriage, there is no purpose at all to the tensions and complications of the love-triangle. Why not create some other Christian knight either for her or for Clorinda? Or make the vision of Clorinda into a figure like Creusa's ghost, offering assurances of her salvation and well-being, comfort for the loss, and prophetic admonitions about a terrestrial future with another woman?

What Clorinda does say when she comes to bring a measure of peace to the sleeping Tancredi is in quite a different vein. She speaks not only of her own salvation, but of his, so long as he avoids the snares of the flesh. She does not say as long as he continues to lead a generally upright Christian life, but as long as he avoids the sin of lust, a sin for which his falling in love with her must have argued some propensity. Now, Tasso does not distinguish between licit and illicit sexual enjoyment. As the scenes in Armida's garden make abundantly evident, he had a very just appreciation of the joyful possibilities of sex, and for this reason he believed they had to be restrained. Sexuality is a trap because it distracts people from God and from a holy life. It is possible, as he points out in <u>Il padre di famiglia</u>, to create a sexual institution consistent with a godly life, but such an institution must explicitly deny free rein to the senses. The letter to Scipione Gonzaga makes it clear that to Tasso there is a difference between a "happy ending" and a "good ending," where the latter is one that serves the needs of the Christian religion. And no ending that involves full sexual consummation could possibly be "good" in this sense.

<u>Armida: The Limits of Redemption</u>

Erminia's love is ardent and, in the normal course of events, should find expression in a proper marriage. But Erminia is a virgin, which means that, for all her eagerness, her sexuality has a negative definition. (Indeed, one of her chief concerns when Antioch is captured and, again, when she is wandering about the Holy Land by herself, is the preservation of her chastity.) Similarly, when she becomes involved in the Crusaders' cause, it is not through military action, but through the transmission of information and the practice of medicine. Despite the relative passivity and malleability of her nature, however, Erminia can only be incorporated into the Christian ranks by the exercise of a certain narrative equivocation.

The problems Tasso faced in assimilating Armida to the Christian world were all the greater in that she lacks Erminia's gentle flexibility. It was necessary for him to confront those problems because Armida represents the female character in its most aggressive form: sexually active, spiritually demonic, and militarily engaged. Just as the word "feminine" is the most common--and the most irresponsibly applied--description of Erminia, so the most frequently used word in analytic discussions of Armida is "woman." To the extent that "woman" can imply this complex of sexual, religious, and military assertiveness--as well as the capacity to be moved and eventually dominated by love--its use is not inappropriate, for the challenge Tasso faces is precisely that of female nature at its most positive. He devotes a great deal more attention to the range and intricacies of her personality than he does to those of Clorinda and Erminia because the material is more stubborn, more insistently itself. Yet the resolution he devises, on the narrative plane, is almost identical to that achieved by Erminia: submission to the man, acceptance of Christianity, and, on that double basis, a new, but realistically inconclusive relationship with the beloved.

Sozzi calls Armida an essentially tragic character.[48] I think it is closer to the truth to say that she is a tragic character whose tragedy is not allowed to occur--because

---

[48] B. T. Sozzi, "Il magismo nel Tasso," in Studi sul Tasso (Pisa: Nistri-Lischi, 1954), p. 330.

that kind of defeat is incompatible with the message of Christian salvation as Tasso and the Counter Reformation itself interpreted it. What all three heroines of the <u>Liberata</u> have in common with one another and with the classic tragic hero is that their drama unfolds from within and that the source of its resolution lies in their own most dominant characteristics. Thus, for Armida, salvation derives from the same force that caused her to sin as courtesan, witch, and warrior, her capacity for sexual love.

At first, Armida's sexuality is almost indistinguishable from her identity as a witch, since her assigned role is both to seduce and to enchant the Crusader knights. Tasso's initial description of her at the court of her uncle Idraote conflates the two aspects of her character:

> Donna a cui di beltà le prime lodi
> Concedea l'Oriente, è sua nepote:
> Gli accorgimenti e le più occulte frodi,
> Ch'usi o femina o maga, a lei son note...
> (Canto IV, 23)

Her uncle's instructions are founded on the same assumptions about her nature and, more generally, about the operation of female sexuality:

> Vanne al campo nemico: ivi s'impieghi
> Ogn'arte feminil ch'amore alletti;
> Bagna di pianto e fa' melati i preghi;
> Tronca e confondi co' sospiri i detti:
> Beltà dolente e miserabil pieghi
> Al tuo voler i più ostinati petti:
> Vela il soverchio ardir con la vergogna,
> E fa' manto del vero a la menzogna.

MONSTROUS REGIMENT

> Prendi, s'esser potrà, Goffredo a l'ésca
> De' dolci sguardi e de' be' detti adorni,
> Sì ch'a l'uomo invaghito omai rincresca
> L'incominciata guerra, e la distorni.
> Se ciò non puoi, gli altri più grandi adesca:
> Menagli in parte ond'alcun mai non torni
>
> (Canto IV, 25-26)

From this point on, Armida's actions are completely autonomous. We tend to think of her as a queen, not the dependent niece of a king. Yet in fact she alone of Tasso's three heroines does not choose her own mission and her own role in the poem. It is also significant that in this initial mandate there is no reference to Armida's possession of special powers. The magic Idraote speaks of her practicing is the magic of sexuality and it is this, in the long run, that defines her character. For, while the other Christian knights are attracted by sexuality and dispatched by magic, Rinaldo, her most important victim, is the prey of passion alone.

The first witchery Armida exercises is the attractive power of the sophisticated court lady who takes love for "un gioco di società" and whose vanity and self-esteem are increased by each new conquest.[49] Tasso clearly believes there is a kind of black magic in this alone since, like the more direct practices of witchcraft, it is enmeshed in falsehood and trickery. But, in addition, there is the further mystery that envelopes Armida and that derives from powers beyond those of the ordinary seductress. It is important to distinguish, here, among the different sorts of allegory, for the other knights are captured and held pris-

---

[49] Pool, p. 120.

oner by forces that <u>represent</u> the snares of lust, while, in Rinaldo's case, although the garden itself is artificial, sexuality stands for itself. What works to transform the relationship between Armida and Rinaldo is the natural magic of human sexual relations. In this sense, Armida's story may be seen as a struggle between Nature and Art, where each party to the struggle must also be apprehended dialectically.

Because Armida is the active agent in the affair, and because she is the one whose character grows as it were organically, the real struggle takes place within her. When DeSanctis seeks to glorify Armida as archetypal Woman, he succeeds only in absurdly reifying her and revealing his own sentimental bias. He does perceive, however, that there is a contradiction as well as a collaboration between her witchcraft and her sexuality, and that it is love that makes the latter victorious and points the way to real salvation. Thus, he tells us that Armida is the last magical apparition in poetry (by which he means Italian poetry), and that she is also the most interesting "because of the clearness and truth of her life as a woman." As an apparition she is "penetrated [sic] by man and by Nature. She is the supernatural overcome and dissolved by the strongest laws of Nature."[50] Not only is she originally manipulated into her role as seductive witch, but she becomes a victim of her own witchcraft. "Ma la donna vince la maga e finisce donna."[51]

---

[50] See DeSanctis, 660-61 and, for more of the same sexual enthusiasm, Sozzi, "Il magismo," p. 329. A. Bartlett Giamatti, however, sees the garden as Nature overcome by Grace, represented by the City of God. (See <u>The Earthly Paradise and the Renaissance Epic</u> [Princeton: Princeton University Press, 1966], pp. 184-85.)

[51] De Leval, p. 159. See also DeSanctis, 659, where almost the same words are used.

The sexual indulgence of Rinaldo and Armida is unbridled passion and, hence, one of the most natural forms of human expression. But the Garden of Armida is the symbol, as well as the site, of their relations, and Tasso is at pains to inform us that this beauty is artificial. Birds, trees, and flowers abound in lovely harmony there, but they are not the creations of nature:

> ...quel ch 'l bello e 'l caro accresce a l'opre,
> L'arte, che tutto fa, nulla si scopre.
>
> Stimi (sì misto il culto è co 'l negletto)
> Sol naturali e gli ornamenti e i siti.
> Di natura arte par, che per diletto
> L'imitatrice sua scherzando imìti.
> L'aura, non ch'altro, è de la maga effetto,
> L'aura che rende gli alberi fioriti:
> Co' fiori eterni eterno il frutto dura,
> E mentre spunta l'un, l'altro matura.
> (Canto XVI, 9-10)

The garden is delightful, nonetheless. It is not Tasso's intention to derogate the products of art, but rather to remind us that demonic arts can produce the illusion of beauty. Indeed, the antithesis between appearance and reality constitutes an underlying motif of the entire episode--one that the repeated imagery of mirrors and their substitutes brings into striking relief. Yet the love affair that is enacted in this setting is not the result of Armida's machinations in the way that her other encounters are. The difference is that, this time, she, as well the man, has fallen in love.

They are giving something to one another, but, as the

interchange of mirror images also conveys, their relationship is fundamentally selfish. On Armida's part, this is because she is still motivated by the desire to be worshipped, while Rinaldo glories in this service and forgets that he is first of all the servant of God and instrument of His works on earth. As Tasso expresses it:

> L'uno di servitù, l'altra d'impero
> Si gloria, ella in se stessa, ed egli in lei.
> (Canto XVI, 21)

Rinaldo's lapse from duty is readily corrected. Time and psychological process are required, however, for Armida's sin, which is intrinsic to her character, to give way to another kind of love. It is because both sorts of change do occur that their love story is an integral part of the Christian heroic poem as Tasso conceived it.

But, in the garden itself, Rinaldo's dereliction claims our attention. The relationship between seeing and knowing is very important to this episode. When the Cruaders sent to rescue Rinaldo arrive, the first object to meet their eyes is the elaborately sculpted entrance, carved with representations of mythological and historical tales about the incompatibility of sexual love and heroic destiny. Their mission is to remind Rinaldo of this fact, showing him--a man who knows what he is supposed to be--what he has let himself become. Pietro l'Eremita instructs them to wait until Armida leaves him alone, then,

> Vuo' ch'a lui vi scopriate, e d'adamante
> Un scudo ch'io darò, gli alziate al vólto,
> Sì ch'egli vi si spechhi, e 'l suo sembiante
> Veggia, e l'abito molle onde fu involto:

> Ch'a tal vista potrà vergogna e sdegno
> Scacciar dal petto suo l'amor indegno
>
> (Canto XIV, 77)

They follow their orders to the letter, and the effect on Rinaldo's conscience is immediate and thoroughgoing:

> Egli al lucido scudo il guardo gira;
> Onde si specchia in lui qual siasi, e quanto
> Con delicato culto adorno: spira
> Tutto odori e lascivie il crine e 'l manto;
> E il ferro, il ferro aver, non ch'altro, mira
> Dal troppo lusso effeminato a canto;
> Guernito è sì, ch'inutile ornamento
> Sembra, non militar fèro instrumento
>
> (Canto XVI, 30)

The simile Tasso employs to describe Rinaldo's feelings is that of a man waking from a deep slumber and "coming to" again. Twice in as many lines, the poet stresses that what Rinaldo awakes to is _himself_:

> Qual uom, da cupo e gravo sonno oppresso,
> Dopo vaneggiar lungo in sé riviene,
> Tale ei tornò nel rimirar se stesso:
> Ma se stesso mirar già non sostiene:
> Giù cade il guardo...
>
> (Canto XVI, 31)

What he is being shown, of course, is that by sexual indulgence he has become something less than a man--almost, indeed, a woman--and that the way to return to his true self is to be a soldier once again, to cease looking at his luxurious reflection in the polished shield, turning that shield around, instead, and using it once more as a military accessory.

After this, the rupture is inevitable. Tasso takes a couple of stanzas to crow over Armida's downfall, "ch'amo d'essere amata, odio gli amanti," but these verses have their greatest effect later. At this point, the poet's moralistic triumph seems, if anything, rather misplaced, for it is followed by her final pleas to her lover and the final rejection. Her words are proud, but she admits the evil origins of their affair, the depth of her present feeling, and her wish to be with him on any terms. And she is unable to finish, because she burst into tears. Rinaldo's attempts to "reason" with her and his talk of loving memories leave her unimpressed. He is as clumsy as Aeneas in the same situation, she as impassioned as Dido. Her cries and her vows of vengeance are all the more powerful in that, unlike Dido, Armida is not helpless. As Rinaldo points out, their love has left her no less a queen--and, he might have added, no less a witch--so that where Dido can only curse, Armida can threaten and plan revenge:

> Io no'andrò pur, dice ella, anzi che l'armi
> De l'Oriente il re d'Egitto mova.
> Ritentar ciascun'arte, e trasmutarmi
> In ogni forma insolita mi giova;
> Trattar l'arco e la spada, e serva farmi
> De' più potenti e concitargli a prova:
> Pur che le mie vendette io veggia in parte,
> Il rispetto e l'onor stiasi in disparte.
> (Canto XVI, 73)

Armida has returned to her former character with, as it

were, a vengeance. Yet even in this moment of passion and pain, there is the beginning of a new consciousness. For she understands that the role into which she has been forced is unnatural and even, despite its reliance on her sexuality, "unfeminine":

> Non accusi già me, biasmi se stesso
> Il mio custode e zio, che così volse.
> Ei l'alma baldanzosa e 'l fragil sesso
> A i non debiti uffici in prima volse.
> Esso mi fe' donna vagante, ed esso
> Spronò l'ardire, e la vergogna sciolse.
> Tutto si rechi a lui ciò che d'indegno
> Fèi per amore, o che farò per sdegno.
> (Canto XVI, 74)

Armida is like the woman whose sins are forgiven her because she has loved much. But that love and her injured pride lead her through further experiences of sin before she can approach a Christian consciousness. These experiences include her first direct involvement in the military aspect of the Crusade, and it is love that makes a soldier of the witch and courtesan. The eventual conversion and reconciliation take place on the field of battle, in fact, and as a result of what Armida has learned in the course of armed struggle against her Christian lover and his faith.

Yet there remain critics who are uncertain as to which of the lovers has actually undergone the transformation. Brand claims that Rinaldo is the one who develops most in the course of the poem and that the reconciliation with Armida is, in a way, a result of his reconsecration on Monte Oliveto. After that experience Rinaldo must be a model of moral perfection and, rather than continue to follow the example of the heroic--but pagan--Aeneas, he forgives and converts his mistress, instead of deserting her.[52] Donadoni, however, points out the facile nature of Rinaldo's serial conversions, passing "too easily from avenging fury to lasting love, to forgetfulness of woman and to religiousness."[53] It seems to me undeniable that in the great battle scene it is Armida who is wracked by a succession of emotions and that it is she whose consciousness is radically altered in consequence of her suffering. In these scenes, the poetry returns to the lyric and dramatic heights achieved in recounting the original story of love and rejection.

It is the most wretched unhappiness that turns Armida into a warrior, yet her first appearance in that guise-- leading both male and female troops--is magnificent:

>Nessun più rimanea, quando improvisa
>Armida apparve, e dimostrò sua schiera.
>Venìa sublime in un gran carro assisa,
>Succinta in gonna, e faretrata arciera;
>E mescolato il novo sdegno in guisa
>Co 'l natio dolce in quel bel vólto s'era,
>Che vigor dalle; e druda ed acerbetta
>Par che minacci, e minacciando alletta.
>
>Somiglia il carro a quel che porta il giorno,
>Lucido di piropi e di giacinti;
>E frena il dotto auriga al giogo adorno

---

[52] Brand, p. 106.

[53] Eugenio Donadoni, *A History of Italian Literature*, trans. Richard Monges, I (New York: New York University Press, 1969), 266.

MONSTROUS REGIMENT

> Quattro unicorni a coppia a coppia avvinti.
> Cento donzelle e cento paggi intorno
> Pur di faretra gli omeri van cinti,
> Ed a i bianchi destrier premono il dorso,
> Che sono al giro pronti, e lievi al corso.
> (Canto XVII, 33-34)

When she offers her services to the pagan army, she speaks as royalty, declaring that all arts, including those of war, befit her regal rank. But she employs more characteristically feminine weapons, as well, for she offers her hand in marriage to the warrior who will slay Rinaldo; since her sexuality is still her dominant quality, it is the latter offer that is taken seriously, as the Saracen knights vie in their promises of vengeance.

Nonetheless, she persists in what, in her case, is an impious and unnatural military role. She appears at the final battle clad in armor, though surrounded by men who love and have sworn to champion her. Once she sees Rinaldo, she realizes that her love for him is not dead and she no longer completely desires the revenge she has come to win:

> Ella stessa in su l'arco ha già lo strale;
> Spingea le mani, e incrudelìa lo sdegno:
> Ma le placava e n'era amor ritegno.
>
> Sorse amor contra l'ira, e fe' palese
> Che vive il foco suo ch'ascoso tenne.
> La man tre volte a saettar distese,
> Tre volte essa inchinolla, e si ritenne.
> Por vinse al fin lo sdegno; e l'arco tese
> E fe' volar del suo quadrel le penne.

Tasso

> Lo stral volò; ma con lo strale un vóto
> Sùbito uscì, che vada il colpo a vòto.
> (Canto XX, 62-63)

Her arrows do fail and her knights are defeated one by one. Armida realizes that she will lose and cries,

> Or qual arte novella, e qual m'avanza
> Nova forma in cui possa anco mutarmi?
> (Canto XX, 67)

Although several pagan champions still defend her, she has no more faith in magic or military arts. For her, there remain only love and the deepest bitterness. She escapes from the battle and decides to use at least one weapon with honor, to commit suicide. Rinaldo has followed her and grasps the arm with which she is about to stab herself. In her pride, she struggles, but he assures her that he is not saving her from death in order to make her his slave. He promises her a secure throne and, if she will accept conversion, further material rewards, as well:

> --Armida, il cor turbato omai tranquilla:
> Non a gli scherni, al regno io ti riservo;
> Nemico no, ma tuo campione e servo.
>
> Mira ne gli occhi miei, s'al dir non vuoi
> Fede prestar, de la mia fede il zelo.
> Nel soglio, ove regnâr gli avoli tuoi,
> Ripôrti giuro; ed oh piacesse al Cielo
> Ch'a la tua mente alcun de' raggi suoi
> Del paganesmo dissolvesse il velo,
> Com'io farei che 'n Oriënte alcuna

> Non t'agguagliasse di regal fortuna.--
> (Canto XX, 134-135)

Her rage disappears and is replaced, at this moment of conversion, by a submissive love, as she echoes the Virgin Mary's words of acceptance and consummation:

> --Ecco l'ancilla tua; d'essa a tuo senno
> Dispon, gli disse, e le fia legge il cenno.--
> (Canto XX, 136)

The conclusion of Erminia's story is obscure because it is so subtle; she simply fades into the Christian sphere. With Armida, the resolution is spelled out, and I have traced it in some detail because, on the narrative level, it is nonetheless just as obscure as the other. Armida is defeated and, according to the fundamental laws of Christian salvation, she has given up her freedom to win her freedom. She abases herself before Rinaldo and before his wish for her salvation. Her ardor and her passion remain, to be placed, now, in the service of the Christian life. But Tasso leaves us entirely in the dark as to the practical consequences of her action.[54]

There is even some critical speculation that his reconciliation with Armida signals Rinaldo's rejection of the purifying experience on Monte Oliveto and a return to a life of sexual indulgence. I think Tasso would have found such an ending intolerable and I see no evidence that it was his

---

[54] Giamatti (pp. 209-10) goes further, to make a convincing case about the permanence of the inner conflicts dramatized in Armida's garden. He says "we wince" at Armida's resignation and considers Tasso's resolution "forced" and desperate.

intention. But, ruling out a renewal of their former relations, what is left for them? Their "new, spiritual love is barely hinted at--it does not move Tasso because it lies outside his experience."[55] More precisely, it does not move him because he can give it no definable social form. If marriage was inconceivable for Erminia and Tancredi, it is all the more so for Armida and Rinaldo, given their voluptuous history and his destruction of the enchanted wood. Marriage is once again part of the poem's "hidden agenda"--and, once again, Tasso cannot grant sacramental sanction to a sexual institution and thus make private love the means for building holiness into human society.

---

[55] Brand, p. 106.

CHAPTER FIVE
SPENSER: THE MATTER OF BRITOMART

The Faerie Queene brings it all together. Unlike Tasso, Spenser secures many of his virtuous couples the fulfillment of marriage; unlike Ariosto, he reflects on this development, acknowledging the social and ideological innovation he is proposing. One result of this awareness is the elaboration within the poem of a philosophical position about the role of sexuality in human experience, a position that encompasses both its spiritual and its political dimensions. Sexual love, as Spenser envisions it, is part of the divine plan for earthly life, not merely because it is essential for the physical continuation of that life, but also because, properly apprehended and governed, it can constitute a means to the spiritual perfection of the individual. The sacrament of marriage, which provides the institutional setting for chaste sexual expression, is also understood as a political phenomenon, simultaneously reflecting and contributing to the good order of society.

I think it would be a mistake, however, to conclude from this that The Faerie Queene is a poem in some sense about matrimony or that Spenser was chiefly concerned with presenting a complex theoretical or mythic justification for the emerging Protestant doctrine of marriage. To do so is to confuse substance and accident, image and content, in a fashion that seriously distorts and limits one's approach to the poem, and that is particularly dangerous for the interpretation of allegory. It seems to me that any reading of The Faerie Queene has to account for the series of fine articulations and interactions on which the poem is constructed--between, for instance, the private and the public, the medieval and the modern, the material and the ideal worlds. And I believe that the locus of all these contradictions and their resolution is the Renaissance state as Spenser understood it.

Spenser himself distinguished the "priuate morall vertues" examined in The Faerie Queene from the "polliticke vertues" that would be embodied in a projected second poem about Arthur as king.[1] But this in no way detracts from the highly political character of the poem we actually have, for the measure of Spenser's politics was always the individual and the personal. Moreover, those elements that contribute to the ideal balance of the polity are situated in what he perceives as typically masculine and feminine qualities of actual male and female figures.

In declaring, as he does in his Letter to Raleigh, that the Queen "beareth two persons," Spenser is not simply acknowledging the contemporary legal doctrine of the sovereign's dual nature, but is expressing something more fundamental, as well, an interplay of personal and civic identity that involves the entire human community. The theme of sexual love (and, to a lesser but nonetheless considerable extent, that of money) creates a nexus between the individual and the polity. In this chapter, I explore the way that

---

[1] See Edmund Spenser, Letter to Sir Walter Raleigh, 23 January 1589, in The Poetical Works of Edmund Spenser in Three Volumes, ed. J. C. Smith (1909; rpt. Oxford: Oxford University Press, 1961), III, 485. All citations from the text of the poem are from this edition. I have not followed modern practice in spelling, but I have eliminated the confusing italics with which the text is sprinkled.

Spenser uses his ideas of sexuality to establish an equilibrium embracing both facets of identity. At the same time, I hope to justify my contention that The Faerie Queene is primarily a public poem and that, for Spenser, private morality assumes its highest terrestrial form when it serves and symbolizes political virtue.

As is evident from my summary of the issues, The Faerie Queene is one enchanted wood in which it is extremely difficult to tell the forest from the trees. Despite the fact that Spenser's poem is the most consistently allegorical work in the heroic tradition, it is not always possible to distinguish between a symbol and what it signifies. Spenser's allegorical method relies, in the first instance, upon personification and iconographic conventions and on this level, of course, there is little problem of interpretation. When the Knight of Chastity passes unscathed through fires encircling the dwelling-place of Lust, while a virtuous but more passionate knight, whose shield bears the image of Cupid, is seriously burned in an unsuccessful attempt to get through, the reader knows just what connections to make. Characters and events that are considerably more complicated are susceptible of similar explanations.

The questions arise when we consider the larger forces and incidents that make up the fabric of the poem. As Rosemary Freeman points out, "allegory presupposes a separation between concept and image, between the idea and the tangible objects in which it is expressed.[2] This is almost tautological, yet when it comes to a continuous allegory like The

---

[2] Rosemary Freeman, Edmund Spenser, Writers and their Work, No. 89 (London: Longmans, Green for the British Book Council and National Book League, 1957), p. 23. On this general question, see also Graham Hough, "Allegory in The Faerie Queene," Chapter VI of A Preface to the Faerie Queene (New York: Norton, 1962).

Faerie Queene, whose narrative does not admit of the sustained reading on the literal level that is possible with the romance-epics of Ariosto and Tasso, it is not a very useful description. Precisely because the allegory is so integral to Spenser's poem, it must be read without the constant oscillaton between a sign and its referent that Freeman's description implies. The allegory is contained in a narrative which of necessity we read as a narrative, and this means that when we come up against a constellaton of ideas about, for example, love, marriage, and the state, we know there is a symbolic relation among the parts, one that links these forces to the more specific "one-to-one" allegories in the poem. But it is not immediately obvious which idea in the cluster is the principal subject in whose service the others function. This ambiguity is what makes it at least possible for me to reverse the usual interpretation and suggest that Spenser's humanism leads him to explore human nature and morality as an approach to broader questions of political morality, rather than the other way round.

The Historical Present

The entire literal level of The Faerie Queene--and particularly the elements of plot and characterization--is clearly of secondary importance to Spenser. It is tempting to assume that the poet's apparent lack of commitment to his narrative is evidence of a more general non-interest in the progress of events, and to conclude, with William Nelson, that "Spenser's overriding concern is with the moral nature of man rather than with happenings or people."[3] To take

---

[3] William Nelson, The Poetry of Edmund Spenser: A Study (New York : Columbia University Press, 1963), pp. vii-viii.

this position to its logical conclusion, however, is to identify literary narrative with history and to ignore the preoccupation with historical process that pervades *The Faerie Queene*.

The broad context of this preoccupation is the cyclical and dialectical sweep epitomized in the Mutabilitie Cantos and reinforced by the generative drama of the Garden of Adonis. But its specific effect is to locate Spenser's story, despite its static, pictorial form, in a human history that is conceived as part of the more general patterns of change and generation. The qualities associated with male and female character are closely related to the ideas of fixity and change, as well as to the generative vision. And the poem's attention to questions of fictive history and dynastic development serves to situate Spenser's allegory in recorded events and in time itself. Moreover, the dynastic theme is the medium through which certain ideas about sexual character and relationships find their way into the poem.

Like his poetic predecessors, Spenser considers dynastic issues simultaneously from the point of view of his own time, which is one sort of "present tense," and the time of the narrative, which is "the present" for his characters. The parallel histories of Britain and Faerie-land make it possible for him to treat this shifting perspective with some subtlety and to link historical progression to the intrinsic stasis of the poem's overall design. In this way, the Trojan origins of Britain are explored as a common past, along with the history of ancient Britain from the time of Brut to that of Arthur. At the same time, the future descendants of Britomart and Arthegall are traced through two different sources. Each of the time periods with which the poem is concerned makes a distinct contribution to the historical vision of *The Faerie Queene*.

Spenser

Spenser's treatment of the Trojan theme differs from the approaches employed by other practitioners of literary epic in that it places far less emphasis on the achievements of Troy, proportionately more on establishing genealogical facts. When Paridell and Britomart discuss the fall of Troy at Malbecco's grudging entertainment, conventional reference is made to the

> famous towne
> Which raignd so many yeares victorious
> And of all Asie bore the soueraigne crowne.
> (III.ix.39)

But even this description occurs in a passage lamenting the fall of the city, and many more stanzas are devoted to the destruction of Trojan civilization than to the civilization itself. No mention is made of Hector or any other Trojan hero, and Aeneas enters the story almost as an afterthought, although acknowledged as the prince who preserved the remnant of the Trojan population that eventually founded Rome.

The lack of attention to what Troy was before its destruction has a two-fold origin: on the one hand, Spenser's overriding concern with the movable mandate of Troy-novant, and, on the other, his very real discomfort with the moral associations of Trojan descent. It is the idea of divinely-ordained empire that intrigues him, rather than the particular nature of earlier states whose destiny it has been to rule. Thus, the Roman _imperium_ is given equally short shrift: The accomplishments recounted in the second half of The Aeneid are summarized here in two brief stanzas, ending with the founding of Rome. And the Roman part of the story is concluded with another stanza:

> There there (said Britomart) a fresh appeard
>   The glory of the later world to spring,
>   And Troy againe out of her dust was reard,
>   To sit in second seat of soueraigne king,
>   Of all the world vnder her gouerning.
>   But a third kingdome yet is to arise,
>   Out of the Troians scattered of-spring,
>   That in all glory and great enterprise,
> Both first and second Troy shall dare to equalise.
>   (III.ix.44)

For Ariosto and Tasso, descent from Troy is important because it also entails descent from imperial Rome. But Spenser is not concerned with acquiring the glories of either vanished empire for the line that Britomart and Arthegall will found. Indeed, the only other time that Rome is mentioned in a dynastic or historical connection, it is as the oppressor of Britain, and Roman emperors are catalogued in terms of the relative cruelty with which they administered Britain or the nature of the resistance they encountered. What clearly attracts Spenser is the notion that human political history is guided by Providence and that his England can share the divine favor--not the specific character-- of its Trojan and Roman ancestors. (For similar reasons, Spenser does not seem to feel that writing of Troy to the "Trojan-descended" Tudors requires any of the anti-Greek partisanship that marks the <u>Orlando furioso</u>. Thus, although the turrets of the House of Alma are compared with the towers of Thebes and Troy, Greece is acknowledged, not much further on, as "the Nourse of all good arts.") The word "Troynovant" is used to designate the British capital in the history that Arthur reads, as well as in Britomart's own relation of historical events. But, more than a specific place name, it is as a living concept that the term exercises its greatest fascination and power.

As I have suggested, Spenser's evasion of Troy as such, as distinct from Trojan origins, is at least partially linked to his distaste for the sexual excess and luxurious sin identified with that city. The fall of Troy and the fate of exiles from the city are first recounted in the context of a banquet at which Paridell, whose behavior echoes that of his ancestor and namesake, Paris, relates the part of the tale that concerns the decline and destruction of the city and the escape of Aeneas. But it is up to Britomart, whose own line is to create a third divinely-ordered state, to tell of the foundaton of Rome as the new Troy.

Britomart is aloof from the tawdry sexual behavior of Paridell and his paramour, much as Aeneas stood apart from the "Oriental" indulgence of sensuous Troy. The Knight of Chastity makes no effort to prevent a development that must be obvious to anyone who can see better than the blindly jealous Malbecco. She fights for Chastity and she exemplifies it, but nowhere does she advance any arguments for so axiomatic a virtue in the Spenserian canon. The actual seduction of Hellenore, in fact, takes place after Britomart leaves, and is accompanied by a diversionary conflagration that is explicitly compared to the fire that burned Troy. Britomart's situation here is analogous to that of Aeneas; both are unable to prevent either the initial trespass or the retribution, but are permitted to save something that is the basis for a new start. The similarity should not be urged too far, of course, especially since Britomart's role in the incident, though ambiguous, is a minor one; the chief character in the episode of Paridell and Hellenore is Malbecco. It is important, however, from both the narrative and allegorical points of view, that Spenser's disapproval of the sexual mores of Troy is expressed in this section of the poem, for he is the first author since Virgil to make positive use of the Matter of Troy while reserving--and exercising--the right of severe moral judgment upon it.

Paridell may trace his ancestry to Paris' days as a shepherd on Mount Ida, but the rulers of Britain are descended from Brut, and, through him, from Aeneas himself. Whenever this first "British" ancestor is mentioned, the narrative focus becomes very precise, and Brut's accomplishments, as well as the fact of his existence and his genealogical role, are part of the narrative. Thus, in <u>Briton Moniments</u>, his settlement of England is portrayed as a truly creative act, one that brings order out of diabolical chaos. Unlike the chaste and austere Italy that Aeneas' coming destroys, primitive Britain is populated by savage giants, half human and half fiend:

> They held this land, and with their filthinesse
> Polluted this same gentle soyle long time:
> That their owne mother loathd their
>   beastlinesse,
> And gan abhorre her broods vnkindly crime,
> All were they borne of her owne natiue slime,
> Vntill that Brutus anciently deriu'd
> From royall stocke of old Assaracs line,
> Driuen by fatal error, here arriu'd,
> And them of their vniust possession depriu'd.
>   (II.x.9)

Brut brings not only order, but civilization, for he constructs the literal and figurative Troynovant. As Britomart tells the assembly around Malbecco's table:

Spenser

> The Troian Brute did first that Citie found,
>   And Hygate made the meare thereof by West,
>   And Ouert gate by North: that is the bound
>   Toward the land; two riuers bound the rest.
>   So huge a scope at first him seemed best,
>   To be the compasse of his kingdomes seat:
>   So huge a mind could not in lesser rest,
>   Ne in small meares containe his glory great,
> That Albion had conquered first by warlike feat.
>   (III.ix.46)

The ruling line from Brut through Uther Pendragon is described in <u>Briton Moniments</u>. Use of the book-device to recount chronicle history has the advantage of making Spenser's reader the reader of history. It provides us, moreover, with a situation, rare in this tradition, in which the person who is audience to one of these oral, written, or pictorial chronicles makes a response. Arthur's irritation at having the narrative stop with his father's accession to the throne is overshadowed by the patriotic emotions aroused by the text itself:

>   that so vntimely breach
>   The Prince him selfe halfe seemeth to offend,
>   Yet secret pleasure did offence empeach,
> And wonder of antiquitie long stopt his speach.
>
> At last quite rauisht with delight, to heare
>   The royall Ofspring of his natiue land,
>   Cryde out, Deare countrey, O how dearely deare
>   Ought thy remembraunce, and perpetuall band
>   Be to thy foster Childe, that from thy hand
>   Did commun breath and nouriture receaue?

MONSTROUS REGIMENT

> How brutish is it not to vnderstand,
> How much to her we owe, that all vs gaue,
> That gaue vnto vs all, what euer good we haue.
> (II.x.68-69)

That history is a rather conventional recital of wars, rebellions, conflicts, and struggles remarkable only for its detailed length and for the unusual prominence of women within it. It is true, of course, that the reader already knows there is a link in Spenser's imaginative construct between sexuality and the long sweep of history, but references to the female role in specific events are too numerous and too varied for it to be a case of their simply being more noticeable because the general subject is on our minds.

For instance, although Ariosto and Tasso put both passionate jealousy and women warriors into their poems, they have nothing that compares with Spenser's story of Queen Guendolene's response to her husband's unfaithfulness:

> The noble daughter of Corineus
> Would not endure to be so vile disdaind,
> But gathering force, and courage valorous,
> Encountred him in battell well ordaind,
> In which him vanquisht she to fly constraind:
> But she so fast pursewd, that him she tooke,
> And threw in bands, where he till death
>   remaind;
> Als his fair Leman, flying through a brooke,
> She ouerhent, nought moued with her piteous looke.
> (II.x.18)

Although this remarkable woman slays her husband's mistress and the latter's guiltless daughter, Spenser does not define her as an irrational or hysterical creature. Indeed, after she dispatches her enemies, she proceeds to govern as regent until her young son attains his majority:

> During which time her powre she did display
> Through all this realme, the glorie of her sex,
> And first taught men a woman to obay:
> But when her sonne to mans estate did wex,
> She surrendred, ne her selfe would lenger vex.
> (II.x.20)

Far from being unbalanced, Guendolene demonstrates a fine, balanced sense of justice, both in her conduct of government and her readiness to relinquish the throne when the rightful heir comes of age.

Nor does the chronicle invariably assign passionate behavior to female characters. Relating the history of King Lear, Spenser makes Cordelia its hero, ending the story with her raising an army to restore her father to his throne, which he then occupies until his death from old age:

> And after wild, it should to her remaine:
> Who peaceably the same long time did weld:
> And all mens harts in dew obedience held:
> Till that her sisters children, woxen strong
> Through proud ambition, against her rebeld,
> And ouercommen kept in prison long,
> Till wearie of that wretched life, her selfe she hong.
> (II.x.32)

It is worth remarking that Cordelia not only succeeds her father, but that she is a good ruler. Spenser's concern, throughout, is not simply to demonstrate that some women do hold power legitimately, but also to show that legitimate female power means virtuous government.

Thus, two great law-givers--one of each sex--are mentioned in <u>Briton Moniments</u>. The first is Donwallo, whose leadership unites Britain after internecine conflict has destroyed Brutus' descendants and who, after being elected king himself, proceeds to defeat his enemies and establish an orderly "ciuill gouernaunce":

> Then made he sacred lawes, which some men say
> Were vnto him reueald in vision,
> By which he freed the Traueilers high way,
> The Churches part, and Ploughmans portion,
> Restraining stealth, and strong extortion.
> (II.x.39)

Donwallo's work is completed by the woman who marries his great-grandson:

> Dame Mertia the fayre,
> A woman worthy of immortall prayse,
> Which for this Realme found many goodly layes,
> And wholesome Statutes to her husband brought;
> Her many deemd to haue beene of the Fayes,
> As was Aegerie, that Numa tought;
> Those yet of her be Mertian lawes both nam'd and
> thought.
> (II.x.42)

In none of the instances that the chronicle cites, is there anything about the way the women rulers exercise authority that is specific to their sex, any intrinsically "feminine" contribution that they make to government. With Mertia, to be sure, there is the suggestion of supernatural aid, but Donwallo's precepts are also said to have been the product of revelation. Spenser supplies no details about the "goodly layes and wholesome Statutes" the queen devises, but his mention of their survival would seem to indicate that he considers them sound and appropriate.

Perhaps the most impressive woman who appears in <u>Briton Moniments</u> is the queen Spenser calls Bonduca who, seeing the Roman forces profit from a divided Britain, gathers an army to resist foreign tyranny:

>   And taking armes, the Britons to her drew;
>   With whom she marched streight against her
>   foes,
> And them vnwares besides the Seuerne did enclose.
>
> There she with them a cruell battell tride,
>   Not with so good successe, as she deseru'd
>   By reason that the Captaines on her side,
>   Corrupted by Paulinus, from her sweru'd:
>   Yet such, as were through former flight
>   preseru'd,
>   Gathering againe, her Host she did renew,
>   And with fresh courage on the victour seru'd:
>   But being all defeated, saue a few,
> Rather than fly, or be captiued her selfe she
>   slew.
>
> O famous moniment of womens prayse,
>   Matchable either to Semiramis,
>   Whom antique history so high doth raise,
>   Or to Hypsiphil' or to Thomiris:

> Her Host two hundred thousand numbred is;
> Who whiles good fortune favoured her might,
> Triumphed oft against her enimis;
> And yet, though ouercome in hapless fight,
> She triumphed on death, in enemies despight.
>   (II.x.54-56)

Although Spenser's version places a somewhat false emphasis on the place of women in British history, he writes about female leaders whose historicity—or at least whose position in national legend—is assured. Furthermore, the poet may exaggerate the achievements of some of the other women he mentions, but Bonduca gets no more than her due.[4]

In this way, Spenser injects the idea of a female presence, though not of a characteristically female contribution, into the historical-dynastic movement of *The Faerie Queene*. The only antecedents Ariosto and Tasso could claim for their women warriors are literary ones, and, in any event, the relationship between the classic Amazon-figure and the heroines of romance-epic is strictly iconological. Britomart, however, has been provided with a line of activ-

---

[4] It must have been difficult for Spenser, as a reader of the classics, to achieve a British perspective on the last stages of Roman conquest. The *Annals* and the *Agricola* of Tacitus, reports from the partisan viewpoint of the eventual victors, are the principal sources for events surrounding the uprising of Boadicea. (Spenser employs a variant of the queen's name for its etymological significance. As her name implies, she is a good leader.) Tacitus' description of the slaughter of Romans and their "allies" (British collaborators) suggests to Winston Churchill "an inexpiable war like that waged between Carthage and her revolted mercenaries two centuries before." (*The Birth of Britain, A History of the English-Speaking Peoples* [New York: Dodd, Mead, 1956], p. 26). As Tacitus also chronicles, in literature's first reference to the city of London, it was Boadicea's troops who burned "Troynovant" nearly to the ground.

ist women from whom she can claim familial and national, as well as ideological descent. When Glauce conceives the idea of her charge's riding forth to seek Arthegall, she refers to this tradition:

> And sooth, it ought your courage much inflame,
> To heare so often, in that royall hous,
> From whence to none inferiour ye came,
> Bards tell of many women valorous
> Which haue full many feats aduenturous
> Performd, in paragone of proudest men:
> The bold Bunduca, whose victorious
> Exploits made Rome to quake, stout Guendolen,
> Renowmed Martia, and redoubted Emmilen.
>
> And that, which more than all the rest may sway,
> Late dayes ensample, which these eyes beheld,
> In the last field before Meneuia
> Which Vther with those forrein Pagans held,
> I saw a Saxon Virgin, the which feld
> Great Vlfin thrise vpon the bloudy plaine
> ....
> Faire Angela (quoth she) men do her call,
> No whit lesse faire, then terrible in fight:
> She hath the leading of a Martiall
> And mighty people dreaded more then all
> The other Saxons, which do for her sake
> And loue, themselues of her name Angles call.
>   (III.iii.54-56)

As we know, when Britomart assumes the martial role, she makes use not only of the "ensample" but also the armor of the Saxon queen.

Although the plan for Britomart's becoming a knight originates in Glauce's "foolhardy wit" and matchmaking propensities, Spenser does not seem to consider it an improper course of action. For, in thus aggressively seeking out the man she is destined to marry, Britomart establishes not only the fact but the conditions of their meeting, assuring that the military and public element will enter into their courtship. At the same time, by learning "the dreadful speare and shield to exercize" and by employing them in the causes she supports, she is turning herself into a fit ancestor for the British rulers whom Merlin foresees as her progeny. Her action and its results are a literal enactment of the "hard begin" that the wizard tells the love-sick girl will culminate in her dynastic triumph.

Merlin's prophecy itself draws the analogy between the vicissitudes Britomart undergoes on her way to founding a dynasty, and those the British people will experience in the course of fulfilling their national destiny. The prophet's general theme is the cyclical and Providential nature of historical process. Thus, although the stanzas devoted to Britomart's (Welsh) descendants for some generations to come are full of bloodshed, betrayal, and defeat, their overall vision is a satisfying one. Its recurrent theme, like that of <u>Briton Moniments</u>, is expressed in Merlin's words:

> Then woe, and woe, and euerlasting woe,
>   Be to the Briton babe, that shalbe borne,
>   To liue in thraldome of his fathers foe;
>   Late King, now captiue, late Lord, now
>   forlorne,
>   The worlds reproch, the cruell victors scorne,
>   Banisht from Princely bowre to wastfull wood:
>   O who shall helpe me to lament, and mourne

Spenser

> The royall seed, the antique Troian blood,
> Whose Empire lenger here, then euer any stood.
> (III.iii.42)

Whereas <u>Briton Moniments</u> breaks off in mid-sentence, "without full point, or other Cesure right," Merlin's vision encompasses a triumphant future, although still emphasizing that the progress of history is not linear:

> ...when the terme is full accomplishid,
> There shall a sparke of fire, which hath
>   long-while
> Bene in his ashes raked vp, and hid,
> Be freshly kindled in the fruitfull Ile
> Of Mona, where it lurked in exile;
> Which shall breake forth into bright burning
>   flame,
> And reach into the house, that beares the stile
> Of royall maiesty and soueraigne name;
> So shall the Briton bloud their crowne againe
>   reclame.
>
> Thenceforth eternall vnion shall be made
>   Betweene the nations different afore,
>   And sacred Peace shall louingly perswade
>   The warlike minds, to learne her goodly lore,
>   And ciuile armes to exercise no more:
>   Then shall a royall virgin raine, which shall
>   Stretch her white rod ouer the Belgicke shore,
>   And the great Castle smite so sore with all,
> That it shall make him shake, and shortly learne
>   to fall.

> But yet the end is not...
>
> (III.iii.48-50)

This consummation is reminiscent of the way Antiquitie of Faerie lond concludes. In contrast to Briton Moniments, the chronicle that Guyon reads at the House of Alma is a tale of creative energies well and peacefully spent in generative, societal, and material endeavors. Although the book is longer than the record of Britain's tempestuous history, Spenser's summary of it is much shorter, rapidly listing the elfin rulers and their accomplishments: the continents under their sway, the cities established by them, the monuments constructed on their orders. It ends with a rather rosy version of Tudor domination. After seven hundred rulers have serenely followed one another to the throne, Elficleos--Henry VII--is made king.[5] In this account, there is nothing remarkable or out of order about his accession, and his reign is magnificent even for Faerieland. Then, we learn that

> He left two sonnes, of which faire Elferon

---

[5] Spenser's use of the Roman name, Mona, for the Island of Anglesey, whence the Tudors returned to England, once more brings Tacitus to mind. Historically, the prelude to Boadicea's uprising was the conquest of Mona. In fact, Suetonius and his army were still carrying out "mop-up" operations there when recalled to deal with the more serious revolt. As the Romans approached Mona initially, they saw the shore lined with the enemy: "a dense host of armed men, interspersed with women clad in black, like the Furies, with their hair hanging down and holding torches in their hands...These strange sights terrified the soldiers...At last, encouraged by the general and exhorting each other not to quail before the rabble of female fanatics, they advanced their standards, bore down all resistance, and enveloped the enemy in their own flames." (Tacitus, Annales, trans. G. G. Ramsay, cited Churchill, p. 23. Italics are mine.)

Spenser

> The eldest brother did vntimely dy;
> Whose emptie place the mightie Oberon
> Doubly supplide, in spousall and dominion.
>
> Great was his power and glorie ouer all,
>   Which him before, that sacred seate did fill,
>   That yet remaines his wide memoriall:
>   He dying left the fairest Tanaquill,
>   Him to succeede therein, by his last will;
>   Fairer and nobler liueth none this howre,
>   Ne like in grace, ne like in learned skill;
>   Therefore they Glorian call that glorious flowre,
> Long mayst thou Glorian liue, in glory and great powre.
>
> (II.x.75-76)

Both the faery-chronicle and the magician's forecast thus conclude with the reign of Elizabeth. Since <u>Antiquitie of Faerie lond</u> is history up to what is the present time in the narrative, whereas Merlin's prophecy includes events <u>from</u> that time through the sixteenth century, the poet's own present time, the fact that both culminate in Elizabeth reinforces Spenser's sense of historical development. As will be evident in my discussion of the Garden of Adonis and the generative vision, I believe it is highly significant that the poem communicates the idea that historical time and sexual time (which is to say, biological time mediated by human relations) are the same quantities, and that the dynastic myth is the concrete link between them.

The Queen's Presence

The Faerie Queene differs from other literary epics in the degree to which its patron is also its subject. For, in its political, sexual, and moral dimensions, Spenser's epic is a poem *about* Queen Elizabeth. By contrast, Virgil's allusions to Augustus are extremely subtle, restricted as they are to the dynastic issue itself and to certain specific matters of policy. The propaganda function of the *Aeneid* is very generally ideological, supporting those attitudes and values that the Emperor and his partisans perceived as essential to their new order. Both Ariosto and Tasso are more direct in their address to the Estensi as regards questions of descent and proposed courses of action. Tasso chooses his moments--although not his diction--with some discretion, and the motif of praise or advice for Alfonso d'Este is present through most of his poem only by implication. The Este family, Cardinal Ippolito in particular, looms much larger, of course, in the *Orlando furioso*. Nonetheless, the two Italian romance-epics tend to limit the patrons' function to the poems' political and dynastic dimensions, and to treat them as somewhat peripheral to the general design. The Estense role in both poems is like that of the portraits of the artist's patron often included in Renaissance religious paintings, where the prelate or prince or merchant who commissioned the picture will be shown rather incongruously kneeling before his saintly namesake and adding a stiff, anachronistic note to the whole. Only in *The Faerie Queene* and through the complex mediation of Spenser's allegory is the royal patron able to break out of her marginal role and participate in the full range of content that the poem affords.

For Elizabeth, however, as for Augustus and the members

of Casa d'Este, the dynastic subject remains an important way of linking her to the poem's action. The theme of his queen's ancestry inspires Spenser with an awe that echoes but far overshadows Ariosto's reaction to writing about the Este lineage. When Arthur takes up <u>Briton Moniments</u> and Spenser is about to summarize the contents of that chronicle, he speaks in his own voice about his unworthiness to treat this elevated subject and his despair at ever finding words to encompass its glory:

> Argument worthy of Moeonian quill,
>   Or rather worthy of great Phoebus rote
> Whereon the ruines of great Ossa hill,
> And triumphes of Phlegraean Ioue he wrote,
> That all the Gods admird his loftie note.
> But if some relish of that heauenly lay
> His learned daughters would to me report,
> To decke my song withall, I would assay,
> Thy name, O soueraine Queene, to blazon farre
>   away.
>
> Thy name O soueraine Queene, thy realme and race,
>   From this renowmed Prince derived arre,
> Who mightily vpheld that royall mace,
> Which now thou bear'st, to thee decended farre
> From mightie kings and conquerours in warre,
> Thy fathers and great Grandfathers of old,
> Whose noble deedes aboue the Northerne starre
> Immortall fame for euer hath enrold;
> As in that old mans booke they were in order told.
>   (II.x.3-4)

Even more pointed are the opening stanzas of the third Canto in Book Three, the Canto in which Britomart learns of her destiny and rides out to meet it halfway. The previous Canto ended with Glauce's unavailing spells against the love-sickness that consumes her nursling, and the narrative is to continue with the old woman's concern and her decision to ask Merlin's help. Before taking up this story in the new Canto, Spenser interrupts it to apostrophize the spirit of history, and concludes by addressing its Muse:

> Begin then, O my dearest sacred Dame,
>   Daughter of Phoebus and of Memorie,
>   That doest ennoble with immortall name
>   The warlike Worthies, from antiquitie,
>   In thy great volume of Eternitie:
>   Begin, O Clio, and recount from hence
>   My glorious Soueraines goodly auncestrie,
>   Till that by dew degrees and long protense,
> Thou haue it lastly brought vnto her Excellence.
>   (III.iii.4)

In both passages, Spenser makes it very clear that the principal reason for recounting dynastic history is to glorify Elizabeth's ancestry. His willingness not merely to suspend, but apparently to forget the particular narrative occasion is one of the features of the poem that sometimes make it difficult to tell which elements within it are the symbols, which the things symbolized.

But the Queen's participation in the poem is not simply as the descendant of the legendary and historical persons who are its characters. Through the figures of Belphoebe and Mercilla, Spenser brings her directly into his allegorical statements about chastity, justice, and mercy. When we explore the sexual and political values that make up the fabric of *The Faerie Queene*, it will be essential to recall the relationship of Elizabeth to those themes and their anticipated influence on state policy or ideology.

Although Gloriana is not an active character in the poem--or at least in the part of it that was actually produced--*The Faerie Queene* remains a most appropriate title. For, in so far as Gloriana stands for Elizabeth, both queens may be said to dominate and draw together the moral allegory that provides the poem's framework. It is Prince Arthur who embodies Magnificence, the virtue that in the Aristotelian system perfects and contains all the others.[6] Yet Elizabeth is explicitly referred to as the possessor and exemplar of each virtue, although, in a larger sense, each knight represents an aspect of the moral character ascribed to the sovereign, and Arthur, as Magnificence, *is* that character.

Thus, the induction to each Book contains some allusion to the Queen's excellence in the quality "sette forth" within it or her relation to the allegorical structure through which the virtues function. Because of Elizabeth's conceptual centrality in Spenser's work, as well as the different modes in which the references are made, they are never reduced to an entirely conventional expression. In the induction to the First Book, Spenser does not elaborate on the virtue of holiness; indeed, he invokes the Muses and three pagan deities--Venus, Cupid, and Mars--before addressing the Queen, who is the nearest thing to an object of Christian veneration that he includes:

> And with them eke, O Goddesse heauenly bright,
>   Mirrour of grace and Maiestie diuine,
>   Great Lady of the greatest Isle, whose light

---

[6] Letter to Raleigh, p. 486.

> Like Phoebus lampe throughout the world doth
>   shine,
> Shed thy faire beames into my feeble eyne,
> And raise my thoughts too humble and too vile,
> To thinke of that true glorious type of thine,
> The argument of mine afflicted stile:
> The which to heare, vouchsafe, O dearest dred
>   a-while.
>   (I.Induction.4)

The Second Book is introduced by the famous apologia for the invention of Faery-land, with its reference to newly-discovered lands (significantly including the Amazon and Virginia) that previous generations would have considered equally imaginary. He then proceeds to discuss his use of allegory in this connection:

> And thou, O fairest Princesse vnder sky,
> In this faire mirrhour maist behold thy face,
> And thine owne realmes in lond of Faery,
> And in this antique Image thy great auncestry.
>
> The which O pardon me thus to enfold
>   In couert vele, and wrap in shadowes light,
> That feeble eyes your glory may behold,
> Which else could not endure those beames
>   bright,
> But would be dazled with exceeding light.
>   (II.Induction.4-5)

When he comes to the Book of Chastity, Spenser recognizes that he is dealing with the quality most directly built into the Queen's public myth, and he is explicit about that virtue's relation to her and hers to the poem:

> It falls me here to write of Chastity,
>   That fairest vertue, farre aboue the rest;
>   For which what neeeds me fetch from Faery
>   Forreine ensamples, it to haue exprest?
>   Sith it is shrined in my Soueraines brest,
>   And form'd so liuely in each perfect part,
>   That to all Ladies, which haue it profest,
>   Need but behold the pourtraict of her hart,
> If pourtrayd it might be by any liuing art.
> ....
> But if in liuing colours, and right hew,
>   Your selfe you couet to see pictured,
>   Who can it doe more liuely, or more trew,
>   Then that sweet verse, with Nectar sprinckeled,
>   In which a gracious seruant pictured
>   His Cynthia, his heauens fairest light?
>   That with his melting sweetnesse rauished,
>   And with the wonder of her beames bright
> My senses lulled are in slomber of delight.
>
> But let that same delitious Poet lend
>   A little leaue vnto a rusticke Muse
>   To sing his mistresse Prayse, and let him mend,
>   If ought amis her liking may abuse:
>   Ne let his fairest Cynthia refuse,
>   In mirrours more then one her selfe to see,
>   But either Gloriana let her chuse,
>   Or in Belphoebe fashioned to bee;
> In th'one her rule, in th'other her rare
>   chastitee.
>   (III.Induction.1,4-5)

Elizabeth's role in the Book of Friendship is more directly spiritual than it was in that of Holinesse. Spenser begins by speaking of love as a serious part of statecraft and other weighty concerns, not a diversion from them. The "Stoicke censours" who fail to understand this, therefore, are not the audience to whom he sings:

> But to that sacred Saint my soueraigne Queene,
> In whose chast breast all bountie naturall,
> And treasures of true loue enlocked beene,
> Boue all her sexe that euer yet was seene;
> To her I sing of loue, that loueth best,
> And best is lou'd of all aliue I weene:
> To her this song most fitly is addrest,
> The Queene of loue, and Prince of peace from
>   heauen blest.
>   (IV.Induction.4)

The prologue to Book V is somewhat longer, encompassing Spenser's theories about both history and government, as well as the origins of Justice itself. In the last stanza, he turns from this "most sacred vertue" to its most sacred embodiment:

> Dread Souerayne Goddesse, that doest highest sit
>   In seate of iudgement, in th'Almighties stead,
>   And with magnificke might and wondrous wit
>   Doest to thy people righteous doome aread,
>   That furthest Nations filles with awfull dread,
>   Pardon the boldnesse of thy basest thrall,
>   That dare discourse of so diuine a read,
>   As thy great iustice praysed ouer all,

Spenser

> The instrument whereof loe here thy Artegall.
> (V.Induction.11)

Finally, the Book of Courtesy opens with an apostrophe to the Queen that draws together a number of the themes that have occurred in the various inductions:

> But where shall I in all Antiquity
>   So faire a patterne finde, where may be seene
>   The goodly praise of Princely curtesie,
>   As in your selfe, O soueraine Lady Queene,
>   In whose pure minde, as in a mirrour sheene,
>   It showes, and with her brightnesse doth inflame
>   The eyes of all, which thereon fixed beene;
>   But meriteth indeed an higher name,
> Yet so from low to high vplifted is your name.
>
> Then pardon me, most dreaded Soueraine,
>   That from your selfe I doe this vertue bring,
>   And to your selfe doe it returne againe:
>   So from the Ocean all riuers spring,
>   And tribute backe repay as to their King.
>   Right so from you all goodly vertues well
>   Into the rest, which round about you ring,
>   Faire Lords and Ladies, which about you dwell,
> And doe adorne your Court, where courtesies excell.
> (VI.Induction.6-7)

In all of these passages, Spenser makes it clear that he is doing more than paying lip-service to the preeminence of Elizabeth as an ideological and moral force. Rather, he states her connection to his theme and to his symbolic approach, employing her simultaneously as subject and image. It is a method that requires both effort and caution in the interpretation, but one that creates the foundation for the kind of interaction between individual qualities and larger public or historical forces that I perceive as the substance of the poem.

The Female of the Species

The long cycles of human and natural history constitute one of Spenser's overriding concerns in The Faerie Queene. Moreover, the motif that creates the framework for each Book of the romance-epic involves a quest and a journey to its fulfillment. Motion through time and space thus shapes the poem's entire content. Yet Spenser's method and style encourage descriptions of his work that stress its pictorial and static qualities. My interpretation is based on a similar assumption about the formal nature of the poem: I proceed as if reading The Faerie Queene were rather like putting together a jigsaw puzzle, each of whose pieces has its own internal consistency and integrity, but little apparent relation to the others, until all the pieces are in place and the whole interlocking design is apparent. Thus, having discussed the historical-dynastic thrust of the poem and its particular relation to Elizabeth, I realize that the next cluster of issues I propose to discuss, the roles and politics Spenser associates with gender, seems almost like a new beginning, unconnected to what went before.

Spenser's system involves a fixed set of polarities between masculine and feminine qualities or attributes. He makes use of these concepts as if they were forces of nature, capable of being dedicated to good ends or perverted to evil ones, but nonetheless fully defined and stable in themselves. Like Ariosto and Tasso, he presents a wide range of feminine types and female possibility. But, whereas the two Italian poets present such a range in order to explore questions about its scope and content, he considers those questions already answered. Spenser includes so much material about women characters and the character of woman in The Faerie Queene because he is trying to redress the imbalance of natural forces that has been falsely imposed upon human society.

The notion of balance is central to the development of Spenser's ideology as it is communicated in the poem. And it is clear, throughout, that, as in the Orlando furioso and the Gerusalemme liberata, it is intimately linked to the nature of the female character and to the relations, both personal and institutional, between the sexes. What is not clear from Spenser's treatment of the matter is whether he believes, as he seems to be saying part of the time, that the ideal balance of an individual psyche or the state comes from its harmonious inclusion of qualities represented in his female characters, or whether, as he appears to be saying the rest of the time, a single female character like Britomart can already embody in herself the perfect equilibrium of gender-defined forces and thus not be an element in the establishment of balance, but actually be ideally balanced. In the middle Books of the poem, where the issue arises most forcibly, a tension is maintained between the two positions.

Although Spenser's principal focus has to do with balance--however ambiguously defined--his attention in the poem is to the female side of the equation. Masculine character and characteristics tend to be defined negatively or through contrasts with what is feminine or what is balanced.

His emphasis on the feminine experience is one of the ways that Spenser attempts, within the argumentative structure of the poem, to compensate for a prevalent literary and political model of society that is based on an unexamined masculine norm.

As I have observed, however, Spenser is never interested in presenting a number of feminine types in order to define femininity; he knows what he means by the concept, and the function of that theme in his narrative is on a more theoretical--or even philosophical--level. Furthermore, though femininity is a ubiquitous notion in The Faerie Queene, strongly presented and urged by vivid, memorable characters, the tacit definition with which Spenser appears to be working is a passive or a negative one. For example, the poet does his best to present chastity as a positive, indeed aggressive virtue. In linking it to marriage and providential generation, he makes it clear that chastity means the regulation of sexual life, not abstention from it. And, in the persons of Belphoebe and Britomart, it has exemplars and defenders who are certainly active and forceful people.

But Britomart is most forceful when she is Britomart, not when she is Chastity. In those instances where her purity enables her to accomplish something that a male knight, morally incapacitated by his sexuality, cannot do, Britomart seems to represent an ideal that is not simply chaste, but asexual. She never succumbs to the temptations of the flesh because she is never tempted. We see her almost overcome by love before Merlin explains the origin and purpose of her feelings, and we see her bearing her sorrow within her even after she undertakes her quest. Once she is betrothed to Arthegall and her sexual energy is more focused, we see her give way to irrational jealousy when she learns that he is with Radigund; it is only after she has vented her immediate feelings that she is able to hear out the story of her lover's captivity and form the determination to rescue him. Emotional restraint, in short, is not Britomart's strong point, only sexual restraint, and that within rather narrowly conceived limits.

Chastity is the only virtue represented by a female knight and, in the Induction to Book Three, it is explicitly identified as a feminine attribute. Obviously, if it is to be understood in a positive sense, it has to be apprehended and practiced by both sexes. But in its proper exercise and its extreme excesses, it is portrayed as applying only to women. Moreover, those very excesses constitute part of Spenser's underlying definition of femininity, for the imposition on young women of responsibility for their own chastity leads to a degree of fearfulness and shrinking that clearly cripples them as people and that certainly, to keep the argument in Spenserian terms, stunts their moral development. Spenser seems to acknowledge this in his depiction of Amoret's responses, for she shrinks from Scudamour, at first, quite as much as she does from Busirane. Her lover relates how he won her, admitting that

> She often prayd, and often me besought,
> > Sometime with tender teares to let her goe
> > Sometime with witching smyles: but yet for
> > > nought,
> > That euer she to me could say or doe,
> > Could she her wished freedome fro me wooe
> > > (IV.x.57)

Even more exaggerated is Florimell's reaction to almost every male she encounters. Her fear of sexual assault is so great that it deranges her mind and makes her suspend her judgment. All men are attracted to Florimell, but in some she arouses the desire to rape, in others the desire to protect her; the terror into which she is cast by the need to preserve her chastity and avoid violence renders the young beauty incapable of distinguishing between good men and evil. This is a state of affairs that Spenser's values would normally cause him to deplore in the strongest terms. The two young women, moreover, do not actually learn anything in the course of their experiences. Their stories end with their being united in loving marriages, but this has not come about through any progressive development in their understanding or, indeed, through any agency of their own.

In his portrayal of Amoret and Florimell, Spenser appears to be saying something about imbalance and excess in individual terms that would complement his views about imbalance in social and institutional situations. But it is not entirely clear that he considers their hysteria excessive. The emphasis, throughout, is on female modesty and "shamefastness" carried to a degree that would be pathological if interpreted literally. In fact, however, there is no display of feminine modesty in the poem, however wrongheaded or misdirected, that the poet criticizes or condemns. Personification of this attribute is always in a female form and, indeed, she is one of the "beuie of fayre damzels" grouped with Womanhood at Venus' feet

> ...next to her sate goodly Shamefastnesse,
> Ne euer durst her eyes from ground vpreare,
> Ne euer once did looke vp from her desse,
> As if some blame of euill she did feare,
> That in her cheekes made roses oft appeare
> (IV.x.50)

Guyon, whose own modesty is part of his nature as the Knight of Temperance, is nonetheless astonished at the timidity of one of the damsels at the House of Alma and fears that he has unintentionally affronted her. Alma's explanation sets out the two sexes' relationship to the virtue and, through it, to each other, as well as, perhaps, to other predominantly "feminine" qualities. Guyon begins by asking how he has offended, but

> She answerd nought, but more abasht for shame,
>   Held downe her head, the whiles her louely face
>   The flashing bloud with blushing did inflame,
>   And the strong passion mard her modest grace,
>   That Guyon meruayld at her vncouth cace:
> Till Alma him bespake, Why wonder yee
>   Faire Sir at that, which ye so much embrace?
>   She is the fountaine of your modestee;
> You shamefast are, but Shamefastnesse it selfe is shee.
>
>   (II.ix.43)

In examining Spenser's apparent preference for the negative or "froward" aspects of womanly comportment over the more active ones, one might also consider the way he describes the adoption of Crysogone's infant daughters by two goddesses. Diana names her child Belphoebe, after that aspect of her own personality most closely associated with her chastity, taking her "to be vpbrought in perfect Maydenhed." Venus, meanwhile, names the other twin Amoretta, after the vagrant Cupid who has run away from her and about whose behavior, unsupervised, she is most uneasy. She takes the child "to be vpbrought in goodly womanhed." (Both III.vi.28; emphasis added.) There is a qualitative—indeed, a spiritual--difference between the two adjectives that aptly conveys a sense (the Garden of Adonis and Spenser's views on marriage notwithstanding) of the relative merits of the two modes of life they represent.

The same priorities determine the alteration in Britomart's character after she is betrothed to Arthegall. She was his equal in chivalry while her love remained one-sided, but, once her beloved shares her feelings and enters into an engagement with her, she sits quietly at home and awaits his return from active duty. Her clinging to him before his departure is "feminine" behavior in the pejorative literary sense, though even here she does not plead with him to take her along and he does not think to invite her.

It is true, of course, that Britomart's assignment is rather different from that of the other knights, since even her major chivalric feats--the rescue of Amoret, for example--are incidental to her goal, which is to win Arthegall. She does, however, undertake various knightly tasks and contests, performing most creditably in all of them, and these accomplishments are not ideologically incidental. Although she never loses sight of her goal, she clearly enjoys knight-errantry as a way of life, and it is rather surprising to see her revert to a more traditional female role as soon as she has got her man. The plot of Book Five, to be sure, demands that she not be present when Arthegall meets and is defeated by Radigund, but it does not require her to be doing nothing in the meantime. (Bradamante's behavior, as she spends almost the entire length of the Furioso waiting for Ruggiero, is one model of how a betrothed lady warrior might be passing the time.) In the Fifth Book, Britomart's conduct as a soldier is meant as a contrast--and reproach--to both Radigund and Arthegall, and as such it is surely sufficient. If anything, her having to come out of "womanly" retirement in order to defeat Radigund confuses the issue, because it makes it harder to discern <u>which</u> qualities of hers are actually brought to bear in her triumph over the Amazon.

But the behavior, active or passive, of a woman warrior is necessarily an exception to the female condition. By contrast, the most common action performed by women in <u>The Faerie Queene</u> is the making of peace. When their ladies encourage Blandamour and Paridell to fight to the death, Spenser remarks that

> ...that which is for Ladies most besitting,
> To stint all strife, and foster friendly peace,
> Was from those Dames so farre, and so
> vnfitting,
> As that in stead of praying them surcease,
> They did much more their cruelty encrease.
> (IV.ii.19)

It is more usual for one of Spenser's women to stop men from fighting, even when she is the subject of their quarrel. Motives and methods mark the principal difference between different women. Phaedria, for instance, interposes her body between Guyon and Cymochles and exhorts them to relinquish their duel. The kind of contest she proposes as a substitute is one that Spenser himself could hardly endorse:

> Another warre, and other weapons I
> Doe loue, where loue does giue his sweet
> alarmes,
> Without bloudshed, and where the enemy
> Does yeeld vnto his foe a pleasant victory.

> Debatefull strife, and cruell enmitie
>   The famous name of knighthood fowly shend;
> But louely peace, and gentle amitie,
> And in Amours the passing houres to spend,
> The mightie martiall hands doe most commend;
> Of loue they euer greater glory bore,
> Then of their armes: Mars is Cupidoes frend,
> And is for Venus loues renowmed more,
> Then all this wars and spoiles, the which he did
>   of yore.
>   (II.vi.34-35)

Although the lady's "mirthful" description of amorous encounters is not consistent with Spenser's elevated sexual code, he accords her peace-making endeavors the same respect he would show to entreaties made on a different basis. It is her sex and what is due it, rather than any specific arguments, that carry conviction, and Spenser describes the result in most conventional courtly terms:

> ...They though full bent
> To proue extremities of bloudie fight,
> Yet at her speach their rages gan relent,
> And calme the sea of their tempestuous spight,
> Such powre haue pleasing words: such is the
>   might
> Of courteous clemencie in gentle hart.
>   (II.vi.36)

Sometimes it takes more than exhortations, however. The arrival of the beautiful Cambina in a chariot drawn by two lions creates the briefest of pauses in the duel between her beloved Cambell and her brother Triamond. They greet her and return to their combat; she is thus forced to escalate her means of persuasion, employing first human and then supernatural techniques:

> They lightly her requit (for small delight
>   They had as then her long to entertaine,)
>   And eft them turned both againe to fight,
>   Which when she saw, downe on the bloudy plaine
>   Herselfe she threw, and teares gan shed amaine;
>   Amongst her teares immixing prayers meeke,
>   And with her prayers reasons to restraine
>   From blouddy strife, and blessed peace to
>   seeke,
> By all that vnto them was deare, did them beseeke.
>
> But when as all might nought with them preuaile
>   Shee smote them lightly with her powrefull
>   wand.
>   Then suddenly as if their hearts did faile,
>   Their wrathfull blades downe fell out of their
>   hand,
>   And they like men astonisht still did stand.
>   Thus whilest their minds were doubtfully
>   distraught
>   And mighty spirites bound with mightier band,
>   Her golden cup to them for drinke she raught,
> Whereof full glad for thirst, ech drunk an harty
>   draught.
>
> Of which so soone as they once tasted had,
>   Wonder it is that sudden change to see:
>   Instead of strokes, each other kissed glad,
>   And louely haulst from fare of treason free,

And plighted hands for euer friends to be.
(IV.iii.47-49)

The female, according to Spenser, is "soft and tender...by kynde." As such, her most characteristic activity is the prevention of violence, the exhortation to settle disputes by peaceful reason and love.

The Dialectic of Gender

That remark of Spenser's about the character of woman is actually more ambiguous than my brief excerpt admits. For his full description involves not only the static "nature" of the sex, but the social context in which it is displayed. The stanzas in which the poet makes these observations are apparently conventional in expression. They represent, however, the nucleus of a complex and frequently contradictory set of atttitudes about the politics of relations between men and women:

> Ye gentle Ladies, in whose soueraine powre
> Loue hath the glory of his kingdome left,
> And th'hearts of men, as your eternall dowre,
> In yron chaines, of liberty bereft,
> Deliuered hath into your hands by gift;
> Be well aware, how ye the same doe vse,
> That pride doe not to tyranny you lift;
> Least if men you of cruelty accuse,
> He from you take that chiefedome, which ye doe abuse.
>
> And as ye soft and tender are by kynde,
> Adornd with goodly gifts of beauties grace,

Spenser

> So be ye soft and tender eeke in mynde;
> But cruelty and hardnesse from you chace,
> That all your other praises will deface,
> And from you turne the loue of men to hate.
> (VI.viii.1-2)

The power and sovereignty that women exercise in the realm of love is conditional on their not abusing it and thus offending the God who created it. Moreover, the way not to abuse it is not to exercise it. Being "soft and tender...in mynde," eschewing "cruelty and hardnesse" means granting to the male the same sovereignty in sexual relations that he enjoys in all other areas of life. More to the point, it means acknowledging that the conventions of courtly literature are no more than figures of spech, metaphors increasingly inappropriate to interpersonal relations in sixteenth-century society.

The poet's position on the whole question is somewhat more dialectical than this passage would imply. It is dialectical in containing mutually contradictory views and also in perceiving the resolution in contradictory terms. Spenser is preoccupied by the concept of balance between masculine and feminine elements, but, as I have indicated, he wavers between representing balance as an interaction of those elements as they occur in the two sexes and representing them as an androgynous ideal exemplified in a single person. The matter is further complicated by the conflicts he experiences with regard to certain crucial aspects of female nature. On the one hand, he states that, because men have controlled the means of expression, women's achievements have historically not been accorded their proper place of respect, and that male domination of society has now greatly limited the opportunities for such accomplishments:

> Here haue I cause, in man iust blame to find,
>   That in their proper prayse too partiall bee,
> And not indifferent to woman kind,
> To whom no share in armes and cheualrie
> They do impart, ne maken memorie
> Of their braue gestes and prowesse martiall;
> Scarse do they spare to one or two or three,
> Rowme in their writs; yet the same writing small
> Does all their deeds deface, and dims their glories all.
>
> But by record of antique times I find,
>   That women wont in warres to bear most sway,
> And to all great exploits them selues inclind:
> Of which they still the girlond bore away,
> Till enuious Men fearing their rules decay,
> Gan coyne streight lawes to curb their liberty;
> Yet sith they warlike armes haue layd away,
> They haue exceld in artes and pollicy,
> That now we foolish men that prayse gin eke t'enuy.
>   (III.ii.1-2)

In addition to recording women's achievements in the spheres that men have taken for their own, Spenser clearly places a high value on the more traditionally feminine activities and characteristics. His comprehensive idea of doing justice to the sex is to give credit for public actions, but also to assimilate the private ones and the personal qualities that inform them into the public world.

Spenser

At the same time, Spenser is clearly uneasy with what he most admires about the eternal feminine. The gentleness, the willingness to be guided by emotion, the yielding softness, the warmth he associates with femininity at its best are inextricably linked with the intrinsic instability of womankind. Mutabilitie herself is a female--a warlike one, at that--and in describing her Spenser makes use of all the conventions about women's changeability in both body and mind. The idea of constant change--decay, even if followed by renewal--is one for which Spenser evinces the deepest moral and spiritual repugnance. The concluding fragment of the poem as we have it fully expresses both his feelings and his fervor:

> When I bethinke me on that speech whyleare,
>   Of Mutability, and well it way:
>   Me seemes, that though she all vnworthy were
>   Of the Heav'ns Rule; yet very sooth to say,
>   In all things else she beares the greatest
>   sway.
>   Which makes me loath this state of life so
>   tickle,
>   And loue of things so vaine to cast away;
>   Whose flowring pride, so fading and so fickle
> Short Time shall soon cut down with his consuming
>   sickle.
>
> Then gin I thinke on that which Nature sayd,
>   Of that same time when no more Change shall be,
>   But stedfast rest of all things firmely stayd
>   Vpon the pillours of Eternity,
>   That is contrayr to Mutabilitie:
>   For, all that moueth, doth in Change delight:

> But thence-forth all shall rest eternally
> With Him that is the God of Sabbaoth hight:
> O that great Sabbaoth God, graunt me that Sabaoths sight.
>
> (VII,viii.1-2)

The declaration in which he puts his faith is Nature's assertion of her own just rule:

> But time shall come that all shall changed bee,
> And from thenceforth, none no more change shall see.
>
> (VII.vii.59)

Now, not merely Spenser's own personification, but the entire catalogue of conventional wisdom identifies the female with instability, motion, mutability, and change, the male with stability, immobility, immutability, and firmness. Moreover, that flexibility is, as I have indicated, the very source of what the poet most values and wishes to glorify in the feminine constitution. In the materials and design of Alma's castle, the elements are ideally combined, but form, by definition, a temporary structure. It is

> Not built of bricke, ne yet of stone and lime,
> But of thing like to that Aegyptian slime,
> Whereof king Nine whilome built Babel towre,
> But O great pitty, that no lenger time
> So goodly workemanship should not endure:
> Soone it must turne to earth; no earthly thing is sure.
>
> The frame thereof seemed partly circulare,

> And part triangulare, O worke diuine;
> Those two the first and last proportions are,
> The one imperfect, mortall, foeminine;
> Th'other immortall, perfect, masculine.
>   (II.ix.21-22)

The allegorical representations, here, are most elaborate, particularly since one reads the passage in a context that constructs several levels of interlocking symbolism. Alma's castle, standing as it does for the body that harbors the human spirit, is built on a plan that unites masculine steadfastness with feminine flexibility. It is, at best, a delicate balance, and Spenser realizes that that means no balance at all, for combining the changeable with the immutable means that the whole mixture unavoidably takes on the tendency to impermanence. (This is the same reasoning that makes Virgil, Tasso, and Spenser apply the term "effeminate" to men engaged in illicit heterosexual relationships. At a time and in a situation where their heroes are certainly demonstrating their virility, the poets argue that the indulgence of passion and, for that matter, the entire business of pleasing a woman sexually makes one more *like* a woman.) In the architectonic metaphor, the temporary nature of the equilibrium is symbolized by the use of a building material that soon will cause the whole structure to crumble back to earth. If true balance is to be attained, it must be through means beyond the flesh.

A number of events and images throughout the poem testify to Spenser's sense of outrage at those who threaten the existing sexual balance. Sometimes the menace comes from a reversal of sex roles or even of gender-linked characteristics, sometimes as an attack on the equilibrium of an individual constitution. In the otherwise rather confusing episode concerning the death of Ruddymane's parents, for instance, Nelson perceives their fate as resulting from a contradiction between their sex-defined character and their present behavior. Thus, since the husband succumbs to lust and the wife to aggressive jealousy, what happens is that "the bold, forward male dies through weakness, the weak, retiring female through bold fury."[7]

Again, in one of several passages in which Spenser examines the nature of avarice, the woman Munera, who is an accomplice, but by no means the instigator, in a money-gouging operation, comes in for exceptionally strong censure. Her sex is responsible for her being so heavily blamed, in that gross materialism signifies a greater fall in her than it would for a man. Woman's nature is supposed to lead her to human concerns, and a preoccupation with wealth and power directly violates the feminine mission and hence the unstable equilibrium of the natural world.

Arthegall's first encounter in Book Five ends with his avenging another kind of imbalance, one that has been aptly called "a crime against the fullness of the psyche."[8] The Knight of Justice pursues Sir Sanglier, whose name reflects his brutal nature. Seeing a lady he liked better than his own, Sanglier offered to trade with the knight escorting the more attractive one, and when this was refused, threw the one lady off his horse, snatched up the other and made a break. The other knight tells Arthegall what followed:

> Which when his Ladie saw, she follow'd fast,

---

[7] Nelson, p. 190.

[8] Elizabeth Bieman, "Britomart in Book V of The Faerie Queene," University of Toronto Quarterly, 37 (1968), 159.

> And on him catching hold, gan loud to crie
> Not so to leaue her, nor away to cast,
> But rather of his hand besought to die.
> With that his sword he drew all wrathfully,
> And at one stroke cropt off her head with scorne,
> In that same place whereas it now doth lie.
>
> (V.i.18)

If the lady may be thought to contain her "masculine" elements in her head, what Sanglier does in committing this murder and severing mind from body is to tear "the balancing masculine function from woman."[9] (I need not elaborate, I hope, on the fact that what Sanglier does is a literal, as well as a figurative crime, and that in the narrative he is punished for decapitating the lady, not for destroying psychic balance.)

Because of the discontinuity in Spenser's thought between social and personal balance, it is useful to consider the views expressed in The Faerie Queene about both spheres. On the public level, the practices of Radigund and her Amazon troops afford an example of what can happen when government is founded on an "unnatural" sexual order. On the plane of individual consciousness and behavior, The Faerie Queene is full of cautionary tales about people who either assume the habits of the opposite sex or, what is equally wrong, betray an immoderate preponderance of the qualities associated with their own. Over and against both kinds of error is an androgynous ideal, as expressed in the tentative image of the hermaphrodite and the character of Britomart.

The major instance of injustice in the Fifth Book of

---

[9] Ibid.

The _Faerie_ _Queene_ is the Amazon rule of Radigund. It is one of those cases where there is an apparent interaction between the image and what it symbolizes, such that power relations between the sexes, being accepted by Spenser's readers as a natural fact, serve to show what happens when the natural hierarchy is violated. At the same time, the disorder and tyranny that result from the Amazon hegemony serve to reinforce the received assumptions about the appropriate balance of power between the sexes.

Although the framework and the metaphor are political --as is Spenser's basic motivation--there is a direct connection made between the injustice being enacted and the sin of lust, the absence of chaste moderation. Radigund's vendetta against the male sex originates in a frustrated love that presumably remained unrequited because she pursued it too aggressively:

> The cause, they say, of this her cruell hate,
>   Is for the sake of Bellodant the bold,
>   To whom she bore most feruent loue of late,
>   And wooed him by all the waies she could:
>   But when she saw at last, that he ne would
>   For ought or nought be wonne vnto her will,
>   She turn'd her loue to hatred manifold,
>   And for his sake vow'd to doe all the ill
> Which she could doe to Knights, which now she doth fulfill.
>
> (V.iv.30)

Once she holds Arthegall captive, she is sexually attracted to him and attempts to win _him_ over. Spenser calls this feeling lust and one reason it is an illicit emotion is that her feelings do not subdue her "pride" and make her willing

Spenser

to be dominated by him, as is "right" in this relation:

> The warlike Amazon,
> Whose wandring fancie after lust did raunge,
> Gan cast a secret liking to this captiue straunge.
>
> Which long concealing in her couert brest,
> She chaw'd the cud of louers carefull plight;
> Yet could it not so thoroughly digest,
> Being fast fixed in her wounded spright,
> But it tormented her both day and night:
> Yet would she not thereto yeeld free accord,
> To serue the lowly vassall of her might,
> And of her seruant make her souerayne Lord:
> So great her pride, that she such basenesse much abhord.
>   (V,v.26-27)

It is Clarin's lust for Arthegall, moreover, that foils Radigund's harsh wooing.

Nor is Arthegall exempt from the illicit passion, for, although his imprisonment opens his eyes to Radigund's true nature and he is not tempted to win his "freedom" as she would wish, it was not always so. He was originally defeated in a scene that parallels and parodies his enamorment with Britomart, in which he is unmanned by the discovery of Radigund's beauty. Spenser summarizes the sexual and political situation that results:

> So was he ouercome, not ouercome,
> But to her yeelded of his owne accord.
>   (V.v.17)

333

Spenser obviously considers this servitude a violation of the proper order of things. For woman to be the master of man is itself a perversion. It is less simple, however, to identify what the poet considers the natural condition. Some commentators maintain that Britomart's role in Book Five means that the goal is not a complete reversal of the situation, but a correction of it. According to this interpretation, Britomart represents an ideal that is distorted by Radigund and her followers, the ideal of "woman as equal and companion of man."[10] As my discussion of Britomart will show, I do not believe that this is the lady knight's significance; she is, rather, a cluster of uneasy contradictions and is intended as an exception to the female condition, not a norm for it.

The Radigund episode itself points to a less liberal conclusion. Radigund is a tyrant, and Spenser makes it clear that her unjust rule originates in the more fundamental sexual injustice that placed state power in her hands:

> Such is the crueltie of womenkynd,
> When they haue shaken off the shamefast band,
> With which wise Nature did them strongly bynd,
> T'obay the heasts of mans well ruling hand,
> That then all rule and reason they withstand,
> To purchase a licentious libertie.
> But vertuous women wisely vnderstand,
> That they were borne to base humilitie,
> Vnlesse the heauens them lift to lawfull
>   soueraintie.
>   (V.v.25)[11]

---

[10] Harry Berger, "Faerie Queene Book III: A General Description," *Criticism*, 11 (1969), 252.

Women's unfitness to govern is linked not only to their sex, but to their sexuality. Aggressive seizure of power is a crime against feminine chastity, and it is bound to result in sexual license--an impression that is enhanced by the previous stanza's comparison of Arthegall's position with Hercules' willing slavery:

> In which forgetting warres, he onely ioyed
> In combats of sweet loue, and with his mistresse toyed.
> (V.v.24)

The shamefastness that accompanied Amoret while she sat in the lap of Womanhood awaiting fulfillment as a virtuous wife is now revealed as not simply a personal but a political attribute. As it was the chief virtue of the individual woman in guiding her relations with men, so too is it the chief virtue of the female sex in its collective or social manifestations.

It is for this reason, of course, that Britomart's role in the episode is so significant, for the Knight of Chastity is the only one who can render true justice in such a situation. Her function as the exemplar of chastity is what makes Britomart a Good Woman and thus able to overcome the lustful Amazon; Britomart's chastity also ofers the only salvation for Arthegall once he is entangled in the toils of lust. Politically, however, there is no implication that the Britomarts of the world have a more legitimate claim to

---

[11] Most scholars agree that the reference to "lawfull soueraintie" for some women is a sop to Elizabeth. On Spenser's use of exceptional females to "prove" otherwise oppressive rules, see Ellen Cantarow, "A Wilderness of Opinions Confounded: Allegory and Ideology," College English, 34 (1972), especially pp. 232-4.

rule than the Radigunds. In fact, the equation of female sovereignty with unchastity makes such a claim logically impossible.

When Britomart fights Radigund, the contest is very different from the one that Arthegall loses. For one thing, the lady knight contemptuously rejects Radigund's "streight conditions" and will fight only according to the established and just rules of knighthood:

> For her no other termes should euer tie
> Then what prescribed were by lawes of cheualrie.
> (V.vii.28)

There is a great deal of sexual reference in the duel itself. Both women lose control and allow sheer force to replace martial skill. In their ferocity, which Spenser compares to that of a tiger and a lioness, they

> spared not
> Their dainty parts, which nature had created
> So faire and tender, without staine or spot,
> For other vses, then they them translated;
> Which now they hackt and hewd, as if such vse they hated
> (V.vii.29)[12]

Similarly, Radigund reveals the nature of her passion when she strikes Britomart, saying:

---

[12] "Though Britomart fights by manly rules, this struggle agianst another woman bears little resemblance to her jousts against male adversaries," Bieman, pp. 170-71.

> This token beare
> Vnto the man, whom thou doest loue so deare;
> And tell him for his sake thy life thou gauest.
> Which spitefull words she sore engrieu'd to heare,
> Thus answer'd; Lewdly thou my loue deprauest,
> Who shortly must repent that now so vainely brauest.
> (V.vii.32)

Britomart's symbolic function and its political limitations are best revealed in the description of how she restores justice to the land after she accomplishes the downfall of Radigund's tyranny. While she and Arthegall are recuperating from their respective experiences at Radigund's hands

> she there as Princess rained,
> And changing all that forme of common weale,
> The liberty of women did repeale,
> Which they had long vsurpt; and them restoring
> To mens subjection, did true Iustice deale:
> That they all as a Goddesse her adoring,
> Her wisedome did admire, and hearkned to her loring.
> (V.vii.42)

It is significant, of course, that, in her capacity as both princess and goddess, Britomart acts to restore power to men, placing Arthegall on the throne and making "magistrates" of the knights who had been his fellow-prisoners.

An important aspect of the Radigund episode is its emphasis on the reversal of gender roles through the symbolic assignment of female clothing and "women's work" to Arthegall. This penalty reflects the general "unnaturalness" of political domination by the wrong sex and, at the same time, emphasizes the function of misdirected sexuality in that situation. On one level, because of the way Arthegall is taken captive, his story may represent "the diversion of the gentleman from his proper work in the world by the power of feminine beauty."[13] At the same time, it reinforces the idea that a man who succumbs to lust for a woman becomes womanish. Mercury's taunts to Aeneas in Carthage and his comrades' demonstration to Rinaldo in Armida's garden are expressed here through the ignominious transfer of apparel and labor. At this point, Arthegall really is a member of the weaker sex.

Britomart, who spends so much of her time in male attire, is not only shocked but deeply ashamed to see her beloved in female garments. She knows that he has been defeated, imprisoned, and enslaved, that he could not have been saved without her help, yet it takes the evidence of his "womanishe attire" for her to understand that he has also been <u>unmanned</u>:

> At sight thereof abasht with secrete shame,
> She turnd her head aside, as nothing glad,
> To haue beheld a spectacle so bad:
> And then too well beleeu'd, that which tofore
> Iealous suspect as true vntruely drad,
> Which vaine conceipt now nourishing no more,
> She sought with ruth to salue his sad misfortunes sore.

---

[13] Nelson, p. 272.

> ....
> Ah my deare Lord, what sight is this (quoth she)
>   What May-game hath misfortune made of you?
>   Where is that dreadfull manly looke? where be
>   Those mighty palmes, the which ye wont t'embrew
>   In bloud of Kings, and great hoastes to subdew?
>   Could ought on earth so wondrous change haue
>   wrought?
>   As to haue robde you of that manly hew?
>   Could so great courage stouped haue to ought?
> Then farewell fleshly force; I see thy pride is
>   nought.
>   (V.vii.38,40)

Most scholars reject F. S. Boas' contention that transvestism "had an irresistible fascination for the Elizabethans, which we find it difficult to appreciate today."[14] In fact, the implications of cross-dressing are far more complex than that and, in any event, vary according to which sex is wearing the garments of the other and whether the exchange of clothing is voluntary. Britomart's restoration of his clothing to Arthegall is symbolic of restoration of his manhood and hence of his sovereignty. There has been no period in Western culture when loss of manhood held much positive fascination for the majority of men. Britomart in this scene has been compared to a mother dressing her child in the proper clothing. The simile is particularly apt in that if Arthegall has not precisely been feminized upon being temporarily emasculated, he has certainly been infantilized. The scene also adds another dimension to the

---

[14] F. S. Boas, Sir Philip Sidney: Representative Elizabethan (London: Staples Press, 1955), p. 65.

series of men in the middle Books of The Faerie Queene who "are either defeated or rescued by women."[15]

The labor Arthegall is forced to perform is also significant. After he has been dressed in "womans weedes," he is shown the other captive knights at work:

> Spinning and carding all in comely rew,
> That his bigge hart loth'd so vncomely vew.
> But they were forst through penurie and pyne,
> To doe those workes, to them appointed dew:
> For nought was given them to sup or dyne,
> But what their hands could earne by twisting
>   linnen twyne.
>
> Amongst them all she placed him most low,
>   And in his hand a distaffe to him gaue,
> That he thereon should spin both flax and tow;
> A sordid office for a mind so braue.
> So hard it is to be a womans slaue.
>   (V.v.22-23)

According to the social division of labor that Spenser deems natural, it is humiliating for a man to have to do "women's work"--more particularly, to have to do it as a woman's slave. But Arthegall and his companions are not precisely slave-labor, in that they are said to be earning their bread. Theirs is prison-labor and they are wage slaves, probably the first in literature. The significance of this observation ought not to be exaggerated or it may be easily reduced to absurdity. Yet, Spenser might not have multiplied

---

[15] Richard A. Lanham, "The Literal Britomart," Modern Language Quarterly, 28 (1967), 442.

and extended to a whole group of prisoners the single image of Hercules at the distaff, were it not that the mode of textile production in England was rapidly being transformed into something like the factories described in the bourgeois paeans of Thomas Deloney, and that this transformation was bringing about a change in the nature and definition of work itself. What is important about all this for a reading of The Faerie Queene is that Spenser explicitly equates the female sex and people who work for wages, considering the activity appropriate to both groups unworthy of a "mind so braue" as that of an aristocratic soldier.

The Androgynous Potential

Imbalance caused by an improper reversal of sexual forces in the body politic yields only to corrective imbalance in the other direction. Britomart has brought her qualities--epitomized in the chastity she represents--to bear on the situation, but only as a temporary measure. There is apparently no way to retain her feminine attributes and still keep things working in accord with Spenser's idea of Justice. At least not in the Land of the Amazons. But Spenser sometimes seems to imply that the ideal balance of sexual forces is to be attained on a human, not a public scale. The hermaphrodite image that concluded the first edition of Book III (and hence the first published segment of the poem) is of great significance in translating the ideal into the terms of a love relationship. And the character of Britomart, the lady knight, suggests the possibility of uniting the best of both sexes in a single human consciousness.

Harry Berger maintains that, although individual instances are the vehicle, the thematic impetus of Book Three is essentially impersonal--generic and archetypal--in that it is directly related to Spenser's generalizations about the masculine or feminine character:

> The feminine fears and fantasies which contribute to the power of Busirane are not caused by the particular responses of Amoret or Britomart, but by 'wavering wemens wit' in general. They are the products of tendencies inherent in the female psyche and encouraged by the existing climate of customs, institutions, traditions and literature. ...Finally, the problems posed by opposition of chastity and eros in III seem to be those which can be resolved by happy <u>sexual</u> union...Chastity no less than eros aims at the moment of embrace exemplified in the rejected first ending of Book III.[16]

In the long run, the "happy sexual union" to which Berger refers must be portrayed in institutional--and hence in political--terms. Its initial expression, however, is through a static visual image. Britomart has released Amoret from her imprisonment and torture at the hands of Busirane. Scuadmour rushes to his beloved, and the embrace is described in language that freely intermingles the sensuous and spiritual elements of their coming together:

> Lightly he clipt her twixt his armes twaine,
>   And streightly did embrace her body bright,
>   Her body, late the prison of sad paine,
>   Now the sweet lodge of loue and deare delight:

---

[16] Berger, "Faerie Queene Book III," p. 234.

> But she faire Lady ouercommen quight
> Of huge affection, did in pleasure melt,
> And in sweet rauishment pourd out her spright:
> No word they spake, nor earthly thing they felt,
> But like two senceles stocks in long embracement dwelt.
>
> (III.xii.45, 1590 edition)

The simile follows, rendered as graphic as possible by its reference to a particular statue unearthed in the Renaissance period, rather than to the concept of androgyny in general:

> Had ye them seene, ye would haue surely thought
> That they had been that faire Hermaphrodite,
> Which that rich Romane of white marble wrought,
> And in his costly Bath causd to be site:
> So seemd those two, as growne together quite,
> That Britomart halfe enuying their blesse
> Was much empassiond in her gentle sprite,
> And to her selfe oft wisht like happinesse,
> In vaine she wisht, that fate n'ould let her yet possesse.
>
> (III.xii.46, 1590 edition)

By addressing the reader as a possible witness to the scene, then shifting the focus to Britomart, the actual witness, and *her* emotional response to what she sees, Spenser enhances the visual impact of the description itself.

The significance of comparing two lovers at the moment of reunion with an artifact uniting the characteristics of both sexes has been explored from both Christian and neo-

Platonic perspectives. It seems to me most important to underscore Spenser's choice of an image suggesting physical unity and integrity in order to demonstrate how completely the lovers fuse into one. The hermaphrodite, after all, is not a phenomenon that is achieved by <u>combining</u> masculine and feminine features, but one that, possessing both, is greater than the simple sum of its (sexual or spiritual) parts. In their embrace, then, Amoret and Scudamour reflect something that is indivisible, because it is a single whole, not a joining of two other things.

It should be borne in mind that Spenser discarded the five stanzas that originally concluded Book Three and in which the hermaphrodite image is contained. He abandoned the static picture and the sense of at least temporary resolution it conveys, replacing it with a new set of problems that draw us forward into Book Four. The lovers' embrace no longer recalls the ideal blending of sexual opposites because there is no embrace, no reunion. Britomart takes Amoret out of captivity and leads her to the spot where Scudamour was waiting, but the knight has disappeared, and the Book ends on a note of affective and narrative uneasiness. In the Fourth Book, moreover, the reader learns that the initial abduction of Amoret had taken place at the couple's betrothal feast, so that one broken narrative occurs within the framework of a larger unresolved condition. Spenser placed the image of the hermaphrodite before us, and it is not improper to try to understand its function. But he also removed it and any interpretation must take into account that the hermaphrodite is eventually replaced by a situation of narrative instability, where male and female, far from being joined in a single form, are still embroiled in their frustrated quest for one another, caught up in the "desire and pursuit of the whole."

Spenser

In the character of Britomart, Spenser explores the question of an androgynous human nature far more thoroughly than in his more explicit reference to the sculpted hermaphrodite. Although the image of the statue is more ephemeral, its materiality also makes it less ambiguous than the full-scale treatment. That is, the sexual unity of the Roman sculpture is literal and physical; of course, Spenser uses it as a symbol of the spiritual affinity between two lovers who have been restored to one another, but that affinity is itself celebrated by a physical embrace. Now, the statue in Spenser's simile is defined as a hermaphrodite because it possesses sexual parts of both male and female. In the material world and its aesthetic representation there is no doubt about which organs are masculine, which are feminine, and the hermaphrodite itself is a complete and unambiguous figure.

But in the social world these certainties are reversed. There are no qualities of character or temperament that are as unequivocally "feminine" as the vulva or as "masculine" as the penis. As a <u>social</u> category, androgyny, in contrast to hermaphroditism, is always to some extent metaphorical, and the androgynous personality, containing sexual qualities that are ill-defined except in their antithesis to one another, is necessarily ambiguous. The problem for understanding Britomart is whether, in creating her, Spenser demonstrates that he accepts the rigid gender-based definitions of human nature, behavior, and roles that is the origin of androgyny as a social ideal, or whether, on the contrary, his portrayal of the lady knight reflects a new flexibility of sexual definition.

The general effect of allegory in <u>The Faerie Queene</u> is to simplify the already schematic treatment of character that occurs in the traditions of epic and romance. With

Britomart, however, Spenser broaches a far more complex set of issues and problems than has been attempted by the other poets in this vein. To the essential polarity between male and female and the further opposition, within the feminine character, of the "maidenly" and the "womanly" elements, Spenser adds a possible equilibrant in the person of Britomart. Resolution of the tension between Amoret and Belphoebe, respectively the foster-children of Venus and Diana, calls merely for someone who is a fuller person than these rather limited characters. To embody and transcend the contradiction between male and female, however, would require someone superhuman--lacking, among other things, those weaknesses that are intrinsic to Britomart as Spenser presents her. Yet he is able to use the character and her apparently androgynous qualities to explore some basic questions about the nature of both sexes and the way they interact.

Interpretations of Britomart usually begin by underscoring her "femininity." The outline of her character, most commentators agree, may have started on the model of Penthesilea or Camilla, but it has been "feminized on the pattern of Ariosto's Bradamante."[17] Even more than with Bradamante, the "feminization" of this warrior figure is understood as a softening, rather than broadening of her personality. Spenser's martial maid, we are assured, "is no Amazon. Beneath the armour of the Saxon Queen there beats a very tender heart."[18] The range of Britomart's character, however, and the issues the poet engages by means of it, make it difficult to identify that tenderness as her sole

---

[17] Lanham, p. 427.

[18] M. Pauline Parker, The Allegory of the Faerie Queene (Oxford: Oxford University Press, 1960), p. 176.

womanly attribute. If Spenser contributes to a stereotype of femininity it is at least one that incorporates his heroine's moral and physical courage. Indeed, she has been described as harmonizing "sweetness and power in a way that is above all things womanly."[19]

But the contradictions in Britomart's nature cannot be resolved by recourse to a formula about womanhood, because such sentiments do not adequately explain her positive assumption of a masculine identity, along with male clothing and a male role. In this regard, it is worth noting that Britomart is mistaken for a male knight more frequently and for longer periods than any other military heroine. She is involved in many situations in which her sex is revealed only belatedly and a number in which it never is. Moreover, she is the only woman warrior in the literary tradition--be she Amazon leader or lady knight--who has apparently established no reputation in her own right. Thus, there is no equivalent in The Faerie Queene for the scene early in the Furioso where an unknown knight, initially referred to with masculine pronouns, unhorses Sacripante and, after departure, is identified as the much-celebrated Bradamante. Nor is there any analogy to the proud affirmation with which Clorinda's announcment of her identity can constitute in itself a safe-conduct or a challenge. What Spenser creates instead are scenes like the tourney in Book Four, in which Britomart outshines the other knights present and is awarded the prize for manly valor. On the one hand, the poet makes it clear than she genuinely--if temporarily--deserves the title she has won; but, in another sense, her victory is as meaningless as snowy Florimell's being granted the prize for

---

[19] Herbert E. Cox, Edmund Spenser: A Critical Study, University of California Publications in Modern Philology (Berkeley: University of California Press, 1917), p. 198.

womanly beauty. One is left with an impression of sustained and deliberate ambiguity.

Richard Lanham observes that Virgil's Camilla, in so far as she is "three-dimensional" at all is "a kind of Diana. Physically a woman, emotionally she was a man." But in the creation of Britomart, he continues, Spenser was trying "to preserve both emotion and physique of both male and female."[20] His success in this endeavor should not be overestimated, but, as I have indicated, Spenser does take some pains to elaborate a masculine persona for Britomart that embraces physical and temperamental qualities. It is mainly through her military role--that is, through the militancy of her nature, as well as her dress and bearing--that these qualities are expressed. As a woman, she is more fully realized than either Belphoebe or Amoret, whose primary aspects she combines. In the Books Spenser actually produced, she has not yet developed as a wife, the role that would emphasize the side of her personality that bears affinity with Amoret, and thus she is seen principally in her capacity as chaste warrior. But Britomart differs from Belphoebe in that role, as well, not only in being more "feminine," but also in being more "masculine." Some of the polarities within her personality can be understood as applications of conventionally male character structure, although this structure itself is in tension with other contradictions arising out of her femininity. Thus, "the cuteness of the maiden trying to tease Red Cross into praising Arthegall bears only a tenuous relationship to the maiden diseased with passion. And the relation of the martial Britomart to the diseased-with-love one is logical on a

---

[20] Lanham, p. 429.

narrative level only if we think of both as a <u>man</u>."[21]

Spenser's boldness in effecting this fusion is underscored by contrasting Britomart to Bradamante, who also encompasses the languishing maiden and the intrepid warrior within her nature. But, when she is suffering most from her lovesickness, her military involvement in duels unrelated to her immediate preoccupations is perfunctory, whereas her performance is exceptionally forceful in situations where she sees herself as fighting for her love or what it signifies. Indeed, a "modern" aspect of the way Ariosto's heroine practices chivalry is precisely this connection between the cause for which she undertakes a fight and the commitment and energy she displays in it. Except in the confrontation with Radigund, however, Britomart's actions as a soldier are never motivated by her lovelorn condition. Rather, her psychic makeup attempts to combine the elements more directly and consistently. She is always yearning for Arthegall and she is always yearning for a good fight. On the literal level, at least, this kind of behavior and the chivalric situations it implies do tend to be associated with the male personality.

In another sense, however, the military role is as much an adjunct of Britomart's femininity as it is of Bradamante's. For Spenser explicitly recognizes something that has been an unacknowledged theme in the other poems we have been considering: the intimate bond between sexual passion and violence. Britomart embodies that bond in relations between men and women. From this perspective, the differences between Spenser's lady knight and her Ariostan model appear as vivid on the allegorical as on the literal level. That is, Britomart's manner of fulfilling her military role

---

[21] <u>Ibid</u>., p. 436.

and, in particular, the way her militancy articulates with the sexual emotion, is shaped by her being the Knight of Chastity.

In this sense, the aggressive mode is not only compatible with a masculine typology, but is also an expression of basic female experience. The virtue that she possesses and represents is, as Berger points out, "not the only virtue women need; it is fundamental not only because essential, but also because rudimentary. Embattled woman, threatened from within and from the outside, needs this militant virtue if she as well as her lover is to be fulfilled."[22] Britomart figures forth Chastity in the abstract, but there is no suggestion that she represents Woman in any similarly general sense. In fact, the forcefulness of her championship is a magnificent exception to the largely negative expressions of chastity that Spenser allows other female characters.

I think it is sounder, although certainly less provocative, to perceive Britomart's militancy as feminine, in so far as it is a defensive response to her situation. "She protects herself against aggressive male warfare by wearing armor, against aggressive male passion by wearing disguise and against the assaults of eros by using the forms of male aggressiveness as an outlet."[23] It may be that the excess of militant zeal she frequently displays is a result of this defensiveness. And that is an excess, as I think I have indicated, that may be read as either masuline or feminine —or both. Thus, rather startlingly, an aspect of her character that would appear to strengthen one side of the sexual contradiction represented by Britomart may tend, instead, to

---

22 Berger, "Faerie Queene, Book III," pp. 238-9.
23 Ibid., p. 251.

enhance the impression of androgyny that she creates. Even more remarkable is the fact that Spenser has succeeded not only in portraying a character who is, at least at times, plausibly androgynous, but in using that character to represent married love.

One reason for this success is precisely that chaste love, leading, in Christian marriage, to sexual procreation, is an explicit subject of Spenser's poem, whereas the concept of androgyny is an interpretive tool. Nowhere does the poet allude to the idea of the hermaphrodite except in the single discarded simile that has attracted so much attention, and in one image of Venus. Any impression of Britomart's personality as the living expression of the androgynous ideal must be derived by the reader's putting together what Spenser has to say--as it were, discretely-- about its feminine and masculine facets. His achievement is particularly impressive in that he is able to inject into the illustrations of traditionally male or female characteristics some suggestion of the attributes of the other sex, as well.

There are some few passages in which Spenser himself appears to be underscoring his heroine's androgynous nature. Commenting, for instance, on Britomart's ability to resist material temptation, Nelson observes that "as she scorns Marinell's wealth because she possesses that of which it is only a shadow, power, so she is moved not by beauty of appearance but by its essence, beauty of spirit."[24] This remark is meant as an elaboration upon the way that the young warrior combines the womanly and maidenly qualities identified with the two daughters of Chrysogone. The repeated insistence on Britomart's insusceptibility to female

---

[24] Nelson, p. 232.

beauty reminds us that she is a woman herself and thus presumably immune, but tend, nonetheless, on a level beneath the narrative, to evoke admiration for this exercise of "manly" restraint.

Moreover, her contempt for material wealth is couched in similarly masculine terms. She has bested Marinell in battle, and his fall is compared to that of the ox slaughtered for a sacrifice. The references to that creature's "gilden hornes and flowry girlonds" and to the perfumed atmosphere of the temple, seem to identify Britomart's antagonist with his possessions: "So fell proud Marinell vpon the pretious shore." Having conquered its owner, she rides unconcernedly over the jeweled strand and out of the picture, for she

>   would not stay
> For gold, or perles, or pretious stones an
>   howre,
> But them despised all; for all was in her powre.
>   (III.iv.18)

The sexual ambiguity of Britomart's encounter with Marinell is pointed up by the same dramatic irony that comes into play whenever she resists the lures of an attractive woman while only the reader, aware of her true sex, knows that she is not really tempted at all. Here, the superiority of martial and moral power is displayed against a background of Cymoent's grief and confusion. Marinell's mother, by shielding him from sexual encounters, believes she has protected her son from his prophesied defeat at the hands of a woman. Even as she bewails the fate that has overtaken him, it does not occur to her that he has indeed been vanquished by a woman, although by one employing traditionally masculine means of "undoing" a foe.

Most of the scenes in which Britomart appears explore either the "masculine" or the "feminine" side of her character and do not bring them into explicit relation with one another. Thus Lanham, obedient to one of the oldest dogmas in Western literature, describes even the militancy of the literal Britomart as a feminine characteristic, representing "woman's desire to dominate, whether married or not."[25] It seems to me that, even on the literal level, the lady knight evinces no ambitions of this sort. She does not allow Marinell's wealth to tempt or deflect her from her quest and, after she has succeeded in that quest, she regards her mission among the Amazons as one of restoring her man and the rest of his sex to their traditional hegemony.

In this light, Britomart's aggressiveness is not merely the defensive violence required of Chastity in a world defined by masculine sexual aggression. Rather, it is "feminine" because it serves her sexual destiny as the consort of Justice and mother of the Tudors. It is true that she suffers a diminution in the course of the narrative: "she who has been the foremost of human knights is now fully resigned to her womanly role."[26] "Resignation" strikes the wrong note, however, for, from the viewpoint that Spenser himself espouses, Britomart's fate is one that both she and her creator regard as complete personal and ideological fulfillment. Her sense of historical mission, although it is somewhat belatedly attached to her awakened sexuality, makes her actions in behalf of Chastity part of a larger and richer definition of that virtue. Hers is not "the chastity

---

[25] Lanham, p. 440.

[26] Bieman, p. 172.

of Diana, Camilla, or Belphoebe. She is...eager to open herself to the future."[27] Thus, her militancy, her chastity, and her womanliness are not to be understood as three incongruous facets of the same personality, but rather as complementary or even identical features of a single destiny.

At the same time, Spenser makes use of the character of Britomart to explore a range of possibilities not usually available to the female. It is not clear, for instance, whether her conquest of Arthegall should be understood as the "feminine conquest" many commentators have called it, or whether the poet is attempting to add another dimension to the idea of conquest as a description of human relationships. Similarly, Britomart herself is the best exemplar of the admonitory graffiti she discovers at the House of Busirane:

> And as she lookt about, she did behold,
> > How ouer that same dore was likewise writ,
> > Be bold, be bold, and euery where Be bold,
> > That much she muz'd, yet could not construe it
> > By any ridling skill, or commune wit.
> > At last she spyde at that roomes vpper end,
> > Another yron dore, on which was writ,
> > Be not too bold; whereto though she did bend
> > Her earnest mind, yet wist not what it might
> > > intend.
> > > > (III.xi.54)

As Nelson points out, "she is mystified, but she need not have been. Her sword is her boldness, her shield restraint.

---

[27] Harry Berger, "The Structure of Merlin's Chronicle in The Faerie Queene III (iii)," Studies in English Literature, 9 (1969), 50.

Scudamour is only bold."[28] Of course, Scudamour's excessive boldness is motivated by his passionate love, but he would be more effective and no less a man if he exercised restraint as well. Moreover, because he is so intemperate, Britomart, who is endowed with "manly" self-restraint, must go alone to rescue Amoret and, in so doing, experience a process of education about sensuality that is part of her perfection in the virtue she champions. It is both her boldness, a conventionally male attribute, and her purity, conventionally female, that enable her to enter upon a process that contributes to the proper understanding of sexuality on which chaste married love is based.

The Anatomy of Love

Spenser's vision of conjugal love requires for its exposition a central image that can convey the fusion, rather than the mere juxtaposition of the male and female principles. Britomart's sexually integral nature serves this purpose in the poem better than any relationship between characters could be expected to do. (In their different ways, the other couples united in the Third and Fourth Books represent the extremes of masculine and feminine personality types. Amoret is womanly, Scudamour manly, in both the positive and negative sense of those terms. Florimell exaggerates and eventually caricatures the shamefast chastity that marks Amoret's femininity, and Marinell, the man with whom she is matched, mirrors and distorts Scudamour's hearty, straightforward maleness with his own bluff machismo. Even Paridell and Hellenore reflect the different effects of erotic aggression on the character of their re-

---

[28] Nelson, p. 234.

spective sexes.) Relations between Arthegall and Britomart are at once too complex and too undeveloped to convey the particular union Spenser had in mind. A single image--and that, significantly, the image of Chastity as represented by Britomart--was needed to embody within the narrative the constellation of ideas represented iconographically by the obscured statue of Venus:

> The cause why she was couered with a vele,
>   Was hard to know, for that her Priests the same
> From peoples knowledge labour'd to concele.
> But sooth it was not sure for womanish shame,
> Nor any blemish, which the worke mote blame;
> But for, they say, she hath both kinds in one,
> Both male and female, both vnder one name:
> She syre and mother is her selfe alone,
>   Begets and eke conceiues, ne needeth other none.
>   (IV.x.41)

This image of the goddess, concrete and yet withdrawn, is at the center of the Temple of Venus, very much as the Temple itself is at the center of Spenser's theory of love. It is this theory that requires Britomart's chastity to have both more integrity and more aggressiveness than that of Amoret or Florimell, for the eventual expression of that chastity in licit marital love has to be literally and symbolically credible. Yet, in exploring the meaning of chastity, either extreme is easier to depict than the balance between them. In the Second Book's Bower of Bliss, Spenser has already delineated the forbidden joys of sexual excess. Book Three examines two essentially negative alternatives to such bestial delights. On the one hand, there is the timorous shrinking and desperate flight of virgins like Amoret and Florimell. On the other hand, there is the chaste belligerence of Belphoebe and Britomart, which is not only a more forceful approach to the same problems, but a way of expressing sexual tension. The stage of sexual development reached in this Book is one that Berger calls precourtship: "In this phase eros naturally manifests itself as hate, i.e. martial or erotic aggression--warfare and hostility, the struggle to possess and devour or to break free from possession, the urge to keep one's elemental condition pure and not mingle or merge with one's opposite except on one's own terms."[29]

In order to take sexual love to a more mature plane, Spenser elaborates two further themes: the myth of generation and the idea of friendship. Like the statue of Venus, under whose protection Scudamour finds his beloved, the Garden of Adonis is introduced into the narrative as part of Amoret's story. In both passages, however, it is Britomart and not Amoret who carries their full ideological weight into the process of the poem. The chief ideas make their appearance in allegorical and cosmic forms; only later does Spenser attempt to translate them into historical and institutional terms.

When Venus adopts one of Chrysogone's orphaned twins, she takes the child to the Garden of Adonis. Instead of continuing his narrative by discussing Amoret's upbringing in "goodly womanhead," the poet proceeds to a lengthy description of the background against which it takes place. Only after some twenty stanzas does the infant Amoret re-enter the poem, when we are informed that Venus

...vnto Psyche with great trust and care

---

[29] Berger, "Faerie Queene Book III," p. 237.

>   Committed her, yfostered to bee,
>   And trained vp in true feminitee:
>   Who no lesse carefully her tendered,
>   Then her owne daughter Pleasure, to whom shee
>   Made her companion, and her lessoned
>   In all the lore of loue, and goodly womanhead.
>   (III.vi.51)

This setting for the process of becoming a woman thus serves as an extended metaphor for the process itself. Not only do Venus and her paramour indulge themselves here in endless sexual delights, but Cupid and Psyche, recently reconciled, are similarly engaged. And a great many nameless lovers, although ruled by the tyranny of Time, share for a while in the joy of the immortals:

>   For here all plentie, and all pleasure flowes,
>   And sweet loue gentle fits emongst them
>   throwes,
>   Without fell rancor, or fond gealosie;
>   Franckly each paramour his leman knowes,
>   Each bird his mate; ne any does enuie
>   Their goodly meriment, and gay felicitie.
>
>   There is continuall spring, and haruest there
>   Continuall, both meeting at one time:
>   For both the boughes doe laughing blossomes
>   beare,
>   And with fresh colours decke the wanton Prime,
>   And eke attonce the heauy trees they clime,
>   Which seeme to labour vnder their fruits lode:
>   The whiles the ioyous birdes make their pastime
>   Emongst the shadie leaues, their sweet abode,

And their true loues without suspition tell
abrode.
(III.vi.41-42)

These delights are openly illicit, yet they constitute an environment in which Amoret is trained in bridal modesty, and through which the reader is prepared for Britomart's championing of married love. Spenser legitimates them by placing them in the larger context of biological and cosmic history. At least one commentator speaks testily of the poet's "puritan inability to enjoy frank pleasures without giving them fancy names," and claims that, in contrast to the denizens of the Bower of Bliss, "the people in the Garden, while enjoying the same pleasures on no discernibly higher moral plane, are able to enjoy their pleasures only by insisting on their holier-than-thou attitude."[30] If anyone is sanctimonious, however, it is not his characters, but Spenser himself, and it is myopic to apply so narrow a judgment to something he genuinely attempts to sanctify. For the open copulation of the Garden occurs in a place that is primarily the breeding-ground and temporary harbor of all sentient souls:

> Infinite shapes of creatures there are bred,
> And vncouth formes, which none yet euer knew,
> And euery sort is in a sundry bed
> Set by it self, and ranckt in comely rew:
> Some fit for reasonable soules t'indew,
> Some made for beasts, some made for birds to weare,

---

[30] Harold Fromm, "Spenserian Jazz and the Aphrodisiac of Virtue," <u>English Miscellany</u>, 17 (1966), 63, 62.

> And all the fruitfull spawne of fishes hew
> In endless rancks along enraunged were,
> That seem'd the Ocean could not containe them there.
>
> (III.vi.35)

The Garden is the cradle of life itself, which, according to the system that Spenser develops in these passages, is generated from Chaos and borrows various material forms in which to express its material essence. Human souls are part of this process, involved in a (significant) millennial cycle, implemented by the "double-natured" Genius who is its gate-keeper:

> He letteth in, he letteth out to wend,
> All that to come into the world desire;
> A thousand thousand naked babes attend
> About him day and night, which doe require,
> That he with fleshly weedes would them attire:
> Such as him list, such as eternall fate
> Ordained hath, he clothes with sinfull mire,
> And sendeth forth to liue in mortall state,
> Till they againe returne backe by the hinder gate.
>
> After that they againe returned beene,
> They in that Gardin planted be againe,
> And grow afresh, as they had neuer seene
> Fleshly corruption, nor mortall paine.
> Some thousand yeares so doen they there remaine;
> And then of him are clad with other hew,
> Or sent into the chaungefull world againe,
> Till thither they returne, where first they

grew:
So like a wheele around they runne from old to new.

(III.vi.32-33)

Human sexuality is thus explicitly linked to reproduction--which is hardly an innovation on Spenser's part--and to the entire range and pattern of life in the universe. The reproductive act acquires thereby a philosophical status that dignifies it and the women who are its indispensable instruments, without resorting to a denial or "transcendence" of its fleshly basis. (As Chrysogone's experience shows, generative nature can assume the paternal role, but apparently knows no substitute for the mother.) At this point in The Faerie Queene, the assertion is still essentially theoretical. Only as Spenser elaborates his theory of friendship and marriage does this description of the generative process acquire further concretion, linking up with the political themes concentrated in the figure of Britomart: the definitions of justice in the Fifth Book and the dynastic history in the Second.

Throughout this Canto, Venus appears in her most unambiguously "feminine" aspects: as mistress, mother, and foster-mother. (Contextually speaking, she is a grandmother, as well, of course since her son Cupid is the father of Psyche's child, Pleasure.) The next time she is referred to, however, it is in Scudamour's history of how he won Amoret, taking his beloved from the temple of her divine protectress. And this is where the representation of Venus is hermaphroditic, a quality that Nelson interprets as a symbol of the Legend of Friendship.[31] Similarly, heterosex-

---

[31] Nelson, p. 237.

ual lovers disport themselves in the temple grounds, but another kind of love binds the chaste pairs of friends whose love is perceived as no less passionate because it is not expressed sexually:

> And therein thousand payres of louers walkt,
> Praysing their god, and yeelding him great
> thankes,
> Ne euer ought but of their true loues talkt,
> Ne euer for rebuke or blame of any balkt.
>
> All these together by themselues did sport
> Their spotlesse pleasures and sweet loues
> content.
> But farre away from these, another sort
> Of louers lincked in true harts consent;
> Which loued not as these, for like intent,
> But on chast vertue grounded their desire,
> Farre from all fraud, or fayned blandishment;
> Which in their spirits kindling zealous fire,
> Braue thoughts and noble deedes did euermore
> aspire.
>
> Such were great Hercules, and Hylas deare;
> Trew Ionathan, and Dauid trustie tryde;
> Stout Theseus, and Pirithous his feare;
> Pylades and Orestes by his syde;
> Myld Titus and Gesippus without pryde;
> Damon and Pythias whom death could not seuer:
> All these and all that euer had bene tyde
> In bands of friendship, there did liue for
> euer,
> Whose liues although decay'd, yet loues decayed

neuer.
(IV.x.25-27)

It is, significantly, in the Fourth Book that the love affairs announced in the Third achieve their resolution. Nelson observes that, just as the Legend of Chastity is chiefly concerned with the power of love, "the Legend of Friendship is an anatomy of the relationships which love creates.[32] It examines both sorts of relations expressed in the temple grounds, taking each on its own terms, although Spenser announces his unequivocal conclusion as to which love is best:

> Hard is the doubt, and difficult to deeme,
>   When all three kinds of loue together meet,
>   And doe dispart the hart with powre extreme,
>   Whether shall weigh the balance downe; to weet
>   The deare affection vnto kindred sweet,
>   Or raging fire of loue to woman kind,
>   Or zeale of friends combynd with vertues meet.
>   But of them all the band of vertuous mind
> Me seemes the gentle hart should most assured bind.
>
> For naturall affection soon doth cesse,
>   And quenched is with Cupids greater flame:
>   But faithfull friendship doth them both suppresse,
>   And them with maystring discipline doth tame,
>   Through thoughts aspyring to eternall fame.
>   For as the soule doth rule the earthly masse,

---

[32] Ibid., p. 236.

> And all the seruice of the body frame,
> So loue of soule doth loue of bodie passe,
> No lesse then perfect gold surmounts the meanest
>   brasse.
>
>   (IV.ix.1-2)

It is interesting to observe that Spenser employs the same accepted analogy of relations between the soul and the body to glorify chaste friendship that Tasso used to justify patriarchal power within the household. Unfortunately for the purity or consistency of Spenser's argument, the dynastic imperatives of history, as well as the generative demands of cosmogony, make it impossible for him to create a pair of heterosexual lovers who transcend their physical relationship. His couples must find their way by means of their sexuality, not around or above it. The best Spenser can do is to situate their union in a context defined as the Book of Friendship, and to utilize that Book to explore neither sexual love nor loving friendship, but, as Nelson indicates, the nature of love <u>relationships</u>.

I think it is worth noting, in this regard, that there is one other relationship that the poet takes into account when he weighs the merits of various kinds of love, and that is "naturall affection," the emotion that subsists within the family. But Spenser dismisses the love of kindred by explaining that it is superseded, in the normal course of events, by sexual love, whose strengths and limitations he then proceeds to detail. Even this momentary inclusion of family feeling, however, serves to point up a surprising shortage of such relationships in <u>The Faerie Queene</u>. Siblings are usually brought in with a strictly allegorical function--to reinforce an antithesis, for example. And, with the exception of the two over-protective mothers whose sons fall for Florimell, parents are altogether missing from the narrative. Spenser's heroes possess ancestors, lineage, social status, all attributes derived from their parents, but the actual mothers and fathers do not appear. The family is represented as a dynasty: forebears on the one side, descendants on the other. In the present generation, it is seen only in potential, as isolated individuals whose institutional involvements go no further than the formation of couples. This concentration on the couple as a unit and hence on the erotic and affective bonds they establish, is one of the clearest marks of the new bourgeois sensibility that shapes Spenser's poem. It is no wonder that there is a discrepancy between the historical and narrative need for the family as an institution and the ideological need to recast that institution; what is remarkable is that Spenser can handle the contradiction at all.

Of the three kinds of human love that Spenser recognizes, therefore, he analyzes only two. And he is entirely consistent in the assertion that friendship is the higher and more lasting form. Yet it is love, heterosexual love with an erotic basis, that commands most of his attention, even in the Legend of Friendship. Where friendship is the central theme, moreover, it is never subjected to the kinds of careful consideration and discussion evoked by sexual love. (I expect that I am not the only specialist in this field--to say nothing of the general reader--who has some trouble recalling the very names of Friendship's two knights.) By maintaining the superiority of friendship and by bringing his love stories to fruition in that context, I think Spenser is doing something even more significant. He is suggesting that the kind of relations that exist between lovers should approach the condition of friendship. And this recognition is fundamental to the theory of marriage elaborated in The Faerie Queene.

With Marriage Meet

Earthly love in its various manifestations is the subject of Spenser's two central Books. In the Legends of both Chastity and Friendship, a series of antitheses is established that enable the poet to explore the full range of each experience he examines. Thus, chastity is explored in two manifestations--celibacy and conjugal faith--and is also counterposed to lust. Lust is not simply the stylized opposite of chastity, but is contrasted with both love and friendship. It is not so much lust as a <u>state</u> that interests Spenser, as the character of personal relations to which that state leads; thus the tale of Paridell and Hellenore or the adventures of the Snowy Florimell are set over against the loving betrothals and loyal friendships that characterize the chaste personalities of the Fourth Book. What Spenser, has to say about marriage, therefore, occurs between the boundaries defined by lust, on the one side, and friendship, on the other.

It has frequently been pointed out that Spenser regards marriage as "the only acceptable form of surrender to the instinct for procreation."[33] Referring to sexual desire as a reproductive instinct, however, glosses over one of the poet's few clear distinctions between licit and illicit sexuality. Without procreation as a motive, one is at a loss to understand why the Bower of Bliss must be destroyed while the Garden of Adonis is a flourishing ideal. There is some tendency to read the poem as if sexuality in the Gar-

---

[33] Judith Ramsay, "The Garden of Adonis and the Garden of Forms," <u>University of Toronto Quarterly</u>, 35 (1966), 206.

den, which is certainly described in extremely appealing terms, is all right because Spenser says it is, while what goes on in the Bower, which is made equally attractive to the senses, is wrong for the same arbitrary reason. This way of thinking can be extended to the fact of marriage itself, for there is no immediate elucidation within <u>The Faerie Queene</u> of exactly how and why matrimony sanctifies sexual expression.

The only explanation for any part of the problem lies in the contrast between the sterility that characterizes the Bower of Bliss and the fertility that is essential to the Garden of Adonis. A great deal of the sexual activity in the Bower does not involve any sort of relationship beyond the erotic, and sometimes does not even bring people into direct contact with one another. Its chief modalities are voyeuristic and onanistic--hence unproductive. Human relations are entirely defined by lust and there seems to be no pairing off into couples except to the limited extent and for the brief duration required by physical acts themselves. By contrast, the Garden of Adonis, as the source of generation, is <u>about</u> fertility. And the sexuality that takes place in this context, like that in the grounds of Venus' temple, happens between established couples. These paired lovers are not necessarily married, but they have developed relationships in which both the emotional and the erotic elements participate and enrich each other.

In the Garden of Adonis, the connection between procreation and acceptable erotic expression is communicated only by juxtaposition. No explicit causality is asserted, and marriage as a social form to contain sexual relations is present in the Garden only by implication. What is conveyed here is a strong sense that the poet is trying to "make human designs and actions conform to an ideal system, a program of life."[34] Spenser's theory of human and divine generation has a theological underpinning, maintaining, as it does, that "sexual passion is part of the heavenly scheme of things, and obedience to heaven's behests can only be virtuous."[35] It is in this sense, as Nelson points out, that the "anatomical reference of the Mount of Venus," otherwise rather lugubrious, "becomes not only appropriate but inevitable, as the process of generation in the terrestrial world is the natural metaphor for the process by which that world is conceived."[36] Once this pattern is understood, moreover, the reader can perceive another dimension to the sexual allegories in the Legend of the Redcross Knight. The marriage between the Knight and Una parallels that union of Christ and His Church that Christian interpreters assert is celebrated in the Song of Songs. And their relationship prior to this happy resolution is anatomized by the poet through the images of affectionate caresses, lovers' separations, and sexual unfaithfulness.

The natural analogue to this cluster of symbols is the marriage of the Thames and the Medway, which is introduced into the story of Florimell and Marinell on the slenderest of narrative pretexts, and which occupies all but a few stanzas of one Canto. It is, of course, the kind of set piece in which Spenser delights, but, like his other passages of description and pageantry, the watery wedding has an evident thematic function. His roll-call of the guests at Proteus' feast for the couple is one of the few places

---

[34] Glen Alton Newkirk, "The Public and Private Ideal of the Sixteenth Century Gentleman: A Representative Analysis," *Dissertation Abstracts*, 27 (1967), 1034A (Denver).

[35] Nelson, p. 222.

[36] *Ibid.*, p. 218.

in *The Faerie Queene* where Spenser calls upon the Muse to assist his memory and his poetic powers, a fact that, in itself, suggests that the catalogue has real significance. The sexual analogy is only mildly hinted at through the relations of personified rivers that are being joined in wedlock:

> Long had the Thames (as we in records reed)
> Before that day her wooed to his bed;
> But the proud Nymph would for no worldly meed,
> Nor no entreatie to his loue be led;
> Till now at last relenting, she to him was wed.
> (IV.xi.8)

Sensuous imagery is much more abundant in the lush recapitulation of bridal attendants and well-wishers, and its procreative element is made explicit in Spenser's summary:

> O what an endlesse work haue I in hand,
>   To count the seas abundant progeny,
>   Whose fruitfull seede farre passeth those in
>   land,
>   And also those which wonne in th'azure sky?
>   For much more eath to tell the starres on hy,
>   Albe they endlesse seme in estimation,
>   Then to recount the Seas posterity:
>   So fertile be the flouds in generation,
> So huge their numbers, and so numberlesse their
>   nation.
>
> Therefore the antique wisards well inuented,
>   That Venus of the fomy sea was bred;
>   For that the seas by her are most augmented.

> Witnesse th'exceeding fry which there are fed,
> And wondrous sholes, which may of none be red.
> Then blame me not, if I haue err'd in count
> Of Gods, of Nymphs, of riuers yet vnred:
> For though their numbers do much more surmount,
> Yet all those same were there, which erst I did recount.
> (IV.xii.1-2)

The catalogue of rivers also incudes a brief and curious animadiversion on sexual and imperial politics:

> Rich Oranochy, though but knowen late;
> And that huge Riuer, which doth beare his name
> Of warlike Amazons, which doe possesse the same.
>
> Ioy on those warlike women, which so long
>   Can from all men so rich a kingdome hold;
>   And shame on you, O men, which boast your strong
>   And valiant hearts, in thoughts lesse hard and bold,
>   Yet quaile in conquest of that land of gold.
>   But this to you, O Britons, most pertaines,
>   To whom the right hereof it selfe hath sold;
>   The which for sparing litle cost or paines,
> Loose so immortall glory, and so endlesse gains.
> (IV.xi.21-22)

The exhaustive shower of names serves principally to connect this wedding to all of geography and history, since each guest is identified by a wealth of interlocking topographical and associative connections. Thus, a sexual event, the wedding, provides the occasion for bringing a whole world of reference rhetorically to bear on the events in Book Four. At the same time, since that wedding is a strictly allegorical event, we readers are expected to bring what we know about sexuality to bear on a description of inanimate nature. In this sense, the sexual background of the catalogue turns the passage into an exaltation of landscape that parallels the hymn to sentient life in the Garden of Adonis.

In the Books where they are the main subject, human relations that have the potential for procreation are explicitly linked to the larger framework of creation. The poem's overall structure--or as much as we have of it--also links sexuality to the scheme of human history. The dynastic chronicles of the Second Book and Merlin's prophecy in the Third all depend for their fulfillment on the marriage of Britomart and Arthegall, a sexual relationship that is also at the basis of the political theory embodied in Book Five. Although it is predicated on this expanded context, Spenser's acceptance of marital sex is by no means grudging or contingent. "Like Calvin, Spenser appears to believe that marriage _graces_ the sexual union between spouses so that there remains nothing about it unacceptable to God."[37]

The Faerie Queene has been taken, along with the _Prothalamion_ and the _Epithalamion_, as reflecting an essentially Protestant vision of marriage as "the basis of Christian social life...an order useful to society as a whole."[38] Such a belief is certainly consistent with the ideas Spenser

---

[37] JoAn Elizabeth Chace, "Spenser's Celebration of Love: Its Background in English Protestant Thought," _Dissertation Abstracts_, 29 (1969), 226A (California, Berkeley).

[38] Ibid.

lays out, and the deep sense of resolution achieved by the betrothals of the principal pairs of lovers. I think it is important to recognize, however, that this social content is present largely by implication. For all its length and its complex structure, The Faerie Queene, like the two shorter poems, is about wedding, not about marriage. (In fact, the Thames and the Medway come closer to a consummation than the human couples, for they are actually married in the course of the poem, while the others are merely betrothed.) Spenser does not use his poem to explore the state or the relationship of marriage, yet it is upon the fact of matrimony that he places the narrative and ideological weight of his epic. Which would suggest that marriage, the sexual politics the poet associates with it, and the female character as expressed through it, all have an allegorical dimension for Spenser. Marriage exists in the poem not so much as a "real-life" social institution towards which symbolic events tend, but as a human event symbolic in itself of larger social forces.

Of Polliticke Vertues

The strongest integrative force in the narrative of The Faerie Queene, bringing together the poem's various strains, its theological background, its dynastic rationale, and its political framework, is the marriage of Britomart and Arthegall. Spenser's handling of this subject has a significance, therefore, beyond the immediate situation it resolves, and should be examined in some detail. Throughout Book Three, where she is at the center of the action, Britomart has been languishing for Arthegall. The events represented in the Legend of Chastity bring her closer to the ideological basis of their union, but not to the union itself. Then, in Book Four, "the saluage knight" appears on the last day of the tournament and overthrows one knight after another, threatening the victory of the Knights of Maidenhead. Just after we--but not the other characters in the poem--learn that this new champion is Arthegall, another unidentified knight enters the lists:

> A stranger knight that did his glorie shend:
> So nought may be esteemed happie till the end.
>
> He at his entrance charg'd his powrefull speare
>   At Artegall, in middest of his pryde,
>   And therewith smote him on his Vmbriere
>   So sore, that tombling backe, he downe did slyde
>   Ouer his horses taile aboue a stryde;
>   Whence litle lust he had to rise againe.
>   (IV.iv.43-44)

After besting a number of other knights in rapid succession, this new victor is revealed--once more, to the reader only--as Britomart. Once he has done this, Spenser drops the masculine pronouns employed while the reader shared the participants' automatic assumption that anyone who joined the test of manhood must, in fact, be a man. In making the revelation, Spenser's language suggests the supernatural character of Britomart's prowess:

> Full many others at him likewise ran:
>   But all of them likewise dismounted were,
>   Ne certes wonder; for no powre of man
>   Could bid the force of that enchaunted speare,
>   The which this famous Britomart did beare;

> With which she wondrous deeds of arms atchieued
> And ouerthrew, whateuer came her neare,
> That all those stranger kights full sore
>   agrieued,
> And that late weaker band of chalengers relieued.
>
> Like as in sommers day when raging heat
>   Doth burne the earth, and boyled riuers drie,
>   That all brute beasts forst to refraine fro
>   meat,
>   Doe hunt for shade, where shrowded they may
>   lie,
>   And missing it, faine from themselues to flie;
>   All trauellers tormented are with paine:
>   A watry cloud doth ouercast the skie,
>   And poureth forth a sudden shoure of raine,
> That all the wretched world recomforteth againe.
>
> So did the warlike Britomart restore
>   The prize, to knights of Maydenhead that day
>   (IV.iv.46-47)

The magical origins and power of Britomart's spear are mentioned in the passage where Glauce persuades her young charge "aduent'rous knighthood on her self to don," but they are not alluded to after that, and, in all her fights prior to the duel with her beloved, the emphasis has been on her superior strength and skill. What "magical" powers she possesses, like the ability to pass unmolested through the flames encircling the house of Busirane, are shown to be natural, in that they stem from her virtuous nature. Even here, where her victory over Arthegall has to be attributed to something other than her simply being a better warrior, the implications of her supernatural advantage are transformed by the simile of a providential downpour after a drought. Britomart's power, like the welcome rain, is <u>natural</u> magic, and, at the same time, reflects the actions of grace.

    This first encounter, in which the prospective lovers do not recognize one another, is rapidly followed by a second, after Scudamour and Arthegall decide to join forces against the "unknightly" Britomart. The lady easily overcomes Scudamour. Her contest with Arthegall, however, is more evenly matched and more prolonged. Dramatic irony is very intense, here, for the reader knows the identity of both parties, and this time the duel between them is no martial game, but a fight to the death. After a series of crashing blows on both sides, Arthegall gathers all his strength for one stroke:

> And therewith stroke at her so hideouslie,
>   That seemed nought but death mote be her destinie.
>   (IV.vi.18)

The blow has shattered her helmet, revealing her face to him and his companion. Both Arthegall and Scudamour react almost superstitiously to the discovery of her beauty, kneeling to worship a perfection that can only be celestial. Britomart, who is already in love and aware of their common destiny, is overjoyed to learn her opponent's identity, and Glauce attempts to effect a complete reconciliation:

> And you Sir Artegall, the saluage knight,
>   Henceforth may not disdaine, that womans hand
>   Hath conquered you anew in second fight:
> For whylome they haue conquerd sea and land,

> And heauen it selfe, that nought may them withstand.
> Ne henceforth be rebellious vnto loue,
> That is the crowne of knighthood, and the band
> Of noble minds deriued from aboue,
> Which being knit with vertue, neuer will remoue.
>
> And you faire Ladie knight, my dearest Dame,
> Relent the rigour of your wrathful will,
> Whose fire were better turn'd to other flame;
> And wiping out rembrance of all ill,
> Graunt him your grace, but so that he fulfill
> The penance, which ye shall to him empart:
> For louers heauen must passe by sorrowes hell.
> Thereat full inly blushed Britomart;
> But Artegall close smyling ioy'd in secret hart.
>   (IV.vi.31-32)

While Britomart tells Scudamour what she knows about the fate of Amoret, the instant enamorment of her own destined lover develops into true love. Their relationship is established and their future sealed in two appallingly conventional stanzas:

> In all which time, Sir Artegall made way
> Vnto the loue of noble Britomart,
> And with meeke seruice and much suit did lay
> Continuall siege vnto her gentle hart,
> Which being whylome launcht with louely dart,
> More eath was new impression to receiue,
> How euer she her paynd with womanish art
> To hide her wound, that none might it perceiue:
> Vaine is the art that seekes it selfe for to

deceiue.

> So well he woo'd her, and so well he wrought her,
>   With faire entreatie and sweet blandishment,
>   At the length vnto a bay he brought her,
>   So as she to his speeches was content
>   To lend an eare, and softly to relent.
>   At last through many vowes which forth he pour'd,
>   And many othes, she yeelded her consent
>   To be his loue, and tkae him for her Lord,
> Till they with marriage meet might finish that accord.
>
>   (IV.vi.40-41)

    This is not merely the climax of <u>The Faerie Queene's</u> central love story, it is the last we see of it <u>as</u> a love story. The relationship between Britomart and Arthegall is never developed as a relationship, beyond the purely static fact of their betrothal. And their marriage, which is a major nexus of Spenser's ideas, does not even take place within the existing poem. But Britomart and Arthegall are the principal characters in Book Five, and the evolution of the Legend of Justice makes it clear that their marriage serves allegorical as well as thematic functions within the poem. Spenser's deliberate inattention to the nature of the married love that Britomart and Arthegall stand for and his detailed consideration of the social issues in which they are embroiled reflect the generally symbolic and political status of these questions.

    In a somewhat similar fashion, the wedding of the Thames and the Medway, which I discussed earlier as connecting the natural and generative themes in the poem to the sexual institution of marriage, also has a further level, in which the symbolic marriage of the two rivers also represents "the bond which unites a land under its sovereign."[39] The bridegroom wears the city significantly referred to as "Troynovant" as his marriage crown, and is honored as the chief waterway of Britain by the other rivers of England and even of Ireland. Nelson adds a political interpretaiton to the other symbolism I identified in the gathering of the world's major rivers to pay homage to the new couple: "Their presence raises Britain to the stature of the most famous nation of all time and provides the spur to Englishmen to win immortal glory (and 'endlesse gaines') through the conquest of the golden lands of the new world."[40]

Spenser's nationalism is fundamental to his political philosophy, but it is by no means identical with it. His larger vision of politics is contained in Book Five, where the story of Britomart and Arthegall assumes a social dimension. Interpretation of the Legend of Justice in terms of its attitude towards the state and human governance immediately encounters opposition from the scholarly tradition, which denies that this is the subject. Such a view acknowledges the generally patriotic and nationalistic thrust of Spenser's work, his attachment to the philosophic ideal of harmony as a component of both public and private intercourse, and his reverence for Elizabeth as the source of harmonious national fulfillment. But it relegates any more specific theory of the state to the twelve unwritten Books devoted to Arthur's tenure as king. From this point of view, even the Book of Justice belongs more to the rubric of "ethice" than "politice," since its "discourse deals with

---

[39] Nelson, p. 254.

[40] Ibid., p. 255.

the nature of those who act justly rather than with the nature of just action."[41]

It seems to me essential to consider the significance of Spenser's concentrating on justice chiefly as an individual quality. This concern with perceiving the moral and political universe on a human scale is, itself, one of the principal characteristics of the politics Spenser espouses, and is closely bound up with the didactic function of The Faerie Queene. Spenser's declared purpose, as enunciated in the Letter to Raleigh, is "to fashion a gentleman or noble person in vertuous and gentle discipline."[42] It is clear from the way the word "fashion" is used elsewhere in the explanatory letter that its nearest synonym, here, is something like "portray." But his concern with setting forth each virtue in its most attractive form is also explicitly justified as a means of making the portrayal an acceptable example; in this sense, the poem also "fashions" a gentleman by helping to shape and mold his character.

As the letter proceeds, Spenser compares his own treatment of "ethical" and "political" qualities to what other epic poets from Homer to Tasso have made of this division. At the same time, he compares his method to that of two ancient writers on government, referring to

> the vse of these dayes, seeing all things accounted by their showes, and nothing esteemed of, that is not delightfull and pleasing to common sence. For this cause is Xenophon preferred be-

---

[41] Ibid., pp. 274-5.

[42] Letter to Raleigh, p. 485. See Stephen Greenblatt, Renaissance Self-Fashioning (Chicago: University of Chicago Press, 1980).

> fore Plato, for that the one in the exquisite depth of his iudgement, formed a Commune welth such as it should be, but the other in the person of Cyrus and the Persians fashioned a gouernment such as might best be: So much more profitable and gratious is doctrine by ensample, then by rule.[43]

Spenser's reliance on this analogy implies that he perceived a greater intersection between "ethice" and "politice" than commentators like Nelson normally admit. It would suggest that the nexus of these ideas is precisely the concept of the gentleman that is both subject and object of Spenser's poem. For, in creating a work whose stated intention is to portray and to shape the ideal individual of a certain class, Spenser is making a clear declaration about the form and content of his politics. It is hardly necessary, I imagine, to belabor the point that a phrase like "man or person" is different from the one Spenser actually uses, "gentleman or noble person," and that this difference brings the element of class into the discussion of personal morality. Which, in turn, means that morality immediately assumes a public aspect, for the moral obligations of nobility are societal, based on the _fact_ of nobility, that is, on status, character, and power. No one, I think, would seriously argue that Spenser's use of class-based language is simply fortuitous or conventional; he knew what he meant by a "gentleman," and that was not entirely synonymous with a "person." The difficulty arises in attempting to understand the _significance_ of his class assumptions and the way they influence the poem itself.

---

[43] _Ibid._, pp. 485-6.

The scholarship on this subject tends simultaneously to acknowledge and to deny the special situation created by Spenser's preoccupation with the gentleman. It tells us, for instance, that "under the peaceful Tudors the English knight became a gentleman; there was a shift in emphasis from martial pursuits to civil employments...It was a heraldry of hands, not arms, of noblesse achieved."[44] Surely, not even Spenser's contemporaries, eager as they were to embrace inflated myths about themselves and their imperial destiny, would have recognized their ruling family under the rubric "peacefulness" or their own fiercely competitive, tumultuous, increasingly mercantile society as the one where chivalric swords were being hastily beaten into the plowshares of innocuous civil employment. The civic world reflected in the Legend of Justice is one menaced by bloody conspiracies, rebellious colonies, an insubordinate popular mob, and howling chaos. And the methods employed by the representatives of "justice" to contain or subdue those threats owe as little to diplomatic maneuvering as they do to the decorous choreography of the chivalric code.

Feudalism and the military system that maintained it had, indeed, begun to be replaced by a merchant capitalism that determined productive relations on the land as well as in the urban areas. And the military arm of the new system was assuming a new, national form. Similarly, the social ideal of knighthood had to be transformed into an exemplary type more in keeping with actual social conditions. It is important to bear in mind, however, that chivalry had both a practical and a literary dimension, and that this dualism was intensified in the Renaissance period; the gentry were a

---

[44] Leonard R. N. Ashley, "Spenser and the Ideal of the Gentleman," <u>Bibliothèque d'Humanisme et Renaissance</u>, 27 (1965), 112-13.

creation of historical and material forces, but the <u>gentleman</u> was the creation of literature. <u>The Faerie Queene</u> is one of the principal documents in the history of that class, because it contributed so strongly to defining its ideology.

When Newkirk claims that Spenser fused "the feudal and humanist worlds to form the perfect gentleman," he ignores the poet's use of chivalric conventions to express modern content.[45] Spenser's deliberate archaism is a larger issue than can be responsibly considered here, but, in the more limited terms of Book Five, he certainly employs the assumptions appropriate to a familiar but obsolete system of social relations in the service of new relations and the new values to which they give rise. He has the double task of portraying the nature of the just gentleman and, at the same time, authenticating that gentleman's role as administrator of justice. In other words, he had not only to show the reader what a gentleman was and show the gentleman-reader how best to live up to his status, but to give some ideological reinforcement to the very hegemony of the gentleman and his class.

Any analysis of what happens in the Fifth Book of <u>The Faerie Queene</u> must recognize that Spenser is not simply ringing the changes on a conventional definition of the gentleman. He does something innovative in taking the new class to which he himself belonged and placing it at the center of his epic. And he was assimilating to that class some of the virtues and attributes associated with the feudal ruling class, as if his doing so might further blur the

---

[45] Newkirk, p. 1034. In this argument, I am assuming that Spenser meant a new and specific class when he referred to the "gentleman," rather than simply calling attention to the fundamental division of sixteenth-century society into the "gentlemen" and everyone else.

distinction between the two classes. Throughout the poem, whenever there is a conflict between bourgeois and aristocratic values, Spenser opts for the aristocratic ones. But much more of his energy is spent in resolving such conflicts, for the most consistent political attitude he expresses is that of natural hierarchy and social order. It may be said that the attribute of the old ruling class that he is most eager to secure to the new one is the fact that it (in fact) rules.

Spenser makes use of three interlocking motives to support his image of the gentleman: the feudal or chivalric, the ethical, and the sexual metaphors. The most pervasive of these is, of course, the chivalric theme, since both the narrative and the allegory depend on the character and adventures of knights representing the ethical qualities. As I have indicated, I think this constant recourse to the forms of an earlier time is intended to provide a mask of familiar associations for some dramatically new ideas. But Spenser pays repeated homage in Books Five and Six to the notion of noble birth as the origin of the right to sovereignty. Now this is a view, one would think, that genuinely belongs with the verbal and cultural trappings of feudal aristocracy; it is certainly not one of the "modern" ideas the poet slips into the poem in chivalric dress. I believe that Spenser's focus on political power clarifies the apparent contradiction between this insistence on noble descent and the whole ethical thrust of the poem.

The Faerie Queene's fundamental moral premise is that certain personal qualities are necessary to the character of the individual who governs justly. From this perspective, government is a kind of meritocracy, since ethical fitness to rule is the hallmark of the ruler. The idea that achievement and not birth is the touchstone of greatness is basic, of course, to the political thought of the Renaissance period. When Spenser argues in favor of a noble background, in fact, he does so in terms of the more "modern" values: The man of inherited position is the one who does possess the moral qualities that make a good ruler. Spenser thus relies on the essentially bourgeois notion of individual merit to carry the argument for aristocratic birth and, at the same time, employs "knighthood" and aristocracy as symbols for ethical merit. This is actually another and more subtle use of the same technique I identified earlier, for, here again, the feudal framework of the poem operates in the service of the dominant Renaissance ideology.[46]

In Book Five, where these issues come to the fore, the principal events occur around the confrontation with Radigund and her Amazon realm. The basic metaphors for justice and injustice, therefore, are sexual ones. But the Radigund episode is not the only example of disorder (and hence injustice) that the just figures encounter and set right, nor is it the only use of sexual imagery to convey a class--and hence a political--message. Ellen Cantarow points out that "the subordination of the Amazon society in Book V is only one act of Justice in a range of acts that include the subjugation of Anabaptists, and the crushing of the Irish peasant rebellion." She maintains that in this instance, as in others throughout the poem, "standards of conduct and misconduct...are frequently presented as allegorical types

---

[46] "One of the paradoxes of the age was that...an excessive adulation of ancient lineage took place at precisely the time when political theorists were laying increasing emphasis upon virtue, education and the capacity to serve the state as the supreme test of and justification for a leisure class living off the labours of others," Lawrence Stone, The Crisis of the Aristocracy, 1558-1641 (Oxford: Clarendon Press, 1965), p. 27.

of male and female sexuality...which makes class behavior seem sex-linked, therefore universal and eternal since rooted in Nature."[47] Commenting on this article, Nancy Hoffman argues that in giving so wide a scope to women characters throughout his poem, Spenser is far *less* limited on the subject of female potential than most of his contemporaries, and that the limitations that do exist for his women originate in the class nature of the poem.[48] I would suggest that there is a more direct interaction between sex and class ideology in The Faerie Queene than either commentator acknowledges. The reasoning that inferior status is natural and ordained by God, and that the desired balance is synonymous with the status quo, is the same whether the subject group be the female sex or the Giant's unruly followers. The two sets of arguments reinforce one another precisely because the categories themselves are so closely interconnected.

But it is not as simple as my categorical statements may imply. In the incident at Mercilla's court, for example, we see an unresolved opposition between "masculine" and "feminine" versions of justice. Although neither the ruthless iron man nor the soft-hearted queen is right in this instance, elsewhere, Talus' harsh methods are taken as synonymous with justice. He is nonetheless incapable of overthrowing Radigund and rescuing his master. Only Britomart, a female who contains the sexual contradictions within herself, can constitute an equilibrant force in the unbalanced situation. Furthermore, it is not what she represents in herself that brings down Radigund's kingdom, but her

---

[47] Cantarow, pp. 234, 233.

[48] Nancy Hoffman, Comment on Cantarow, "A Wilderness of Opinions," College English, 34 (1972), 255.

relationship to Arthegall, which motivates her and which replaces the "incorrect" sexual politics of Amazon rule with the proper balance embodied in the conjugal condition. That proper balance, as we have seen, is one that takes all power away from women and restores it to men, its "rightful" possessors. Yet this happens through the aggressive action of the female and the enforced passivity of the male.

The marriage between Britomart and Arthegall never does take place in *The Faerie Queene* as we have it. The betrothed lovers of the Fourth Book do not move, in the Fifth, to a consummation of their personal situation, but to the resolution of a series of problems in the political sphere. To the extent, however, that their new relationship is a paradigm for that resolution, the marriage between Britomart and Arthegall actually is consummated, and most appropriately, through the political and class institutions that it serves to represent and renew.

AFTERWORD

The *Orlando furioso*, the *Gerusalemme liberata*, and *The Faerie Queene* constitute a coherent and, generally speaking, self-contained tradition. When all discernible debts of form, style, and matter are suitably acknowledged, and the contributions of Virgil, Plato, Petrach, Pulci, Boiardo, and Castiglione granted their due weight, it remains clear that there had never been anything quite like our three heroic poems before. Moreover, though all three have been highly influential, their impact, even for immediately succeeding generations, was not of the sort that is reflected in imitation. So there has been nothing quite like them since, either. If it is difficult to summarize and draw conclusions about them, that is because they cover so much ground, in themelves, and because four subsequent centuries of history--both the history of literature and the history of human events--have forced us to reexamine the issues these poems broach and the resolutions they propose.

The composition and publication of the three romance-epics covered almost the whole of the sixteenth century. (When forty Cantos of the *Furioso* came out in 1516, they were already the product of some years' labor, yet the definitive, expanded version that was published in 1532 reflects considerable revision. Tasso's *Rinaldo*, forerunner to his major work, was finished in 1562, and the *Liberata* itself in 1575. Three Books of *The Faerie Queene* appeared in 1590, the rest of the poem as we have it being published in 1596.) Not only are all three poems shaped by the social forces, the tensions and changes, that characterized their times, but they were intended to play their own part in that history. They reflect an emerging ideology, but they were also supposed to contribute to it. Neither reference point is a stable one. The times, moreover, witnessed enormous changes in the structure of human life and in the way people understood their experience. But some of the most far-reaching changes adumbrated in the poetry were still in their earliest and most tentative stages. It is possible to speak of them with any confidence ony because we have witnessed some of the conclusions ourselves.

What is troubling me as I attempt to bring my observations together is the superficial ease of generalization. It is all too easy to speak about a century now four hundred years in the past as if it were a monolithic entity. The structure of literary education has also helped build up the reified concept, "sixteenth century." When the hallmark of a given period is change--in economic, political, ideological, religious, and cultural life--it is especially difficult to gauge which changes had already crystallized by the time a particular poem was written, which were yet to come. And underlying this question is the dangerous assumption that literatue is essentially mimetic--an assumption that does very little to advance a fruitful reading of allegory.

In the heroic poems of Ariosto, Tasso, and Spenser, the idea of sex equality and love-marriage founded on that equality is examined in relation to a set of propositions about government and the human qualities necessary to its conduct. Because the love stories are so attractive, and because they are the nexus of so many other themes, they have to be understood as having something to do with

Afterword

relations between actual men and women before they can be situated in their larger political context. That is, although the lady knights embody the "feminine" qualities required for the administration of government in the mercantile state, they also participate in a love theme that is impossible to ignore and almost equally impossible to interpret.

The difficulty is that the love-marriage theme, as presented, is neither mimetic nor prescriptive. Marriage for love was not only absent from the dominant values, but it was also a rarity in practice, and remained so for some time to come. The marriage of lovers was not unheard of in Western literature, from at least the time of the Greek romances, but in sixteenth-century literature it became an ethical norm; it became increasingly acceptable for literary lovers to marry and, in the fictions of subsequent centuries, it would become unacceptable for them to marry for any motive other than love.

Near the end of the <u>Orlando furioso</u>, the love-match between Bradamante and Ruggiero faces a new obstacle. Parallel to the issues that have already arisen and that are natural developments of the plot--the legitimacy of their betrothal, the consequences of Ruggiero's delayed conversion, the just claims of Leone after the lovers' duel--Ariosto brings in the objections raised by Bradamante's parents. These objections are entirely venal and can be laid to rest only by the assurance that Ruggiero's feats of valor in Eastern Europe have made him an eligible <u>parti</u> from the material point of view. The commentators who mention the passage have been nearly unanimous in attacking it, and a great many of them do so by criticizing the untoward introduction of a "bourgeois" theme into the aristocratic fabric of romance-epic. Some scholars even refer to parent objections to a love match as the bourgeois theme.[1]

Nor are they far wrong. The history of the novel, developed as the bourgeoisie consolidated its economic, social, and, eventually, political hegemony, reflects the establishment and reinforcement of a series of norms about love and marriage, often expressed through the motif of parental manipulation or obstruction and its unhappy results. And the norm became increasingly operative outside of literature, to the point where marriage for love, without material or authoritarian constraints, has become the expected destiny of young women throughout the West. It was no accident that the enthronement of this idea in fiction and in living history should have been a consequence of developing capitalist relations.

As I indicated in the second chapter of this study, the transition to a new mode of productive life was well under way in the sixteenth century, and its impact had already begun to be felt by women and the family. The separation of economic functions into those that were carried on in the cash market and those that were pursued in the household not only reduced the social power of women, but placed relationships inside the family on a different basis. The household remained an economic institution: The dowry and the marriage settlement did not disappear, the family remained essential for material survival among the lower strata of society, and the role of the household as a consuming unit

---

[1] Robert Garnier's tragicomedy, _Bradamante_, expands the Leone-Bradamante-Ruggiero triangle and its subordinate parental-objection plot to constitute the drama itself. It thus provides an interesting illustration of a genuinely bourgeois transformation of this material. See Robert Garnier, _Bradamante_ (1582-85; rpt. Paris: Garnier Frères, n.d.)

Afterword

expanded.[2] But because these economic functions were outside the immediate processes of wage labor and commodity production or exchange, they were increasingly deemphasized. "Family" came to mean a system of personal relationships, rather than signifying those relationships in the institutional framework I have designated by the term "household." And, within this newly private sphere, the heterosexual couple, its material basis denied, gained importance as an emotive entity. As home was increasingly defined as the place where business was not, it had increasingly to become the place where love was. Overcoming whatever obstacles the world of business might establish to fulfillment-through-love in the private realm is, indeed, <u>the</u> bourgeois theme, because it was the bourgeoisie, in the course of assuming power, that created the conditions and the categories that defined the task.

The economic transition and its attendant effects on women were only beginning in the sixteenth century. And the love-marriage and parental-oppositon themes remained relatively undeveloped in comparison with their prominence in the eighteenth- and nineteenth-century novel. But the heroic poetry of the Renaissance period, with its emphasis on the couple themselves, their equality, their love, and their possible marriage, represents one stage of the process. The social and class pressures that were bringing new sexual values into being were also--and rather more rapidly--effecting changes in the process and the concept of

---

[2] See Joan Kelly Gadol, "Did Women Have a Renaissance?" in <u>Becoming Visible: Women in European History</u>, ed. Renate Bridenthal and Claudia Koonz (Boston: Houghton Mifflin, 1977) and my own expansion of some themes of the present study in Lillian S. Robinson, "Woman Under Capitalism: The Renaissance Lady," in <u>Sex, Class, and Culture</u> (Bloomington and London: Indiana University Press, 1978), pp. 150-77.

government. From this perspective, the political and the sexual themes are not distinct, but rather different aspects of the same question. Participation of the lady knights in both elements reflects just how much, their chivalric garb and allegorical functions notwithstanding, the women warriors belong to the future.

BIBLIOGRAPHY

Virgil

Baccelli, Alfredo. *Studi Virgiliani*. Rome: Sapientia, 1932.

Barbu, Nicholas I. "Valeurs romaines et idéaux humaines dans le livre VI de *l'Enéide*." *Vergiliana: Recherches sur Virgile*. Ed. H. Bardon and R. Verdière. Roma aeterna III. Leiden: Brill, 1971. 15-34.

Basson, W. P. "Virgil, Roman History, and the Roman's Destiny. Notes on *Aeneid* VI, 836-53." *Akroterion* 20 (1975): 83-92.

Beaujeu, Jean. "Le mariage d'Enée et de Didon et la causalité historique." *Revue du Nord* 36 (April-June 1959).

Bonds, William Sadler. "Joy and Desire in the *Aeneid*: Stoicism in Virgil's Treatment of Emotion." Diss. U of Pennsylvania, 1978.

Brisson, J. P. "Le pieux Enée." *Latomus* 31 (1972): 379-412.

Bromberg, Anne (Ruggles). "Concordia: Studies in Roman Marriage Under the Empire." Diss. Radcliffe, 1961.

Burke, Paul F. "Virgil's Amata." *Vergilius* 22 (1976): 24-29.

Cairns, F. "Geography and Nationalism in the *Aeneid*." *Liverpool Classical Monthly* 2 (1977): 109-16.

Commager, Steele, ed. *Virgil: A Collection of Critical Essays*. Englewood Cliffs: Prentice, 1966.

Corbett, Percy Ellwood. *The Roman Law of Marriage*. Oxford: Clarendon, 1930.

Costa, Giuseppe. *La psicologia della passione amorosa in Didone (Eneide: libri I e IV)*. Padua: Pesavento, 1930.

Cova, P. V. "Ideologia e semantica di pietas nell'*Eneide*." *Lo stoico imperfetto. Un'immagine minore dell'uomo nella letteratura latina del principato*. Studi e testi dell'antichità 10. Naples: Napolitana, 1981.

DeGraff, Thelma B. "Dido--Tota Vergiliana." *Classical Weekly* 43 (1949-50): 147-51.

Dimochi, G. E. "The Mistake of Aeneas." *Yale Review* 64 (1975): 344-56.

Donato, Alfonso. *Didone: o, Amore di terra lontana*. Naples: Miccoli, 1940.

DuBois, Page. "The pharmakos of Virgil: Dido as Scapegoat." *Vergilius* 22 (1976): 11-23.

Fabbri, Paolo. *Virgilio, poeta sociale e politico*. Milan: Società Editrice Dante Alighieri, 1929.

Finley, M. I. *Aspects of Antiquity: Discoveries and Controversies*. London: Chatto and Windus, 1968.

Forbes, Clarence A. "Tragic Dido." *Classical Bulletin* 29 (1953): 51-53, 58.

Gosling, A. "The Political Level of the Aeneid." *Akroterion* 20 (1975): 42-45.

Gossage, A. J. "Two Implications of the Trojan Legend." *Greece and Rome* 2nd ser. 2 (1955): 23-29.

Gruen, Peter. "Facta Impia and Dido's Soliloquy (*Aeneid* 4.590-629)." *Classical Bulletin* 56 (1980): 65-69.

Hallett, Judith P. "The Role of Women in Roman Elegy: Counter-Cultural Feminism." *Arethusa* 6 (1973): 103-24.

Hanson, J. O. de G. "Creusa, Dido, Lavinia and Aeneas." *Museum Africum* 5 (1976): 65-72.

Horsfall, N. "Virgil, History and the Roman Tradition." *Prudentia* 8 (1976): 73-89.

Bibliography

Hughes, Merritt Y. "Our Virgil?" University of California Chronicle 32 (1930).

Johnson, W. P. "The Broken World: Virgil and his Augustus." Arethusa 14 (1981): 49-56.

---. Darkness Visible: A Study of Virgil's Aeneid. Berkeley: U of California P, 1976.

Knauer, Georg Nikolaus. Die Aeneis und Homer: Studien zu poetischen technik Vergils mit Listen der Homerzitate in der Aeneis. Göttingen: Vanderhoch und Ruprecht, 1964.

Lesueur, Roger. "Civitas et patria: unité ou dualité du message virgilien dans l'Enéide?" Présence de Virgile. Actes du Colloque des 9, 11 et 12 décembre 1976, Paris. Ed. P. Chevallier. Paris: Les Belles Lettres, 1978.

Lewis, C. S. "Virgil and the Subject of Secondary Epic." A Preface to Paradise Lost. Oxford: Oxford UP, 1954.

McLeish, K. "Dido, Aeneas, and the Concept of Pietas." Greece and Rome 19 (1972): 127-35.

Maguiness, J. S. M. "Heroism in Virgil." Proceedings of the Virgil Society 10 (1970-71): 45-56.

Miles, Gary. "Glorious Peace: The Values and Motivation of Virgil's Aeneas." California Studies in Classical Antiquity 9 (1976): 133-64.

Monti, Richard C. The Dido Episode and the Aeneid: Roman Society and Political Values in the Epic. Mnemosyne Suppl 66. Bibliotheca Classica Batava. Leiden: Brill, 1981.

Morris, Brian, "Virgil and the Heroic Ideal." Proceedings of the Virgil Society 9 (1969-70): 20-36.

Oroz de la Consolacion, Fr. Jose, O.R.S.A. "Virgilio, poeta del 'imperium'." Helmantica 4 (1953): 351-77.

Parry, Adam. "The Two Voices of Virgil's Aeneid." Arion 2 (1963): 66-80.

Phinney, Edward, Jr. "Dido and Sychaeus." Classical Journal 60 (1965): 355-9.

Pöschl, Viktor. *The Art of Virgil: Image and Symbol in the Aeneid*. Trans. Gerda Seligson. Ann Arbor: U of Michigan P, 1962.

---. "Dido und Aeneas." *Festschrift Karl Vretska zum 70 Geburtstag*. Ed. Doris von Ableitinger and Helmut Gugel. Heidelberg: C. Winter, 1970.

Préaux, J. "Les sept premiers vers de l'Enéide et les découvertes de Lavinium." *D'Eschyle à nos jours. Lecons d'archeologie, de littérature, de philologie classiques*. Ed. G. Cambier. *Latomus* 37 (1978).

Sainte-Beuve, C.-A. *Etude sur Virgile*. 1856, 2nd edition. Paris, 1870.

Sanderlin, G. "Aeneas as Apprentice: Point of View in the Third *Aeneid*." *Classical Journal* 71 (1975): 53-56.

Stahl, H. P. "Aeneas: An Unheroic Hero?" *Arethusa* 14 (1981): 157-77.

Thompson, David. "Allegory and Typology in the *Aeneid*." *Arethusa* 3 (1970): 147-53.

Thompson, George. *Studies in Ancient Greek Society: The Prehistoric Aegean*, 3rd ed. New York: Citadel, 1961.

Todd, Ruth W. "Lavinia Blushed." *Vergilius* 26 (1980): 27-33.

Tracy, H. L. "*Aeneid* IV: Tragedy or Melodrama?" *Classical Journal* 41 (1946): 199-202.

Vance, Eugene. "Warfare and the Structure of Thought in Virgil's *Aeneid*." *Quaderni Urbinati di Cultura Classica* 15 (1973): 111-62.

Virgil. *P. Vergili Maroni Opera*. Ed. Frederick Arthur Hirtzel. Oxford: Clarendon, 1900.

---. *P. Vergili Maroni Opera*. Ed. R. A. B. Mynors. Oxford: Clarendon, 1969.

---. *Publi Vergili Maronis Aenedos, Liber Quartus*. Cambridge: Harvard UP, 1935.

West, Grace Starry. "Virgil's Helpful Sisters: Anna and Juturna in the *Aeneid*." *Vergilius* 25 (1979): 10-19.

Bibliography

Williams, G. "Some Aspects of Roman Marriage Ceremonies and Ideals." *Journal of Roman Studies* 48 (1958): 16-29.

Wittenberg, Sr. Mary Ste. Therese, S.N.D., "Virgil's Camilla." *Classical Bulletin* 42 (1966): 69-71.

Zarker, J. W. "Virgil's Trojan and Italian Matres." *Vergilius* 24 (1978): 15-24.

Historical and Theoretical Background

Ashley, Maurice Percy. *The Stuarts in Love: With Some Reflections on Love and Marriage in the Sixteenth and Seventeenth Centuries*. London: Hodden and Stoughton, 1963.

Bainton, Roland. *Women of the Reformation in Germany and Italy*. Minneapolis: Augsburg Publishing House, 1971.

Beard, Mary. *Woman as Force in History*. 1946. New York: Collier, 1962.

Blade, Melinda K. *The Education of Italian Renaissance Women*. Women in History 21. Mesquite, TX: Ide House, 1983.

Bridenthal, Renate and Claudia Koonz, ed. *Becoming Visible: Women in European History*. Boston: Houghton, 1977.

Brown, Elizabeth A. R. "The Tyranny of a Construct: Feudalism and Historians of Medieval Europe." *American Historical Review* 79 (1974): 1063-88.

Burckhardt, Jacob. *The Civilization of the Renaissance in Italy*. 1850. New York: Random House, 1954.

Burstein, Diane, ed. *Distaves and Dames: Renaissance Treatises for and about Women*. Scholars' Facsimiles and Reprints 317. Delmar, NY: Scholars' Facsimiles, 1978.

Camden, Carroll. *The Elizabethan Woman*. Houston: Elsevier, 1952.

Cannon, Mary Agnes. *The Education of Women During the Renaissance*. 1916. Westport, CT: Hyperion, 1981.

Carroll, Berenice, ed. *Liberating Women's History*. Urbana: U Illinois P, 1976.

Carter, Charles Howard, ed. *From the Renaissance to the Counter-Reformation: Essays in Honor of Garrett Mattingly*. New York: Random, 1960.

Casey, Kathleen. "The Cheshire Cat: Reconstructing the Experience of Medieval Women." Carroll 224-49.

Castiglione, Baldassare. *Il libro del cortegiano. Opere di Baldassare Castiglione, Giovanni della Casa, Benevenuto Cellini*. Ed. Carlo Cordie. Milan: Ricciardi, n.d.

Chrimes, S. B. *English Constitutional Ideas in the Fifteenth Century*. Cambridge UP, 1936.

Churchill, Winston. *The Birth of Britain*. A History of the English-Speaking Peoples. New York: Dodd, Mead, 1956.

Clark, Alice. *Working Life of Women in the Seventeenth Century*. London: Routledge; New York: Dutton, 1915.

Dobb, Maurice. "Reply to Sweezy." *The Transition from Feudalism to Capitalism.*

DuBois, Page Ann. "'The Devil's Gateway': Women's Bodies and the Earthly Paradise." *Women's Studies* 7 (1980): 43-58.

Elton, G. R. "A High Road to Civil War?" Carter 296-324.

---. *The Tudor Revolution in Government: Administrative Changes in the Reign of Henry VII*. Cambridge UP, 1962.

Fabry, E. "Three Early Renaissance Treatises on Women." *Italian Studies* 11 (1956): 30-55.

Ferguson, Wallace, et al. *Facets of the Renaissance*. New York: Harper, 1959.

Gardiner, Judith Kegan. "The Renaissance Marriage Debate." Third Berkshire Conference on the History of Women. Bryn Mawr College, June 1976.

Gies, Frances and Joseph. *Women in the Middle Ages*. New York: Barnes, 1978.

Godfrey, Elizabeth. *Social Life Under the Stuarts, 1603-1649*. London: Richards; New York: Dutton, 1904.

Bibliography

Harbison, E. Harris. "Machiavelli's Prince and More's Utopia." Ferguson 41-72.

Hare, Christopher. Men and Women of the Italian Reformation. London: St. Paul, 1914.

Hay, Denys. The Italian Renaissance in its Historical Background. Cambridge UP, 1962.

---. The Renaissance. The New Cambridge Modern History I. Ed. G. R. Potter. Cambridge UP, 1964.

Helton, Tinley, ed. The Renaissance: A Reconsideraton of Some of the Theories and Interpretations of the Age. Madison: U Wisconsin P, 1964.

Herlihy, David. "Land, Family and Women in Continental Europe 701-1200." Traditio 18 (1962): 89-120.

Hicks, David L. "The Sienese State in the Renaissance." Carter: 75-94.

Hill, Christoper. Change and Continuity in Seventeenth-Century England. Cambridge: Harvard UP, 1975.

---. Puritanism and Revolution: Studies in Interpretation of the English Revolution of the 17th Century. New York: Schocken, 1958.

Hough, Graham. A Preface to The Faerie Queene. New York: Norton, 1963.

Huizinga, Johan. Men and Ideas: History, the Middle Ages, the Renaissance. London: Eyre and Spottiswoode, 1960.

Kelly (-Gadol), Joan. Women, History and Theory: The Essays of Joan Kelly. Women in Culture and Society. U of Chicago P, 1984.

Kelly Gadol, Joan. Bibliography in the History of European Women. Bronxville: Sarah Lawrence College, 1976.

---. "Did Women Have a Renaissance?" Bridenthal 137-64.

--- "Notes on Women in the Renaissance." Conceptual Frameworks in Women's History. Bronxville: Sarah Lawrence Pub 1976.

Kelso, Ruth. *Doctrine for the Lady of the Renaissance*. Urbana: U of Illinois P, 1956.

King, Margaret L. and Albert Rabil, Jr., eds. *Her Immaculate Hand: Selected Works by and about the Woman Humanists of Quattrocentro Italy*. Medieval and Renaissance Texts and Studies 20. Binghamton, NY: Center for Medieval and Early Renaissance Studies, 1983.

Knox, John. *The First Blast of the Trumpet Against the Monstrous Regiment of Women*. 1558. Ed. Edward Arber. London: Arber, 1878.

Laffin, John. *Women in Battle*. London: Abelard-Schuman, 1951.

McNamara, JoAnn and Suzanne Wemple. "The Power of Women Through the Family in Medieval Europe: 500-1100." *Clio's Consciousness Raised: New Perspectives on the History of Women*. Ed. Mary Hartman and Lois W. Banner. New York: Harper, 1974.

---. "Sanctity and Power: The Dual Pursuit of Medieval Women." Bridenthal 90-118.

Marx, Karl. *The Eighteenth Brumaire of Louis Bonaparte*. 1852. New York: International, 1963.

Mattingly, Garrett. *Changing Attitudes Towards the State During the Renaissance*. New York: Harper, 1959.

---. "Changing Attitudes Towards the State." Ferguson 19-40.

---. *Renaissance Diplomacy*. London: Jonathan Cape, 1955.

---. "Some Revisions of the Political History of the Renaissance." Helton 3-26.

Maude de la Clavière, Marie Alphonse René de. *The Women of the Renaissance: A Study of Feminism*. Trans. George Herbert Ely. Folcroft, PA: Folcroft Library, 1978.

McLaren, Angus. *Reproductive Rituals: Perceptions of Fertility in Britain from the Sixteenth Century to the Nineteenth Century*. New York: Methuen, 1985.

Bibliography

Meinecke, Friedrich. *Machiavellism: The Doctrine of Raison d'Etat and its Place in Modern History*. Trans. Douglass Scott. London: Routledge, 1951.

Monter, E. William. "The Pedestal and the Stake: Courtly Love and Witchcraft." Bridenthal 119-36.

Neale, J. E. *Essays in Elizabethan History*. London: Jonathan Cape, 1958.

Newkirk, Glen Alton, "The Public and Private Ideal of the Sixteenth-Century Gentleman: A Representative Analysis." Diss. U of Denver, 1967.

Painter, Sydney. *Feudalism and Liberty*. Ed. Fred A. Cazel. Baltimore: Hopkins UP, 1961.

Powell, Chilton Latham. *English Domestic Relations, 1487-1653*. New York: Columbia UP, 1917.

Prior, Mary. *Women in English Society, 1500-1800*. New York: Methuen, 1985.

Radcliff-Umstead, Douglas, ed. *The Roles and Images of Women in the Middle Ages and the Renaissance*. U of Pittsburgh Publications on the Middle Ages and the Renaissance 3. Pittsburgh: Center for Medieval and Renaissance Studies, Institute for the Human Sciences, c. 1975.

Rowbotham, Sheila. *Hidden from History: 300 Years of Women's Oppression and the Fight Against It*. London: Pluto, 1973.

---. *Women, Resistance and Revolution*. New York: Random, 1972.

Rowen, Herbert H. "Kingship and Republicanism in the Seventeenth Century: Some Reconsiderations." Carter 420-31.

Stone, Lawrence. *The Crisis of the Aristocracy, 1558-1641*. Oxford: Clarendon, 1965.

---. *Family and Fortune: Studies in Aristocratic Finance in the 16th and 17th Centuries*. Oxford: Clarendon, 1973.

Sweezy, Paul. "Critique of Dobb's *Studies in the Development of Capitalism*." *Transition from Feudalism*.

---. *The Transition from Feudalism to Capitalism*. New York: Science and Society, 1954.

Travitsky, Betty, ed. *The Paradise of Women: Writings by Englishwomen of the Renaissance*. Contributions in Women's Studies 22. Westport, CT: Greenwood, 1981.

Valency, Maurice. *In Praise of Love*. New York: Macmillan, 1961.

Vann, Richard T. "Toward a New Lifestyle: Women in Preindustrial Capitalism." Bridenthal 192-216.

Warnicke, Retha M. *Women of the English Renaissance*. Contributions in Women's Studies 38. Westport, CT: Greenwood, 1983.

Wiesner, Mery E. *Women in the Sixteenth Century: A Bibliography*. Sixteenth Century Bibliography 23. St. Louis: Center for Information Research, n.d.

Wright, Louis B. *Middle-Class Culture in Elizabethan England*. Ithaca: Cornell UP, 1958.

Wyntjes, Sherrin Marshall. "Women in the Reformation Era." Bridenthal 165-91.

The Renaissance Epic: General Studies

DeLuca, Diana M. "Forgetful of her Yoke: The Woman Warrior in Three Renaissance Epics." *DAI* 43 (1982): 5127A.

DeSanctis, Francesco. *A History of Italian Literature*. 1870. Trans. Joan Redfern. New York: Basic Books, 1959.

Donadoni Eugenio. *A History of Italian Literature*. Trans. Richard Monges. New York UP, 1969.

Fichter, Andrew. *Poets Historical: Dynastic Epic in the Renaissance*. New Haven: Yale UP, 1982.

Giamatti, A. Bartlett. *The Earthly Paradise and the Renaissance Epic*. Princeton UP, 1966.

Greene, Thomas M. *The Descent from Heaven: A Study in Epic Continuity*. New Haven: Yale UP, 1963.

Bibliography

Hutchinson, Mary Anne. "The Devil's Gateway: The Evil Enchantress in Ariosto, Tasso, Spenser and Milton." Diss. Syracuse, 1975.

Lentzen, Manfred. "Alcina, Armida und die Jüden von Toledo: Drei Verfurerinnen bei Ariosto, Tasso, und Lope de Vega." Spanische Literatur in Goldenen Zeitalter: Fritz Schall zum 70 Geburtstag. Ed. Horst Baader and Erich Loos. Frankfurt: Klostermann, 1973, 229-68.

Luciani, Vincent. A Brief History of Italian Literature. New York: Vanni, 1967.

Parotti, Philip C. "The Female Warrior in the Renaissance Epic." Diss. U of New Mexico, 1973.

Whitfield, J. H. A Short History of Italian Literature. London: Penguin, 1969.

Wilkins, Ernest Hatch. A History of Italian Literature. Cambridge: Harvard UP, 1951.

Ariosto

Ariosto, Ludovico. Orlando furioso. Ed. Nicola Zingarelli. 6th edition. Milan: Hoepli, 1959.

---. Orlando furioso. Trans. William Stewart Rose, 1823-31. Ed. Stewart A. Baker and A. Bartlett Giamatti. Indianapolis: Bobbs-Merrill, 1968.

Benson, Pamela Joseph. "Independence and Fidelity: The Contributions of the Querelle des femmes to the Orlando furioso." Diss. Columbia U, 1978.

---. "An Unrecognized Defender of Women in the Orlando furioso." Italica 54 (1980): 268-70.

Binni, Walter. Due studi critici, Ariosto e Foscolo. Rome: Bulzoni, 1978.

---. Metodo e poesie di Ludovico Ariosto. 2nd ed. Messina: d'Anna, 1961.

Brand, C. P. Ludovico Ariosto: A Preface to the Orlando Furioso. Writers of Italy 1. Edinburgh U Press, 1974.

Carne-Ross, D. S. "The One and the Many: A Reading of *Orlando furioso*, Cantos 1 and 8." *Arion* 5 (1966): 195-234.

Chesney, Elizabeth A. *The Countervoyages of Rabelais and Ariosto: A Comparative Reading of Two Renaissance Mock Epics*. Durham: Duke University Press, 1982.

Croce, Benedetto. *Ludovico Ariosto*. Part I of *Ariosto, Shakespeare, Corneille* 1920. Bari: Laterza, 1963.

Cuccaro, Vincent. *The Humanism of Ludovico Ariosto: From the 'Satire' to the 'Furioso'*. L'Interprete 18. Ravenna: Longo, 1981.

Garnier, Robert. *Bradamante*. 1582-85. Paris: Garnier Freres, n.d.

Grilli, Alfredo. *Figure muliebre nell'Orlando furioso*. Ferrara: Stabilmento tipografico Estense, 1933.

Hartley, K. H. "Robert Garnier and Ariosto." *Modern Language Review* 56 (1961): 389-91.

Momigliano, Attilio. *Saggio su l'Orlando furioso*. 1928. Bari: Laterza, 1959.

Negri, Renzo. *Interpretazione dell'Orlando furioso*. Milan: Marzorati, 1971.

Piromalli, Antonio. *La cultura a Ferrara al tempo di Ludovico Ariosto*. Rome: Bulzoni, 1975.

---. *Motivi e forme della poesia di Ludovico Ariosto*. Florence: d'Anna, 1954.

Pool, Franco. *Interpretazione dell'Orlando furioso*. Florence: La Nuova Italia, 1968.

Scaglione, Aldo, ed. *Ariosto 1974 in America; Atti del Congresso Ariostesco, diciembre 1974, Casa Italiana della Columbia University*. L'Interprete. Ravenna: Longo, 1976.

Segre, Cesare. *Esperienze ariostesche*. Pisa: Nistri-Lischi, 1969.

Bibliography

---, ed. <u>Ludovico Ariosto: lingua, stile e tradizione: Atti del Congresso organizzato dai comuni di Reggio Emilia e Ferrara, 12-16 ottobre 1974</u>. Milan: Feltrinelli, 1976.

Sestan, Ernesto. "Gli Estensi e il loro stato al tempo dell'Ariosto." <u>Rassegna della Letteratura Italiana (1975)</u>: 19-33.

Tomalin, Margaret. "Bradamante and Marfisa: An Analysis of the Guerriere of the <u>Orlando furioso</u>." <u>Modern Language Review</u> 71 (1976): 540-71.

Tasso

Baldassare, Guido, ed. <u>Tasso: Il Programma letteraria della 'Gerusalemme.'</u> Turin: Paravia, 1979.

---. <u>Inferno e cielo: Tipologia e funzione del meraviglioso nella Liberata</u>. Rome: Bulzoni, 1977.

Ballerini, Carlo. <u>Il blocco della guerra e il suo dissolversi nella Gerusalemme liberata: Il rompersi del blocco conflittuale nell'uccisione di Clorinda e nell'esorcismo della selva mistificata</u>. Bologna: Patron, 1978.

Basile, Bruno. "Fonti culturale e invenzione letteraria nel 'Padre di famiglia' di Torquato Tasso." <u>Convivio</u> 36 (1968): 277-92.

Braghieri, Paolo. <u>Il testo come soluzione rituale: La Gerusalemme liberata</u>. Bologna, Patron, 1978.

Brand, C. P. <u>Torquato Tasso: A Study of the Poet and his Contribution to English Literature</u>. Cambridge UP, 1965.

---. "Tasso, Spenser, and the <u>Orlando furioso</u>." <u>Petrarch to Pirandello: Studies in Italian Literature in Honor of Beatrice Corrigan</u>. U of Toronto P, 1973.

Chiapelli, Fredi. "La costruzione di un personaggio: Clorinda." <u>Lettere italiane</u> 30 (1978): 433-38.

Corrigan, Beatrice. "Erminia and Tancredi: The Happy Ending." <u>Italica</u> 40 (1963): 325-33.

DeLeval, Nicole. "Le coppie più rappresentative dell' Orlando furioso e della Gerusalemme liberata." Revue des langues vivantes 30 (1964): 153-61.

Getto, Giovanni. Interpretazione del Tasso. Naples: Edizioni scientifiche italiane, 1951. Reissued as Malinconia di Torquato Tasso. Collana di testi e di critica 24. Naples: Liguori, 1979

Iovine, Francesco. La licenza del fingere: Note per una lettura della Liberata. Rome: Bulzoni, 1980.

Kates, Judith A. Tasso and Milton: The Problem of Christian Epic. Lewisburg, PA: Bucknell UP; London: Associated University Presses, 1983.

Manetti, Aldo. "Una controversia matrimoniale." Studi tassiani 23 (1973): 109-18.

Montari, Fausto. Riflessioni sulla poesia del Tasso. Savona: Sabatelli, 1974.

Pool, Franco. Desiderio e realtà nella poesia del Tasso. Padua: Liviana, 1960.

Praz, Mario. "Armida's Garden." Comparative Literature Studies 5 (1968): 1-20.

Prisco, Michele. "I personaggi femminile della Gerusalemme liberata." Atti del convegno di Nimega sul Tasso, 25-27 ottobre 1977. Bologna: Patron, 1978: 281-96.

Radcliff-Umstead, Douglas. "Structures of Conflict in Tasso's Pastoral of Love." Studi Tassiani 22 (1972): 69-83.

Sozzi, B. T. Studi sul Tasso. Pisa: Nistri-Lischi, 1954.

Tasso, Torquato. Il Padre di famiglia. In his Dialoghi. Ed. Ezio Raimondi. Florence: Sansoni, 1958.

---. Poesie. Ed. Francesco Flora. Notes Lodovico Magugliani. Milan: Rizzoli, 1950.

Ulivi, Ferrucci. Antologia tassiana: Testi e commenti. Rome: EL e A, 1974.

---. Il manierismo del Tasso e altri studi. Florence: Olschki, 1966.

Bibliography

Spenser

Anderson, Judith. "'In liuing colours and right hew': The Queen of Spenser's Central Books." *Poetic Traditions of the English Renaissance*. Ed. Maynard Mack and George de Forest Lord. New Haven: Yale UP, 1982. 47-66.

Ashley, Leonard R. N. "Spenser and the Ideal of the Gentleman." *Bibliothèque d'Humanisme et Renaissance* 27 (1965): 108-32.

Bean, John C. "Making the Daimonic Personal: Britomart and Love's Assault in *The Faerie Queene*." *Modern Language Quarterly* 40 (1979): 237-55.

Berger, Harry, Jr. *The Allegorical Temper: Vision and Reality in Book II of Spenser's Faerie Queene*. Hamden, CT: Archon, 1967.

---. "*Faerie Queene* Book III: A General Description." *Criticism* 11 (1969): 234-61.

---. "The Structure of Merlin's Chronicle in *The Faerie Queene* III (iii)." *Studies in English Literature* 9 (1969): 39-51.

---, ed. *Spenser: A Collection of Critical Essays*. Englewood Cliffs: Prentice, 1968.

Bernhart, Barbara. "Imperialistic Myths and Iconography in Books I and II of *The Faerie Queene*." Diss. McMaster, 1975.

Bieman, Elizabeth. "Britomart in Book V of *The Faerie Queene*." *University of Toronto Quarterly* 37 (1968): 156-74.

Boas, F. S. *Sir Philip Sidney: Representative Elizabethan*. London: Staples, 1955.

Brinkley, Robert A. "Spenser's Garden of Adonis: The Nature of Infinity." *Massachusetts Studies in English* 4 (1974-75): 3-16.

Burchnose, David W. "The Unfolding of Britomart: Mythic Iconography in *The Faerie Queene*." *Renaissance Papers* (1977): 11-19.

Cantarow, Ellen. "A Wilderness of Opinions Confounded: Allegory and Ideology." College English 34 (1972): 215-52.

Center for Hermeneutical Study in Hellenistic and Modern Culture. Spenser's Arcadia: The Interrelation of Fiction and History. Protocol of the Thirty-Eighth Colloquy, 13 April 1980. Berkeley: The Center, 1981.

Chace, JoAn Elizabeth. "Spenser's Celebration of Love: Its Background in English Protestant Thought." Diss. U California at Berkeley, 1969.

Cheney, Donald. Spenser's Image of Nature: Wild Man and Shepher in the Faerie Queene. New Haven: Yale UP, 1966.

Cox, Herbert E. Edmund Spenser A Critical Study. University of California Publications in Modern Philology. Berkeley: U of California P, 1917.

Cullen, Patrick. Infernal Triad: The Flesh, the World, and the Devil in Spenser and Milton. Princeton UP, 1975.

DeNeef, A. Leigh. "Ploughing Virgilian Furrows: The Genesis of Faerie Queene VI." John Donne Journal 1 (1982): 151-68.

---. Spenser and the Motives of Metaphor. Durham, NC: Duke UP, 1982.

Donno, Elizabeth S. "The Triumph of Cupid: Spenser's Legend of Chastity." Yearbook of English Studies 4 (1974), 37-48.

Dunseath, T. K. Spenser's Allegory of Justice in Book Five of the Faerie Queene. Princeton UP, 1968.

Folsom, Marcia McClintock. "'In Equall Portion': Equality of the Sexes in Spenser's Faerie Queene." Diss. U of California at Berkeley, 1977.

Fowler, Earle P. Spenser and the System of Courtly Love. New York: Phaeton, 1968.

Freeman, Rosemary. Edmund Spenser. Writers and their Work 85. London: Longmans for the British Council and National Book League, 1951.

Bibliography

---. *The Faerie Queene: A Companion for Readers*. Berkeley: U of California P, 1970.

Fromm, Harold. "Spenserian Jazz and the Aphrodisiac of Virtue." *English Miscellany* 17 (1966): 49-68.

Garson, Marjorie Joyce. "Images of the Self: Chastity Figures in *The Faerie Queene*." Diss. U Toronto, 1977.

Geller, Liba. "Spenser's Theory of Nobility in Book VI of *The Faerie Queene*." *English Literary Review* 5 (1975): 49-57.

Giamatti, A. Bartlett. *A Play of Double Senses: Spenser's Faerie Queene*. Landmarks in Literature. Englewood Cliffs: Prentice, 1975.

Green, Paul D. "Spenser and the Masses: Social Commentary in *The Faerie Queene*." *Journal of the History of Ideas* 35 (1974): 389-406.

Greenblatt, Stephen J. *Renaissance Self-Fashioning*. U of Chicago Press, 1980.

Grund, Gary R. "The Queen's Two Bodies: Britomart and Spenser's *Faerie Queene*, Book III." *Cahiers Elisabethains* 20 (1981): 11-33.

Guillory, John. *Poetic Authority: Spenser, Milton and Literary History*. New York: Columbia UP, 1983.

Haller, William. "Hail Wedded Love." *Journal of English Literary History* 13 (1946): 79-97.

Hamilton, A. C. *The Structure of Allegory in the Faerie Queene*. Oxford: Clarendon, 1961.

---, ed. *Essential Articles for the Study of Edmund Spenser*. Hamden, CT: Archon, 1972.

Hannah, Susan, "Womb(an) Power: Or a Faerie Tale of the Good, the Bad, and the Ugly." *RE: Artes Liberales* 5 (1978): 27-35.

Hedley, Eleanor J. "Masculine and Feminine in *The Faerie Queene*: An Ontological Analysis." Diss. Bryn Mawr, 1974.

Hoffman, Nancy. "Comment on Cantarow, 'A Wilderness of Opinions.'" *College English* 34 (1972): 253-55.

Hough, Graham. *A Preface to The Faerie Queene*. New York: Norton, 1963.

Hume, Anthea. *Edmund Spenser: Protestant Poet*. Cambridge UP, 1984.

Kennedy, Judith M. and James A. Reither, ed. *A Theater for Spenserians: Papers of the Interntional Spenser Colloquium, Frederickton, New Brunswick, October 1969*. U of Toronto P, 1973.

Kouwenhoven, Jan Karel. *Apparent Narration as Thematic Metaphor: The Organization of The Faerie Queene*. Oxford: Clarendon, 1983.

Lanham, Richard A. "The Literal Britomart." *Modern Language Quarterly* 28 (1967): 426-45.

McAuley, James. "Politics Versus Art in Book Five of *The Faerie Queene*." *Southern Review* (Australia) 8 (1975): 22-33.

MacCaffrey, Isabel G. *Spenser's Allegory: The Anatomy of Image*. Princeton UP, 1976.

Mendelson, Abbot Jay. "Trumpets Sterne and Oaten Reeds: Martial Duty and Procreative Sex in *The Faerie Queene*." *DAI* 37 (1976): 2898A.

Meyer, Russell J., ed. *Spenser at Kalamazoo 1982. Proceedings of Special Sessions of the Seventeenth International Congress on Medieval Studies, Kalamazoo, Michigan, 6-9 May 1982*. Clarion, PA: Clarion State C. c. 1982.

Miskimin, Alice A. "Britomart's Crocodile and the Legend of Chastity." *Journal of English and German Philology* 77 (1978): 17-36.

Mohl, Ruth. *Studies in Spenser, Milton, and the Theory of Monarchy*. New York: Kings Crown, 1949.

---. *The Three Estates in Medieval and Renaissance Literature*. New York: Columbia UP, 1933.

Moore, Dennis. *The Politics of Spenser's Complaints and Sidney's Philasides Poems*. Salzburg: Institut für Anglistik und Americanistik, Universität Salzburg, 1982.

Bibliography

Nelson, William. *The Poetry of Edmund Spenser: A Study*. New York: Columbia UP, 1963.

Nohrnberg, James Carson. *The Analogy of The Faerie Queene*. Princeton UP, 1976.

Paolucci, Anne. "Women in the Political Love-Ethic of the *Divine Comedy* and *The Faerie Queene*." *Dante Studies with Annual Report of the Dante Society* 90 (1972): 139-53.

Parker, M. Pauline. *An Allegory of the Faerie Queene*. Oxford UP, 1960.

Ramsay, Judith. "The Garden of Adonis and the Garden of Forms." *University of Toronto Quarterly* 35 (1966): 188-206.

Richardson, David A. *Spenser and the Middle Ages*. Cleveland SU, 1976.

Ruedy, Shirley Wallace. "Spenser's Britomart." Diss. Duke, 1975.

Sale, Roger. *Reading Spenser: An Introduction to The Faerie Queene*. New York: Random House, 1968.

Shanley, James Lyndon. *A Study of Spenser's Gentleman*. Diss. Northwestern, 1940.

Shaver, Anne. "Artegall Tamed Too Far." Richardson 135-48.

Spenser, Edmund. *The Poetical Works of Edmund Spenser in Three Volumes*. Ed. J. C. Smith. 1909. Oxford UP, 1961.

Stump, Donald V. "Britomart's Mock Romantic Quest." Richardson 157-66.

Stillman, Carol. "Nobility and Justice in Book Five of *The Faerie Queene*." *Texas Studies in Language and Literature* 23 (1981): 535-5.

Tannier, Bernard. "La Justice dans *The Faerie Queene* de Spenser." *Société francaise Shakespeare: Actes du Congrès 1980*. Ed. M.-T. Jones-Davies. Paris: Touzot, 1981, 9-21.

Vance, Eugene Augustus. "Warfare as Metaphor in Spenser's *Faerie Queene*." Diss. Cornell, 1966.

Wells, Robin Headlam. *Spenser's Faerie Queene and the Cult of Elizabeth*. London: Croom Helm; Totowa: Barnes, 1983.

Williams, Kathleen. *Spenser's World of Glass: A Reading of The Faerie Queene*. Berkeley: U of California P, 1966.

Wood, Robert E. "Britomart in the House of Busyrane." *South Atlantic Bulletin* 43 (1978): 5-11.